Hope and Faith:
A Family History

Robin Milton Stewart

Edited by Andrew Stewart

Dedication

To my father, Robin Stewart, who tirelessly researched our family history over many, many years. His wish was to preserve this history so that we, his direct and extended family, might understand better who we are and where we come from.

In Memorium, Robin Milton Stewart, 5.8.1938 – 31.8.2012

Edited and completed by Andrew Stewart, 2013

Contents

Chapter 1: Introduction 6

Looking Back 6

Interest in Family History 16

Particular Difficulties in Tracing Scottish Ancestors 17

The Highland Tradition in naming of Children 18

Overview of Our Family 18

Chapter 2: The Highland Clan 23

Chapter 3: The House of Stewart 31

Breton Origins 31

From the Duchy of Normandy to the Kingdom of England 1100 32

High Stewarts of Scotland 33

Stewart Coats of Arms 33

Adoption of the Surname of Stewart, or Stuart or Steuart 34

St James of Compostella – Patron Saint of the House of Stewart 35

Succession to the Throne of Scotland 1371 & adoption of the White Rose as an emblem of the Stewarts 35

Main Branches before the Stewart succession to the Throne 36

Main Branches after the Stewart succession to the Throne 37

Senior Branch of the House of Stewart 39

Chapter 4: The Stewarts of Appin 41

Chapter 5: Stewart of Ardsheal 62

Part I: Main Line of Ardsheal 62

Part II Cadet Branches of Ardsheal 67

A: Acharn → Coll: 68

B: Glengalmadale & Stron: 69

C: Other Ardsheal Stewarts 80

Chapter 6: Stewart 1828 Onwards 81

Murdoch Stewart 81

Robert Stewart, 1830 - 1885 87

Children of Robert Stewart & Sophia Ann Boyce 99

Robert Barton Stewart: 1864 - 1908: "Bertie". 108
Guy Milton Stewart 1900 - 1943: 113
Robin Milton Stewart, 1938 - 2011 130

Chapter 7: Ross 139
Ross of Balnagowan: 140
The Rosses of Pitcalnie: 143
Second Ross Line 152

Chapter 8: Boyce 157
The Milton Family Link 167
Northcroft 170
Northcroft Family in New Zealand: 173
Descendants of Henry Thomas Northcroft 175

Chapter 9: Adam 177
Chapter 10: Douglas and Garden 197
The Garden Family: 229

Chapter 11: Jackson including Hartshorne & Rothery 233
The Hartshorne & Rothery families: 236

Chapter 12: Dickson and Collingwood 241
Collingwood Of Great & Little Ryle & Unthank 249

Chapter 13: Earengey, including Steel 254
A Note on the Steel Family 264

Chapter 14: How 270
Ancestry & Family of Rev John Howe 1630-1705: 270

A Note on the Life & Family of Rev George Howe 1815-1899 [2nd son of John & Maria How]: 280
How of Balnacarron, Fife: 283
Family of Viscount, later Earl, Howe: 284
How Family in Devon: 286

Chapter 15: Medhurst 287

Editor's Note

Some explanation for the abbreviations used within this book:

dsp is an abbreviation for the Latin phrase, descessit sine prole ; died without issue. That is, he or she left no heirs

dau is daughter

d means died

b means born

m means married

If you have any questions, corrections or would like to see some of the pictures referenced in the text, please contact Andrew Stewart at andrew@stewarts.eu or adlstewart@me.com.

Andrew Stewart
Bury, 19 November 2013

Chapter 1: Introduction

Looking Back

I was born on 5th August 1938, in Simla, India - the summer capital of the Raj. I was the 3rd child, but the only son of the family. My father, **Guy Milton Stewart** 1900-1943 was a Regular Army Officer. He had been only 8 years old when his own father, **Robert Barton Stewart** 1864-1908 had died, leaving my grandmother to bring up my father and his brother Donald (then less than a month old). There was not much money about. Further, the pressure on teenagers during the First World War was to join the Services upon leaving school. Accordingly Guy went into the Army, and was commissioned on 18th December 1919 into the Royal Engineers. He went to India in December 1922, where he joined the Madras Sappers and Miners. In 1923, he served for a period on survey work in Mesopotamia (Iraq), and returned to India in January 1926. From then until 1939, all his service was in India. At the time of my birth, he was a Major, serving in a staff job at Army Headquarters in Delhi.

My mother, **Elaine Oenone Earengey**, b 1904, was, by the time of her marriage in 1930, a qualified Doctor, with the degree of MD from London University, her doctorate being in Obstetrics and Gynaecology. She was also a talented musician, and had quite seriously considered the possibility of a musical career when in her late teens, for she had a good soprano voice and was an able pianist. In my childhood, we had an HMV gramophone, which had to be wound up like a clock. Each record lasted but a few minutes, and the steel needles had to be changed with great frequency. I still remember the 78 rpm records of Beethoven symphonies, conducted by Toscanini; the recordings of Beethoven's and

Mendelssohn's violin concerti, the former, if not both, played by Kreisler; and my mother playing Chopin on the piano. Music was an important part of my upbringing. But sadly for my mother, increasing deafness deprived her for many years of one of the great joys of her life.

My maternal grandparents were strong believers in the importance of education and qualifications. In my mother's case, her medical qualifications stood her in good stead when my father was killed. She took up part-time practice as a doctor, in schools, and kept this on for quite a number of years, until she became active in family planning.

At the time of my birth, the storm clouds were beginning to gather over Europe, as Hitler was building his Nazi military machine. My father realised that war was coming, and got posted back to England from India in the early summer of 1939. Only 13 months after my birth, the Second World War broke out. Great things seemed to be in store for him. He became Director of Plans at the War Office, working under Field Marshall Lord Alanbrooke (as he became). But in many ways his real chief was the Prime Minister, Winston Churchill, who apparently rated my father highly. But on 29th January 1943, when I was 4½, and my father was only 42, he was killed on active service, flying back from the Casablanca Conference.

Because of the war, I saw, and knew, him only a little. I used to sit on his knee to sip his beer, which I pretended to like, but really hated. But the pretence was important to keep up, for a 3 - 4 year old. I have distant memories of him coming through the front door in uniform, and hanging his cap on the hall stand. He would take no nonsense from a small child, but at the same time was a loving father. The day that he died, my mother had told us that she was going to go to meet him. I now know that when the fateful crash happened, my father was not killed outright, but was admitted to hospital with a broken back. A War Office car was due to pick up my mother early next morning to take her to see him in hospital in Wales. But he died before the car could come. It took me, as a 4 year old to ask bluntly and insistently why she had not gone to meet him, for the facts of the aeroplane crash and of his death to be told to us three horrified, scared, and tearful children.

Hope and Faith

He did not get home a great deal in wartime. So I saw little of him. Though he was posted at the War Office, a London base was essential, because he had to be available at any and all hours for the demands of the Prime Minister, Winston Churchill. So he stayed with my maternal grandparents in Hampstead.

Of wartime England my memory is spasmodic. We lived at Wychwood, Pine Avenue, Camberley, Surrey, a red brick and stucco Edwardian 5 bedroom house. It was set in an acre of sandy land, prolific with rhododendrons. My parents had rented the house in 1940. By the time that they moved in, my father's posting (to be an Instructor at the Staff College) had been changed, but they continued to take the house anyway, and my mother bought it after the war, and remained living there until the 1960s.

We had a Morrison air raid shelter in the house - made of iron, with mesh in the sides, little bigger than a bed, and standing around 3' high. Would it really have protected us had the house been bombed around it? I doubt it. The sirens, warning of coming air raids were a sound associated with terror in my mind for years afterwards. We used to play with the silver foil which was dropped from aeroplanes to foul up radar systems.

Food and clothing were rationed. It must really have been a great struggle to provide properly. None of us children ever went hungry, but we were aware that everything was in short supply - to this day, neither Lynda nor I can bear to see food wasted. Everyone was encouraged to "dig for victory", and our garden was highly productive of vegetables, soft fruit, apples and pears. And the hens produced eggs, some of which were "put down" in buckets containing a solution of isinglass - a useful but unappetising way of securing a supply of eggs throughout the year. As a small child, I could not understand why, when the War was won, rationing did not immediately go. But this did not happen. Clothes remained rationed until 1949, and food until 1952.

Petrol was in very short supply. Most people had their cars put up for the war on blocks. My mother had a limited supply of petrol for her work as a doctor. All other travel however had to be on foot or bicycle. I used to be taken as a pillion passenger on my mother's bicycle to Hawley Lake, several miles away.

The house still had what was probably its original coke boiler - regularly polished up with black lead - and capable of getting red hot if overheated. There was one radiator in the hall. But it was beyond the capacity of the boiler to heat both hot water and the radiator: a choice had to be made between being clean or being warm. We had coal fires down stairs, and the nursery upstairs had an enclosed "Cozy Stove", run on coal, which could be kept in all night. Hair dryers were unknown. Hair was dried before the fire. Sometime I suppose around the end of the War, the nursery was disbanded, and became Rosemary's bedroom. Central heating was not installed until well into the 1950s. Clothes were usually washed by hand, and there was a mangle in the yard outside the back door, with two rollers, turned by a large handle, to squeeze out surplus water. Automatic clothes washers, spin dryers, and tumble dryers, were unheard of then.

Until I was about 4, I had a succession of nannies. One summer's evening, when my father was on leave, I remember being upset about the then nanny, and rushing down stairs, out into the garden to my father, to ask that she leave. What her fault was I do not remember, but leave the next day she did. Until 2 or 3 years after the war, we had a resident cook. From my earliest memories until the end of the War, we had the treasure of Mrs Harriet Stentiford - always known to me as "Stentiford". She was a widow, who was bombed out of her accommodation in London, during, I suppose, the Battle of Britain. The real indignity for her was that the fire brigade had to rescue her from the ruins of her flat, when she was dressed only in her night clothes. My mother's friend Dr Elspeth Madeley knew that we needed a cook and that Stentiford was homeless. So she came to us. My memory is of her well covered figure, dressed in black with a white collar, and grey white hair, always with a smile and a laugh. She would take me by the hand - I suppose I was 3 or 4 at the time - to collect the hens' eggs or to pick vegetables. How delicious freshly pulled raw carrots were. She was the stalwart support of the house until a short time after the end of the War, when she went back to London to make a home for her son when he was demobbed. She died not long after of cancer, but she must then have been quite elderly. She was replaced by a live in maid-cum-cook called Joan Burrows, who had an illegitimate child, Suzanne, then a toddler. She lasted but a year or so, before she was caught by my mother stealing, and was sacked. Thereafter we had no resident staff, only daily help, and a gardener. The gardener during the war and for a few years after was Evans, of whom I remember little save that it was his task to kill and pluck any hen ready for the pot. As children we each had our own pet hen. My mother's fear was that we would learn before the meal that it was our pet that we were eating. Usually we only discovered afterwards, and would then be in floods of tears. Shirley's was called Grizelda. When Grizelda's day came, Rosemary could not contain herself from shouting to Shirley "we're having Grizelda for lunch today". Shirley, in floods of tears, would eat none of it. How my mother contained herself, I do not know. Food was short and a chicken to eat was a rare treat - a luxury.

Some years after the War, Evans retired, and was replaced by Rapley, who with Mrs Jacobs, "Mrs J", the daily, remained for many years. Both were great characters - and real friends to me as I grew up. Rapley was a great story teller - you dared not interrupt him, else he would start all over again. If my mother wanted anything changed in the garden, he would find every reason not to do it, unless he could be persuaded that it was his idea. He did not believe in Banks, but used to tell that he kept all his money in cash in his house. His son "Perce", of whom Rapley was inordinately proud, was a second hand car dealer, with an eye for a bargain. Mrs J was another treasure, always cheerful and happy. Her husband had been a locksmith at the RMA Sandhurst. Every year she carried the flag at the local British Legion Parade. She took great pride in polishing the furniture, and generally in looking after the house and my mother. She would cycle in from Sandhurst, a journey of several miles, and went on working for my mother until she was about 80.

I was sent away to prep school in 1947, to Abberley Hall, Worcestershire. In retrospect, my school days were happy, though I never understood those who promoted the theory that school days are the happiest days of your life. Abberley was set in rolling countryside, with its own home farm. The then headmaster, and owner, was Gilbert Ashton, who had been decorated with a MC in the First World War. He was a man whom everyone admired. The boys held him in some awe, particularly his lessons on "mental arithmetic". It seemed to me at the time that at least half of my contemporaries were the sons of fathers who had been killed in the War. I did not realise until much later that Gilbert Ashton would set a scale of fees to enable war widows to send their children there - at his own cost. While I was at Abberley, the drama of the Berlin Airlift occurred - in 1948 - 49, when the Russians tried to blockade Berlin from the Allies. For nearly 12 months, aircraft poured in to Berlin, at the rate of one every four seconds, until the Russians were forced to admit that they could not win. Gilbert Ashton used to get visitors - his brother Hubert, who was an MP, was one - to come regularly to the school to lecture to the boys on what was going on in international politics. All the speakers were remarkable, for they were able to capture the imagination and interest of the boys. From Abberley, I went to Winchester, to a house where sporting triumphs were keenly looked for - not my forte. To my housemaster's disdain, in my last year in the school, I not only gave up classics for science, but I took members of the house into a singing competition, an unheard of thing for a philistine, sporting, house. Even more to be regretted was that we won the competition, and had the only silver cup on the house mantelpiece that it had that year. It was easy in those days to get into Oxford or Cambridge - a world apart from the present. I opted for New College, Oxford, the first College to offer me a place. I was half in mind to read medicine, but was not a good enough scientist. So I read law instead, on the basis that it should not be too much work, and might be useful one day. Both proved right. New College, or at least most of my friends there, were not keen on organised sports. We found that golf was an ideal pastime, having some "matches" against King's College, Cambridge; but mostly against Cirencester Agricultural College. Their golfers shared the same aim as us - to use a match as an excuse to wine and dine our way round the Cotswolds. We reckoned that there was not a worthwhile restaurant in the Cotswolds that we did not visit.

Hope and Faith

Though I joined the Middle Temple as an undergraduate, I did not then intend to practice law. In my early teens, if not before, I had said that I would follow my maternal grandparents into the law. Thereafter it seemed to be writ in stone that I would do so. I rebelled. But from the influence of my grandparents, as well as my uncle Donald Stewart, I was set on a professional qualification. For 3 months I tried Chartered Accountancy. Donald was a partner in Turquand Youngs in Singapore, and had been a prisoner of war of the Japanese. I was articled to one of his closest friends in the firm, whose name I do not remember. I never even set eyes on him. Those 3 months were the dreariest that I ever spent. The only relief came from my fellow articled clerks. One day I drove off from Camden Town where we were engaged on the audit of Gilbeys, down to Leicester Square for lunch. You could park a car anywhere in London then. I went into one of the small antique shops in Cecil Court, and bought the oil portrait of Bonnie Prince Charlie, which hangs still in our dining room. It was not long after the Goya portrait of the Duke of Wellington had been stolen from the National Portrait Gallery. One wag with whom I worked rang up the Police to say that I had the Goya in my car. As I came out from work, a horde of seedy looking detectives in rain coats surrounded me, cautioned me, and asked whether the portrait was that of Wellington. I had to explain, and physically to demonstrate, that the sizes were different: that the Goya was on wood, whereas mine was on canvas ("how can you tell that?" asked the bemused detectives); and that Wellington had his own hair, whereas Prince Charlie wore a wig. Somewhat non-plussed they left, asking for my address "in case it turns out that this is the Goya after all".

So I read for the Bar instead, and was pupilled to Colin Duncan, then the head of what had been my Earengey grandfather's Chambers, at 1 Brick Court, Temple. Colin was a wonderful man, with an irrepressible sense of humour, and a great fund of stories. He had won an MC at Gallipoli in 1915. He would not say what he had done to win it; but told instead of how terrified he was as a newly commissioned subaltern, going in in the landing craft, with shells landing all around them. One shell exploded within a foot or two of their boat, showering them with water.

Colin had a big burly sergeant, who sat impassively at the back of the boat, merely commenting "Gor, bugger me damn". I suppose that the French equivalent is "putain de bordelles de merde". It put Colin's fears to rest and he went on to win his Military Cross. Colin was the doyen of defamation, and also had a recherche practice in divorce. In one case he was acting as an amicus curiae, the issue being whether some Maltese decree should be recognised in English law. One of the Judges at lunch let slip to Colin "Over my dead body will the Pope win this one". Back in Chambers the message came "Boys, we've got to find a way around this one" - so we did. It was still the custom in those days to pay 100 guineas as a pupillage fee. In the January of my pupillage (1963), Colin earned 20,000 guineas. It hurt to pay the pupillage fee against that.

Colin was one of the great figures of the Bar of his day. He was offered the appointment as Treasury Devil after the war, but turned it down. H L Parker, later Lord Chief Justice, got it instead. Colin was not interested in a "job" on the Bench, though he was Recorder of Bury St Edmunds and then of Norwich. During my pupillage, he took Silk, at the age of 68; not because he really wanted to, but because his Chambers always had a Silk, Neville Faulkes QC had just been made a High Court Judge, and there was no one else in Chambers ready for Silk.

I was Called to the Bar towards the end of my pupillage, in February 1963; and practised for 2 years until 1965, when I took 5 years out in Industry. During that period, in 1966, I followed my grandfather Earengey, by becoming a Liveryman of the Glaziers Company. I returned to the Bar in late 1970, in Chambers at Newcastle upon Tyne. When we lived in Hexham, Northumberland, I was an elected member of Hexham Urban District Council, and then of Tynedale District Council - where I had the amusement of being invited to stand, for the same seat during the same election, for Labour, Liberal, and Conservative. Needless to say, when I stood as a Tory, the other two parties put up opposing candidates. My final foray into politics was to stand as Conservative Parliamentary Candidate for Newcastle upon Tyne West in both General Elections of 1974 - where there was no risk of being elected.

Hope and Faith

In 1975, I was admitted to the Irish Bar - King's Inns, Dublin, because of involvement in a case concerning the painting of Dublin airport (which settled without coming to trial). In 1976, I became Prosecuting Counsel for the Inland Revenue on the North Eastern Circuit, and retained that appointment until I took Silk in 1978. Later on in 1978, I was appointed a Recorder of the Crown Court. It was because I was in Silk, that we moved to York in 1980, that being the geographical centre of the North Eastern Circuit. [We moved back to London, because my practice was there].

In 1988, I was elected a Bencher of the Middle Temple. From 1988-1993, I was a Director of the Bar Mutual Indemnity Fund; a member of the Professional Conduct Committee of the Bar Council 1991-1993, and the first Chairman of the Professional Negligence Bar Association (1991-1993).

Lynda and I met through my cousin Sally, one of the twin daughters of my Uncle Donald Stewart. In advance of the first introduction, each of us was told that the other was the ideal for us. We thought little of it at that stage; but when we met again after a further year or eighteen months, we never looked back. Lynda was the wage earner when we were first married - I was doing my pupillage, and she worked as a radiographer for "Fred" - Dr Campbell Goulding in Harley Street. Fred was a brilliant radiologist, who had made (and married) a lot of money. His consulting rooms in Harley Street were furnished with priceless antiques - delicate chairs, and a splendid Richard Wilson landscape. Oil rich middle easterners would come with their wives to have everything investigated, and Lynda and the others had to get "that fat woman" out of the Queen Anne chairs. With other celebrities, Fred would ensure that the gown of the patient would "accidentally" fall aside, so that he could see whether blonde or ginger hair was the real colour.

It was not my intention then to practice at the Bar, so in 1965 I started 5 years in Industry and Commerce, when we lived in Gerrards Cross - 3 years with EMI in the Record Industry, and a year each with two small American Companies. At EMI I was selected to go to Chile as the successor to their Managing Director there. It would have been highly challenging, and was to have been for a term of 7 years. As events turned out, that would have taken in the democracy of President Allende, and the military takeover by General Pinochet and others. The prospect was in many ways very inviting. Santiago has a climate not unlike the Mediterranean. Children at school would be brought up tri-lingual, English, Spanish, and French. But there was one insuperable drawback - money. In 1968, it was not lawful to take money out of Chile, and inflation was rampant. The need was not just for sufficient pay in Chile to live in the style expected, but for some pay in hard currency, and for a scheme for education when children got to age 11-12. EMI had none, for the then Chairman, Sir Joseph Lockwood, was a bachelor, who viewed woman and children as unnecessary encumbrances. How unlike the big multi-national companies then such as Shell and Unilever. So I left EMI, and after a couple of years I went back to the Bar in 1970, to join Chambers in Newcastle-upon-Tyne. Thus we moved to Hexham, in the Tyne Valley.

I never regretted my 5 years away from the Bar. I saw at first hand the inertia of the large company machine, which was later to frustrate Andrew at Philips, as it did me at EMI. I learnt that much of the talk of "rationalizing" an industry by takeovers, was little but inadequate management realising that if they did not appear to be leaders, they might lose their own jobs. And as a client seeking advice from a leading Barrister, I saw that erudition and learning is of little use, unless the barrister can also couple it with advice on what the client should do.

The head of the Chambers that I joined in Newcastle, was a larger than life character, David Fenwick - who shouted his way through life. Behind the blustering exterior was a kindly man, who took great pride in his practice. I hit lucky, and in 1978 took Silk. We had only the previous year found our ideal Northumbrian house at Southwood, Riding Mill - a stone built house on the side of Prospect Hill, looking south over Hexhamshire. The ever changing light and mood of the countryside looking south, made me wish to have the ability to paint landscapes. Sadly practice in Silk was impossible from rural Northumberland; so we moved to York; and after 9 years, we moved south to be based back in London.

Interest in Family History

I always enjoyed history at school; and I was always curious to know about our family. Perhaps because my father had been killed in the War, I was always interested in the Stewarts. And as I learnt from the start that my Stewart grandmother's family had seen long service in India, the country of my birth, I became interested in them. Granny Stewart, who died when I was 10, told me a little about the family, when I asked. But I was too young to pose the detailed questions which now I would have liked to have asked, such as which ancestor came from which branch of the Appin Stewarts, and when and why our forebears left Appin. Later on, my quest started seriously with the task of identifying the subjects of two small portraits - one a miniature, and one a pen and wash drawing - which came to us from Aunt Emma Adam (Granny Stewart's sister). They were not labeled on the back, and for many years I believed, from what my mother said she had been told by my grandmother, that they were unrelated to each other. Since we knew fairly early on that the pen and wash drawing was of a Douglas uncle killed at Sebastopol, in the Crimean War, we presumed that the miniature was of an Adam forebear. On a visit to Mabel Gray (a cousin on the Douglas side) in Virginia in 1964, we discovered that our two portraits were of mother and son, and that the miniature was of my great-great grandmother Douglas, nee Collingwood Dickson - Mabel even had a photograph of the miniature (her grandmother).

From that start there developed a desire to find out what I could about the family. Delving into family roots is not about grandeur. It is a historical quest, requiring a crossword puzzle mentality, to establish facts - who one's ancestors were; and to trace, insofar as is possible, how their lives were shaped by outside events, such as Wars, the Jacobite Risings, or the Highland Clearances.

Two things I have learnt the hard way. First, caution needs to be exercised before treating as infallible what you are told. Human memory is not always accurate. Second, sources of information should always be recorded. Otherwise it is so difficult to check the accuracy or completeness of what one has noted down.

This family history inevitably concentrates on my Scottish roots, particularly on the Stewarts as the paternal line. There are obvious gaps, and reliance has to be put on traditions where links cannot be proved by documentary evidence. Some of the general material on the Stewarts may ultimately be proved to be of direct ancestral relevance, and some may not. Much of what is set out about the Stewarts, particularly their early history, comes from published sources; but much has come from research, the results of which either have not been published, or have only had limited publication. My aim has been to record as accurately as I can the results of this research. A considerable amount of it derives from the work of the late Dorothy Stewart Linney, and her older sister Bertha - both elderly spinsters when I knew them, living together in Kingskerswell, Devon. They were descendants of the Stewarts of Invernahyle in Appin, and were staunch supporters of the Stewart Society. They had spent many hours tramping around Appin, talking to knowledgeable people, and researching in the General Register Office in Edinburgh. From them I acquired much knowledge about Scottish family history in general, and about the Stewarts of Appin in particular.

Particular Difficulties in Tracing Scottish Ancestors

Tracing Scottish ancestors presents particular problems. Compulsory registration of births, marriages, and deaths did not come in until the mid-19th century. Names were repeated generation after generation; and among cousins [the Ross family - Chapter 7 - illustrates how readily confusion can arise]. According to the family tree of a family of MacDonalds in North Carolina, one Skye minister had three daughters all with the same name. And in the family of Flora MacDonald [who saved the life of Prince Charlie by sailing with him to safety in Skye in 1746] her mother had a daughter by her second marriage, whom she called Florence.[1]

---

[1] See "Flora MacDonald" by Hugh Douglas. 1993

Hope and Faith

After Culloden in 1746, many houses were wrecked and burnt by the victorious Hanoverians, with the loss of their Charters and family papers. One such was Ardsheal House in Appin. Quite apart from that, people got scattered around the Highlands. Some fled for safety. Poverty and deprivation were everywhere to be found. People were forced off the land that their ancestors had held for generations.

Finally, in the Highlands, the tradition was for stories and details about family and ancestry to be handed down orally rather than in writing. This is very much the Celtic - Viking tradition. As a result, once the link has been lost, it is extremely difficult to fill it.

The Highland Tradition in naming of Children

A note on naming children in Scotland is appropriate. The tradition, not universally followed, but the norm in the Highlands, was that the first son was named after his paternal grandfather: the second son was named after his maternal grandfather: the first daughter was named after her maternal grandmother; and the second daughter was named after her paternal grandmother.

Overview of Our Family

Paternally, the family is predominantly Scottish. Typical of many Scots, great emphasis was laid on education. But being in the main without lands or wealth in Scotland, they had pioneered their ways around the British Empire, in search of the ever elusive fortune.

Our Stewart forebears come, by tradition from Appin. I have not been able to prove that to be true; nor have I been able to take the line back beyond the marriage in 1828 in Inverness of my great-great grandfather **Murdoch Stewart** to **Ann Ross**. Murdoch Stewart was a sawyer or shipbuilder - ie a shipwright - in Inverness. My great grandfather, **Robert Stewart** 1830-1885, was a banker, who became the First General Manager in South Africa of the Standard Bank of South Africa. He was the man who made the decision to finance the Kimberley Diamond Mines. One of his first cousins, John MacDonald Ross, was in partnership with Andrew Carnegie in Canada; but ended the partnership, preferring to return to Scotland, just before Carnegie moved down into America and started to make the fortune that made him one of the wealthiest men of his times. My grandfather, **Robert Barton Stewart** 1864-1908, was in the Indian Civil Service. And my father, **Brigadier Guy Milton Stewart**, was a Regular Army Officer, who spent most of his career in India. On the direct paternal line, therefore, I am the first to set out to work in England.

My paternal grandmother, (Frederica Sybil) **"Freda" Adam**1875-1949, was the daughter of **Brigadier General Frederick John Stuart Adam** 1836-1920. He was brought up in France, in Boulogne; with French as his native tongue. His parents had retired there from India, because it was cheaper than England or Scotland. He served in the Crimea, where he was recommended for a commission by the famous Captain Nolan (who was wrongly blamed for the Charge of the Light Brigade, but in fact died trying to stop Lord Cardigan from making his disastrous blunder). He then saw long service in India, including the Mutiny, and the Afghan War of 1879-1880.

The Adam family come from Forfar, in Fife, and can be traced back to the early part of the 13th Century [Chapter 9]. They were friends and allies of the powerful Douglas family. One ancestor, Reginald Adam, who died in 1390, accompanied James 2nd Earl of Douglas, on a successful border raid into Northumberland in 1385. There he captured a lady named Katherine Mowbray "who being of uncommon beauty, he soon after married her". A number of Frenchmen joined in that raid, led by Sir John de Vienne, Admiral of France. This was during the Hundred Years War, but presumably the French went along for a bit of chivalrous sport. Even in those days, "la gloire de la France" caused difficulty. Every English outpost taken on the raid, the French would try to claim for the King of France.

My paternal grandmother's mother was **Mary Isabella Douglas** 1839-1914. Her family's links with service in India go back to the mid 18th century - with my great-great-great grandfather, **Peter Douglas**, being a

Hope and Faith

Captain in the East India Company's Navy. It is through this Douglas line, that I can trace nearly 200 years of continuous connection with India - mine is the 6th consecutive generation to have been born or to have served there. Both of my sisters were born in India too - Rosemary in Bangalore in 1931, and Shirley in Quetta (now Pakistan) in 1934. Mary Douglas' mother came from a wealthy, Lowland Scots naval family - her father being **Admiral Sir Archibald Collingwood Dickson** 2nd Baronet. The Dickson family made their wealth in the 18th century, when James Dickson became a Navy Agent in London. This was something like being an insurer of a ship's cargo, taking the risks of loss from storms, piracy, and war. James Dickson particularly profited from trade between Havana, Cuba, and England. In the next few generations there were a remarkable number of Admirals (one of whom was made a baronet) and Generals (one of whom was one of the earliest recipients of the Victoria Cross). They, perhaps more than any of the other families from whom we descend, were achievers of real distinction.

The Douglas family were of the Queensberry Douglases, scions of the Black Douglases [Chapter 10]. There is an interesting and early connection between the Adam, Douglas, and Stewart families. King Robert the Bruce vowed that if he gained the Kingdom of Scotland, he would go on an expedition to the Holy Land. But the threat of invasion from England was ever present, and it was never safe for him to leave Scotland. When he died in 1329, a party of "Seven Trusty Knights" was led by Sir James of Douglas to fulfill the Bruce's vow, by taking his heart for burial in the Holy Land. One of these Knights was Sir Duncan Adam. The expedition foundered in 1330 in Spain, when they stopped off to help King Alfonso XI of Castile in a battle against the Saracen King of Granada. Sir James of Douglas and Sir Duncan Adam were killed, and the heart of the Bruce was brought back to Scotland and buried in Melrose Abbey. From that expedition, the Adam family adopted the crest of a cross crosslet fitchée surmounted of a sword in saltire, with the motto "Crux mihi grata quies"; and the Douglas family adopted into their arms the human heart (later imperially crowned). Through Princess Marjorie

Bruce the Stewarts gained the Crown of Scotland; for she married Walter, 6th High Stewart of Scotland, and their son succeeded as King Robert II.

My mother's family was a complete contrast - English, solidly respectable, mostly long lived, non-Conformist, with (on her mother's side) a strong Puritanical streak. Her maiden name was **Earengey**. This family came, so tradition has it, from Norway in the early 18th century, and settled in Southern Ireland. In the early 19th century, my grandfather's great grandfather came from Ireland and settled in or near Malmesbury. James Earengey, my great grandfather, was a skilled cordwainer (leather cutter in shoe making). My grandfather **William George Earengey** 1876 - 1961 was a typical, and worthy, product of the old Grammar School system (Cheltenham) - well read, a Classical Scholar, and a cultured man. He always wanted to go to the Bar, but started life as a Solicitor, to earn the capital to enable him to become a Barrister. He became a KC [King's Counsel] and ended as a County Court Judge in London. He was a gentle, upright man, of strong ethics - pre-eminently a man of reason and reasoning. I do not think that I ever heard him raise his voice in anger or frustration. My maternal grandmother **Florence How** 1877-1963, was the daughter of a Cheltenham grocer who had invested and prospered in property. Their roots were Devon Yeomen. The How family was formidable - all well-educated and well read, and great fighters of causes, great or small. Grandma was a suffragette. Her older sister, Edith, was imprisoned as a suffragette, and went on to become one of the first women to get an M.Sc from London University, and one of the first women Labour Candidates for Parliament. Grandma too was a graduate of London University. She was one of the early women called to the Bar, and was for many years a Magistrate. She had a more bubbling, electric personality than my grandfather, and was far more vociferous; but she shared his love of culture and of reason. Behind some of the How family, there was a characteristic of hardness. Whilst Grandma Earengey could properly be described as a "femme formidable", that hard quality rarely surfaced in her, and she was a very loving grandmother. She dominated everything she did, by her magnetism and drive, but it was the quiet reason and ethics of Grandpa Earengey that was in the end probably the stronger influence on me.

Chapter 2: The Highland Clan

The fundamental theory underlying clanship is that every member springs from the founder of the clan; and that the chief, the chieftains, the *duine-uasal* (i.e. those who actually trace their descent to the chiefly line) and the body of the clan, are all of the same kin. Clansmen would gather at the signal of the chief, in family council or for the defence of the *duthus*, called to the side of their "*traist cousin*", the chief, by kinship, not for gold. "Class" feeling, as can occur in England, had no part in Highland clanship (or, for that matter, in the great Lowland families) – or at any rate no part until the clan system was destroyed in the aftermath of the Jacobite defeat at Culloden in 1746.

Many of the chiefs had little wealth. Their houses in the 18th century blended sophistication with the primitive. Frequently they contained good pieces of furniture, fine linen and china, and a surprising number of books, yet the floors would be of mud that turned to quagmires after periods of rain. Dr Samuel Johnson told how he stayed at a house where the furnishings and linen in his room were of the highest quality, but when he undressed to go to bed, he found himself standing in mud on a waterlogged earthen floor.

The clan system bred mutual trusts and responsibilities. When Duncan Stewart 7th of Appin signed away Castle Stalker in the 17th century, to Campbell of Airds, in exchange for a rotten 8 oared boat, and then insisted that honour required him to stand by his bargain, the Clan Members met to consider whether they should depose him as Chief. And when, in the 1860s, the then Stewart of Ardsheal put his estate up for sale, an action was brought in Edinburgh, on behalf of other Stewarts of

Ardsheal descent, to stop the sale, the contention being that the land was in reality held in trust for "the Clan" - all the Stewarts of Ardsheal descent. The action failed. But it was seriously argued in Court. It simply could not have got off the ground in England.

Celtic Society had an early clan system, with territorial kings and chiefs presiding over free and classless men of equal right. But beneath them, there was an underclass of men and women enslaved for punishment, or incomers not of the tribe. Primogeniture played little if any part, for under the Celtic law of Tanistry, succession was linear. A brother or even a cousin had as strong a claim to succeed as a son. As a result, transitions in power were often complex and bloody. In certain respects the system was aristocratic - certain family lines were esteemed, and there was a royal class. But it was in no way feudal. Land belonged to no individual - certainly not the chief - but to the whole clan. Office was hereditary, but confined to families, not to individuals. Clans chose their chiefs by election.

Celtic Scotland was far from a united realm. The Hebrides for example were under the rule of the powerful clan Angus, as Lords or Kings of the Isles. The Orkneys and Shetlands were Norwegian. Of mainland Scotland, the Highlands at least were independent of Lowland Rule, and were broken into separate fiefdoms. Much of Argyll came under the Lordship of the Isles. Then the Vikings began to raid the Highlands and Islands. Raids developed into summer settlements, and then into full time settlements. In 871, after generations of raiding, the Hebrides were conquered by King Harald of Norway, and for the next 370 years, they were ruled by assorted Viking Jarls. A separate Norse Kingdom of the Isles was established, in place of that held by Clan Angus, though still theoretically under the Kingdom of Norway, and Viking control (though not Kingdoms) spread through the western Highlands. At first they held the Celts in thrall, but fairly soon conditions relaxed, Vikings and Gaels intermarried, the Vikings began to speak Gaelic, and Norse or Viking culture was merged with that of the Gaels. The Celtic clan system was then developed under Viking Rule. Its characteristics were classless-ness; democratic decision making; mutual inter-dependence; trust in the Chief;

duty of the Chief towards his clansmen; and land, apart from the immediate surrounds of a homestead, was held for all the clan - it was not held the personal property of the Chief.

There were three important consequences of Viking raids and Viking settlements - first, the Celtic Church was finally broken; second, (inadvertently) they forced the unification of mainland Scotland; and third for nearly 400 years, the Islands (and to a lesser extent the Highlands) were free of the feudal system sweeping in from England and Europe.

The Celtic Church, whatever it was, was not Roman Catholic. The Roman Church was diocesan and episcopal, with authority rigidly held through a hierarchy of bishops. At local level it operated from a church where mass was said by a friar. The Celtic Church was Presbyterian and monastic. It operated from monasteries - communities administered by an abbot or presbyter assisted by elders. There was an office of bishop. But bishops had no authority over the abbots, and no precedence. Their function was consecration and ordination. It was a more fragmented arm of Christendom. The Celtic Church had high regard for the Sabbath, which was kept strictly. Monasteries were not fortresses of refuge from the world, but existed for two purposes - the spreading of learning and education, and evangelism. Above all they acknowledged no head of the Church save "Our Lord". In this, they anticipated post Reformation Presbyterianism.

Two major differences bitterly divided the Celtic and Roman Churches - first, diversity challenged the temporal power of Rome; and second, the dating of Easter was almost explosively controversial. As to that, things came to a head at the Synod of Whitby in 664. It was convened to decide how to date Easter, and came down on the Roman side. From then on, the Northumbrian Church grew distant from Iona, looked southwards, and Roman Catholicism spread throughout England.

In successive raids on Scotland the Vikings slaughtered monks and destroyed monasteries, churches, vestments, and holy books. They destroyed Iona Abbey four times - in 795. 806, 825, and again in 968. As a result of this mayhem, it became impossible to maintain a coherent whole, and Celtic clergy became increasingly solitaries, wanderers, hermits. At the time, the Vikings were of the Teutonic faith, and by nature were tolerant of other faiths. It seems that their slaughter of monks and mayhem of the Celtic Church, done for the greater glory of Odin and Thor, was itself a reaction to the persecution of their own religion in Europe, by Charlemagne. Ironically, in the eleventh century, the Vikings embraced Christianity. But by then it was too late to save the Celtic Church.

By the eleventh century, mainland Scotland was reasonably united under Malcolm III - "Malcolm Canmore". It was his marriage that was the final death-knell of the Celtic Church. He married an English Princess, Margaret, who was a thorough going Romanist, thoroughly English, who had nothing but contempt for the Gaelic language and the Celtic Church. She pressed her husband into wide-reaching Church reforms and innovations. The process was continued by their son, David I. By the end of the twelfth century, the Celtic Church had ceased to be.

For free Norsemen, things were most democratic. Land was held in absolute title by inheritance, not by the goodwill of any feudal superior. It could be bequeathed to children. There was no rent, except civic and occasionally military. A new settler had the right to water and wood, and to as much land as lay within a knife throw of the park – bye land – about his house, his *stadr*, as long as he fenced it within a year. At the centre of every township - *tun* - was the main farm, *bolstadr*; the outlying pasture, beyond the bye-land, was the *saetr*. The collective rights, on common pastures or fishing grounds, were administered by a constable, *hersir*, over a district, *herad*. From this derives the name *na Hearadh*, the *Herries* or Harris.

Measures of land were named and valued on a standard based on weights of silver. Every homestead paid one penny a year as skatt or (civic) rent. Hence "Penny lands".

The Norse governed by a series of Councils, dealing with different spheres of secular and religious life. In these, every freeman had one vote. This included the vote to grant (or withhold) supplies from the sovereign, who thus could not wage war (or make peace) without their consent. Their laws were based on a vigorous democratic morality. Swindling was a serious crime, but a starving man who stole food would not be punished. Chieftainship was elective, not hereditary.

Women had extensive rights, not recovered until the twentieth century. They could own property in their own right and had a recognised share in any marital holding. They could win divorce if they proved ill treatment or brutality by their husband; and they could be divorced for adultery. Otherwise a marriage bond could only be severed by mutual consent.

The Vikings were good farmers, unparalleled seamen, and skilled at sports - hunting, falconry, football, and wrestling . They made music, and delighted in verse and story. They could write, but their stories were in the main handed down the generations by word of mouth, a tradition which continued up to modern times in the Highlands.

Viking rule came under two challenges - in mainland Scotland, the impetus was for development of the Kingdom into a united mainland, as a defence against marauding Norsemen. That was broadly achieved by the eleventh century. Vikings remained, but under the sovereignty of the Kingdom of Scotland. As for their rule over the Isles, in about 1130 Somerled came on the scene. He was born in Ireland in about 1105. His father was Gillebride of Clan Angus, the true (but exiled) King of Argyll. His mother was Norse, a princess, daughter of the King of Man. In about 1130, Somerled returned to Argyll with his father. They roused the people of Morvern, and drove the Vikings out of Argyll. Somerled became King of Argyll, and quickly made his peace with Olav the Red, the new King of Man, and even married his daughter Ragnild. No one went to war with Olav the Red. He was deemed invincible - his power was naval, founded on his fleet of longboats, mighty rowers, skilled navigators, and tough fighting men. Olav died in 1152, and was succeeded by his son Godred, who was a despot. Somerled saw his chance of taking the Hebrides, but first he had to develop a fleet to match those of the King of Man. The Viking longboat had one major weakness: it had no rudder. It was steered by a plank on the right hand side of the ship - the "steering-board" or "starboard". Somerled developed the hinged rudder that enabled him to outmanoeuvre the Viking longboats. On 6th January 1156, they fought off the west coast of Islay. The Vikings were broken - the first sea battle that they had lost. Somerled proposed terms to the King of Man. Godred took the outer Isles, Skye and Raasay. Somerled took everything else: all the Argyll Hebrides and the islands of the Firth of Clyde. Thus he became "Lord of the Isles", with Islay as his base.

When Malcolm IV succeeded David I in 1153, he began to demand the surrender of Somerled's mainland territories to the Scottish Kingdom. Somerled tried to force the issue. He sailed up the Clyde at the head of a fleet of 160 ships and 10,000 men. He marched to Renfrew to meet Walter Fitz-Alan (the First High Stewart). The meeting was cordial, but that night Somerled was murdered in his tent. The schism between Highlands and Lowlands which Somerled had hoped to bridge, became permanent. His three sons split his lands - Ragnall got Islay, Kintyre, and his father's fleet. Dougall took Lorne and the other Argyll Islands. Angus took Arran and Bute. [Ragnall's son, Donald, was the progenitor of Clan Donald - who were to assume the surname MacDonald].

In 1196, William the Lion threw the Vikings out of north Scotland. In 1263 King Haakon of Norway had his last throw. The fleet that he sent was battered to bits in storms, and his army suffered a crushing defeat. King Alexander III seized Skye and the Hebrides. Three years later, Norway formally ceded them in the Treaty of Perth. Angus, King of the Isles, was forced to acknowledge the superiority of the King of Scotland. The feudal system then became imposed on the whole of Scotland.

Feudalism was an import from Europe. It came to England with the Norman Conquest. David I of Scotland, the son of King Malcolm III and Queen Margaret, was brought up in his mother's native England. Before returning to Scotland, he married a wealthy widow, and through her, acquired lands in England, thereby making himself a vassal of the English King. When he returned to Scotland as King, he brought with him a train of some 1,000 Anglo-Norman adventurers, Bruces, Montgomerys, and others, to whom he distributed vast tracts of land, evicting the original owners. He rapidly introduced feudalism to Scotland. Its attractions to a King were obvious. Underlying the feudal system was the theory that the

King was the ultimate power, and that all land was held of the King. Successive grants were made by Feudal Landlords down the chain. But the King's power reached everywhere; and if a feudal tenant committed treason, then his lands were forfeited to the Crown as the feudal superior. When that happened, all those down the chain below the feudal landlord also lost their rights of tenure. This brought great upset and hardship.

Feudalism brought, in theory at least, complete power and control to the Crown. Neither Kings nor Chiefs held office any more by election, but by inheritance. It was a retrograde step for the subjects of the King. It introduced, at its worst, a rigid class system. It denied democracy. Carried to its logical conclusion, it brought the Tudor concept of absolute monarchy, which was developed by James VI & I and by Charles I into the Divine Right of Kings.

Robert I - Robert the Bruce - and the Stewart Kings who succeeded King David II, developed the feudal system remorselessly. Robert I demanded Charters of the Highland Chiefs. They had none, so he granted Charters over lands which had been theirs (including Clan land) by inheritance and by conquest for generations, from times when there were no Kings to grant Charters. In this way, the tentacles of centralised power under the Sovereign replaced the old democracy. Yet despite the feudal system, within the Clan the tradition of equality, classless-ness, and inter-responsibility and inter-dependence continued from the Vikings.

It is ironic that one of the sores which the exiled Stuarts promised to change, if they regained the Crown, was the very feudal system which their ancestors had so determinedly maintained. This was one of the reasons for Jacobite support in the Highlands.

One effect of the '45 was to destroy the old clan system. Kilts and tartans were banned. Chiefs were forced into exile. Slaughter in and destruction of the Highlands was on a massive scale. Estates were forfeited to the Crown. The Forfeited Estates Commission added to this. They wanted longer leases of land to be granted, with larger blocks of land to each lessee (or "tacksman"); and they pursued policies of enclosing land for sheep. It was the start of what would develop into the Highland

Clearances. The triple factors of the drive for higher rents on tacks; bad weather over successive years in the Highlands (especially the Western Isles); and poverty and deprivation, led to large scale emigration to America, starting in the second half of the 1760's and increasing in the 1770's. Our Ross forebears Robert & Catherine Ross [parents of Ann Stewart or Ross, who died 1835-1836] went to Ullapool to emigrate, but then changed their minds [this was probably in the 1780's; Hugh, their oldest son was born in 1787].

But it was not all voluntary emigration. After Culloden, many chiefs had become absentees, leaving estates to be managed by outside Factors or Agents purely for profit. Other estates were sold, bringing in outsiders as Landlords. The old ties were severed, and the tenants at the bottom came to be treated as disposable human trash. Human greed for profit became the driving force. Sheep were brought in to replace humans. Naturally good pasture land, which had been enriched by cattle over generations, became stripped and impoverished. When sheep ceased to be profitable in the 19th century, the sporting estates took over instead, where once there had been settlements of people.

The tenants were cleared off their land often at sword or gun point, often with loss of life. They were denied the benefit of any improvements that they made to land or property. Landlords rigged the system so that abject poverty and sometimes starvation became common place. Many were forced to emigrate to North America in leaky ships brought in by the Landlords, or later to Australia and New Zealand. In some cases, people were herded into ships with no property other than the clothes that they wore; and some were even seized by particularly unscrupulous and unsavoury dealers, and sold into slavery in the Caribbean and elsewhere. The Clan system, with its tradition of duty and responsibility of the Chief towards his Clan, and vice versa, had gone forever.

Chapter 3: The House of Stewart

Breton Origins

The descent of the Stewarts from Fleance, son of Banquo, recounted by Shakespeare in Macbeth, is now considered to be wholly mythical. Shakespeare's source was Hollinshed, who wrote good tales, but was not a sound historian. The scholarship of several generations has now shown that the origin of the Stewarts is Breton.

1. **Hamon, Vicomte of Dinan**, whose castle was at Combourg near Dol, was Lord of Dinan and Dol in the early 11th century. His wife was **Raentlina**. The roots of this family, as rulers of that part of Brittany known as Armorica, go back to Roman times. They had a son **Rhiwallon**, who succeeded to the castle of Combourg, and to the Lordship of Dol. His wife was **Aremburga**, and with the consent of their 4 sons and their daughter, they gave the church of St Mary at Combourg, to the Benedictine Abbey of Marmoutier, near Tours – Charter of 1032-1064. His overlord was named as Conan, Count or Duke of Brittany.

2. **Flaald, Seneschal of Dol de Bretagne** – the progenitor of the Stewarts – was probably a younger brother or nephew of this Rhiwallon. He witnessed the Charter referred to above. He had a younger brother, Haton, who witnessed a Charter of William, Lord of Dol, 1065 – 1070. The office of Seneschal of Dol was of key importance in the household, its essential purpose being to keep the Exchequer in order. Flaald was succeeded by his son:

3. **Alan "dapifer" of Dol** – the food bearer – c.1080 –who also became Seneschal of Dol. This Alan had 3 sons:

    [i]   Alan (the younger), dapifer of Dol, who volunteered for the Crusade called by Pope Urban II in 1095. He fought on this crusade, and was killed on it.

    [ii]   **Flaald**, of whom hereafter.

    [iii]   Rhiwallon, a monk of the Abbey of St Florent de Saumur, near Dol.

From the Duchy of Normandy to the Kingdom of England 1100

1. **Flaald**, son of Alan, attached himself to the rising star of Henry I, the 3rd son of William the Conqueror. When King William died in 1087, his oldest son, Robert Curthose, succeeded only to Normandy, and the second son William Rufus succeeded to England. There followed great rivalry between these two brothers, which was interrupted by Duke Robert going on the First Crusade (1096 – 1101). This accounted for Duke Robert being far away when William Rufus was fatally shot by an arrow in the New Forest in 1100. Henry saw his chance, came over to England, and seized the Kingdom as King Henry 1st. As it happens, 6 years later, at the Battle of Tinchebrai in 1106, Henry conquered Normandy from Robert, and from then up to his death in 1135, he built the Norman Empire into a power greater than was ever again to be seen.

    Flaald Fitz Alan followed Henry to England in 1100, and settled there, acquiring lands in Norfolk, and around Oswestry in Shropshire. By his wife, **Aveline de Hesdin,** he had 3 sons:

    [i]   Jordan Fitz Alan, who succeeded as Seneschal of Dol.

    [ii]   William Fitz Alan, who succeeded as Lord of Oswestrie and died c.1160. His descendants kept the name Fitz Alan, and became (feudal) Earls of Arundel 1290 – 1580, (a feudal earldom being one in which the title follows the ownership of the lands).

Eventually the heiress of the Fitzalan Earls of Arundel married Thomas Howard, 4th Duke of Norfolk – hence Fitzalan Howard, Dukes of Norfolk (and still Earls of Arundel) today.

[iii]   **Walter,** who settled in Scotland, as set out below.

High Stewarts of Scotland

2.   **Walter Fitz Alan, 3rd son of Alan Fitz Flaald, and 1st High Stewart of Scotland,** was in Scotland by 1136. In 1164, he commanded the Scots Army, which either defeated in battle, or murdered in his tent, Somerled, Lord of the Isles. Following this, he was created hereditary High Stewart of Scotland. This was one of the most important offices under the Crown, and involved, just as the office of Seneschal did in Dol, keeping the Royal Exchequer in order.

Walter acquired extensive lands in Renfrewshire and East Lothian. In 1164 he founded Paisley Abbey, a Cluniac Order found also in Shropshire and originating in Brittany. From this base, the Stewart landholdings extended to Cunninghame in Ayrshire, and at a later date included the Earldom of Carrick and the Lordships of Galloway and Bute. He died in 1177, and was succeeded by his son, Alan.

Stewart Coats of Arms

Alan, 2nd High Stewart of Scotland, is known to have used the fesse chequy azure and argent for his Arms, to represent the counting or exchequer board used by the High Stewart, from at least 1190, for they appear on his seal in that year – see Plate 1 of "The Heraldry of the Stewarts" by G Harvey Johnston, published in Edinburgh & London in 1906.

Ever since, all Stewart Coats of Arms have incorporated the "fesse chequy azure and argent" with two exceptions - the Royal Stewarts and the Menteiths. Robert, the 7th and last High Stewart, kept the fesse chequy for his Arms until he succeeded to the throne as King Robert II in 1371.

He then adopted the Arms of Scotland in lieu of the fesse chequy. The Menteiths were the earliest cadets of the House, Walter Stewart, 1st Earl of Menteith, being a son of Walter 3rd High Stewart. Within a couple of generations, they had adopted the surname "Menteith" in lieu of "Stewart", and the fesse chequy in their Arms changed to a bend chequy. [The Heraldry of the Stewarts, Plate VI].

Alan, 2nd High Stewart, died in 1204, and was succeeded by his son, Walter.

Adoption of the Surname of Stewart, or Stuart or Steuart

3. **Walter, 3rd High Stewart,** was the first to adopt a surname for his family and descendants, taking the name "Stewart" from his Office.

"Stewart" being the earliest way of spelling the name, and the spelling that has survived the centuries in Scotland, is the proper Scots spelling. Many Stewarts, however, went and lived abroad – for many centuries up to the French Revolution, for example, there was a Scots Regiment in the French Army. Because the French find a "w" difficult to cope with, the custom came about that those going to work on the mainland of Europe, generally spelt their surname phonetically "Stuart" or "Steuart". One of the earliest examples of the use of such phonetic spelling of the name as "Stuart" in France is provided by the Stuarts of Aubigny – who were of the family of the Stewart Earls of Lennox in Scotland. One of the best known, though least worthy, of that family was Henry Stewart, Lord Darnley (as he was known in England: properly he should have been called the Master of Lennox). He was the second husband of Mary Queen of Scots, and their child succeeded as James VI & I. As it happens, the first Royal Stewart to use the spelling "Stuart" was Mary Queen of Scots, because she was brought up from early childhood in France, her first husband being the Dauphin. Despite school history books, the Royal Stewarts were generally spelt "Stewart" in Scotland, and adopted the phonetic spelling "Stuart" only when living in France, for Mary Queen of Scots, or after James II went into exile living at first in France, and later on in Italy. Even the execution warrant for Charles I referred to the King as Charles Stewart.

One of the reasons why so many bear the name Stewart today, is that it was adopted as a surname so early. Walter, 3rd High Stewart, died in 1246, and was succeeded by his son Alexander.

St James of Compostella – Patron Saint of the House of Stewart

4. **Alexander, 4th High Stewart,** was born in 1214, and died in 1283. He was also known as Alexander of Dundonald, after his castle in Ayrshire. It was he who founded the cult of St James in Scotland, and in around 1252 he went on a pilgrimage to the shrine of St James at Compostella in Spain. Hence St James of Compostella became the patron Saint of the House of Stewart.

   Alexander had a numerous family among who were James 5th High Stewart, and Sir John Stewart de Bonkyl, of both of whom hereafter.

Succession to the Throne of Scotland 1371 & adoption of the White Rose as an emblem of the Stewarts

5. **James, 5th High Stewart,** was born about 1243, married Egidia, sister of Richard de Burgh, Earl of Ulster, and died 1309.

6. **Walter, 6th High Stewart,** who succeeded his father, James, 5th High Stewart in 1309, was born in 1292. He commanded part of the Scots Army at Bannockburn in 1314, and in 1315 he married **Princess Marjorie Bruce**, the daughter of Robert the Bruce (King Robert I). Her only brother was King David II, who in the event was childless.

7. Thus it was that Walter and Marjorie's son, **Robert,** who was born in 1316, succeeded his father as **7th High Stewart,** and subsequently succeeded his uncle David II as King of Scotland. In the meanwhile,

he was declared heir to the throne in 1318, created Earl of Atholl 1342, and Earl of Strathearn 1358.

For many years David II was held captive in England. During his captivity, in 1349, it is recorded that a tournament was held at Windsor. The housings of the Scottish King's charger were of blue velvet

"with a pale of red velvet, and beneath a white rose embroidered thereon".

David II was eventually released from captivity, and returned to Scotland. When he died in 1371, his heir was his nephew, Robert, 7th High Stewart, who succeeded to the throne of Scotland as **King Robert II**. The emblem of the white rose, which was adopted by David II in England, continued in use as an emblem of the House of Stewart. This is the reason why so many Jacobite glasses were engraved with a White Rose and 2 Buds (for James the Old Pretender, and his 2 sons, Bonnie Prince Charlie, and Henry Cardinal Duke of York).

From Robert II are descended all the Royal Stewarts – though no legitimate descendants in the male line survive. The last in the direct line was Henry, Cardinal-Duke of York. When he died in 1807, he left to King George III the coronation ring of James II. By the Scots (Celtic) law of Tanistry, this "legitimated" the Hanoverian succession to the throne.

Main Branches before the Stewart succession to the Throne

1. Though Alexander 4th High Stewart had a number of children, it is only necessary to mention one of the younger sons, **Sir John Stewart de Bonkyl,** who was the forebear of the Stewarts

    [i]   Earls of Angus
    [ii]   Earls of Galloway
    [iii] of Blantyre

[iv]   of Atholl

[v]   **of Lorn and Appin**, of whom hereafter.

[vi]   of Buchan

Main Branches after the Stewart succession to the Throne

1.   King Robert II had several legitimate sons:

[i]   His heir, John, who in 1390 succeeded as King Robert III.

[ii]   Walter, who married Isabella, Countess of Fife, and predeceased his father in about 1362, having no issue.

[iii] Robert, Duke of Albany d. 1420. He had a legitimate son and heir, Murdoch, Duke of Albany, who was beheaded at Stirling in 1425 along with his legitimate sons, Walter & Alexander. Duke Murdoch also had at least 2 illegitimate sons

    I.   James, who was the progenitor of many *Stewarts in Balquhidder*, the most prominent of which now are the *Stewarts of Ardvorlich*.

    II.   Walter, who was the progenitor of the *Earls of Caste Stewart* and of the *Earls of Moray*.

[iv]   Alexander, Earl of Buchan – the Wolf of Badenoch – one of the really bad Stewarts in the history of the House. He had a dispute with the Bishop of Moray concerning certain Church lands, which Alexander wanted. The Bishop had Alexander excommunicated for this and for living in sin with his mistresses. Alexander retaliated by destroying the seat of the Bishop at Elgin, and Elgin Cathedral itself, which was "the mirror of the country and the glory of the Kingdom". Eventually the excommunication was lifted, and when Alexander died, he was buried in Dunkeld Cathedral, where his tomb was inscribed "bonae memoriae". The Wolf left no legitimate heirs, but he was the progenitor of many *Stewarts in*

Atholl, and of many *Stewarts in Aberdeenshire, Banff, and Moray*. His illegitimate sons and their descendants include:

I.   *Alexander Stewart, Earl of Mar*, who died in 1435 or 1436. He married, firstly, in 1404 Isabel daughter of William 1st Earl of Douglas, by Margaret de Mar, heiress of Mar. They had no issue. But through the marriage, Alexander Stewart became Earl of Mar. He married, secondly, Jane, daughter of the Earl of Holland - and again had no issue. He had one illegitimate son, Thomas. Although this Earl of Mar had no legitimate descendants, the cross-crosslet of Mar appears in the arms of many of the descendants of his brothers. It may be that since as Earl of Mar he was granting lands, so the expectation would be that the donees' coats of armour would reflect that the land had been part of the lands of the Earldom of Mar.

II. *Sir Andrew Stewart*, ancestor of the *Stewarts of Auchlunkart, Tannachy, Drummin*. It is notable that Auchlunkart & Drummin had in their arms 3 cross crosslets fitchees in chief, above the usual fesse chequy.

III. *Walter Stewart*, first of the *Stewarts of Kinchardin in Strathspey*, of which he got a Charter in the first year of the reign of Robert III (1390). Their arms were a fesse chequy between 3 open crowns.- see G Harvey Johnston's "Heraldry of the Stewarts". According to Duncan Stewart 1739 *"Most of the Stewarts in Strathspey, Murray, and Inverness are come of Kinchardin"*. Walter Stewart of Kinchardin, mid 17th century had a son, Robert, who married a daughter of Angus Williamson, Tutor of MacIntosh, and had 3 sons:

a. Alexander, father of Baillie John Stewart in Inverness, who died c. 1752

b. John, father of David Stewart, Collector in Inverness.

c. Angus who had several sons

One of the Kinchardin Stewarts was the renowned Jacobite, John Roy Stewart, who was also known for his Gaelic and English verse. He was created a baronet by James VII & II, but ironically the patent was for a baronetcy of "Great Britain" – an entity which the Stewarts had never recognised.

IV. James, from whom descend the Stewarts of Fothergill & Garth and the Stewarts of Balnakeilly.

V. Duncan

Robert II, however, also had many illegitimate sons, amongst whom was Sir John Stewart, Heritable Sheriff of Bute, from whom descend *the Stewarts, Marquises of Bute.*

Senior Branch of the House of Stewart

All descendants of the Royal Stewarts bearing the name Stewart (however spelt) are illegitimate, for instance, the Earls of Moray and the Marquesses of Bute. The senior legitimate branch is that of the Earls of Galloway, who descend from Alexander, 4th High Stewart, through Sir John Stewart de Bonkyl.

Hope and Faith

Notes & Sources:

1. There are a number of books about the origins of the Stewarts, e.g.

   - The Story of the Stewarts – The Stewart Society 1901
   - History of the Stewarts by Duncan Stewart, Edinburgh, 1730
   - The Stewart Dynasty by Stewart Ross (Thomas & Lochar, 1993).

2. On the Breton origin & its details, see the Article by the scholarly George Washington in "The Stewarts" – the magazine of the Stewart Society – Vol XII p. 143.

3. "The Heraldry of the Stewarts", G Harvey Johnston, Edinburgh & London, 1906.

Chapter 4: The Stewarts of Appin

Chapter 1: **Sir John Stewart of Bonkyl** (in Berwickshire) was the second son of Alexander 4th High Stewart. He was born 1246, and was killed at Falkirk 1298. He married Margaret, daughter of Sir Alexander Bonkyl of that Ilk. His issue included:

[i] Sir Alexander Stewart of Bonkyl, whose son John was created Earl of Angus. This title and the estates of Bonkyl ultimately passed to the Douglases.

[ii] Sir Alan Stewart of Dreghorn in Ayrshire, who was killed at the Battle of Halidon Hill in 1333. From him descend:

- the Lords of Darnley & Aubigny; & the Earls & Dukes of Lennox
- the Earls of Galloway & their cadets, the Stuarts of Castlemilk
- the Stewarts of Barclay, Physgill, and Castle Stewart

[iii] Sir Walter Stewart of Dalswinton

[iv] Sir James Stewart of Preston & Warwickhill in Cunninghame. of whom hereafter.

[v] Sir John Stewart of Daldon, who was killed at the battle of Halidon Hill 1333, apparently leaving no issue.

[vi] Sir Robert Stewart of Dalduie in Lanarkshire, from whom descend the Steuarts of Allanton.

[vii] Sir Hugh Stewart, who apparently died without issue.

[viii] Isabel, who married Thomas Randolph, first Earl of Moray.

2. **Sir James Stewart of Preston** (also known as Peristoun or Perston) & Warwickhill in Cunninghame in Ayrshire, who had a Charter of those lands from King Robert the Bruce, was present at the battle of Bannockburn in 1314, and killed at the Battle of Halidon Hill, 19th July 1333. The name iof his wife has not been recorded. He left issue:

[i]   Sir John Stewart of Perston

[ii] Sir Alan Stewart of Ochiltree, in Ayrshire

[iii] Sir Robert Stewart of Schanbothy.

3. **Sir Robert Stewart of Schanbothy** [in Clackmannan] & Lord of Innermeath [now Invermay in Perthshire] third son of Sir James Stewart of Preston, died in 1387, leaving issue:

[i]   Sir John Stewart, of whom hereafter

[ii] Sir Robert Stewart who inherited Schanbothy, ancestor of the Stewarts of Rosyth in Fife & Craigiehall in Linlithgowshire. He married Janet, elder daughter & heiress of John de Ergadia, Lord of Lorn. He subsequently surrendered Lorn to his brother Sir John Stewart, in exchange for Durrisdeer, by a Charter dated 13th April 1388.

4. **Sir John Stewart of Innermeath**, 1st Lord of Lorn, married Isabel de Ergadia, daughter and co-heiress of John MacAlan de Ergadia [or MacDougall] Lord of Lorn. He resigned Durrisdeer to his brother Robert in exchange for the Lordship of Lorn. He also received a confirmatory charter from King Robert II of the lands of Lorn, including Apthane, resigned by his brother. The family of Macdougall of Lorn to whose estates Sir John now succeeded is of great antiquity. And he quartered the galley of the Macdougalls with his paternal coat of arms, giving it precedence in the first and fourth quarters to the fesse chequy of the Stewarts. At the same time he dropped the Bonkyl buckles which had been assumed by his father as a mark of cadency. This John was illustrative of the Royal Stewart policy, of gradually extending their control over the Highlands with their own kin. He had issue:

[i]   Robert, of whom hereafter.

[ii]   Archibald

[iii]   Sir James Stewart, the Black Knight of Lorn, who married Lady Joan Beaufort, grand-daughter of John of Gaunt, and widow of King James II. Their son John was created Earl of Athole in 1457. In 1476, this Earl of Athole was sent by his nephew King James III to subdue the resistance to the royal authority of the last Lord of the Isles. The King bade Athole to "Go forth, have good fortune, and fill the fetters with prisoners". From this the motto of the Lords of Atholl has been ever since "Furth fortune and fill the fetters". Eventually, the heiress of the Stewart Earldom of Atholl married William Murray, 2nd Earl of Tullibardine. Thus the Atholl estate, including Blair Castle, passed to the Stewart Murrays, later Dukes of Atholl.

[iv]   Alexander, 1st of Grandtully, Perthshire.

[v]   William

5. **Sir Robert Stewart** 2nd Lord of Lorn & Innermeath who married in 1409 Margaret, daughter of Robert Stewart, 1st Duke of Albany. They had issue

[i]   John, of whom hereafter

[ii]   Walter Stewart, subsequently of Innermeath

[iii]   Alan, who seems to have had no issue

[iv]   David, Bishop of Moray from 1463 to 1477

[v]   Robert, of whom no records remain.

6. **Sir John Stewart**, 3rd Lord of Lorn, was murdered at Dunstaffnage on 20th December 1463. By his first wife he had 3 daughters each of whom married a Campbell:

[i]   Isabel, m Colin Campbell, 1st Earl of Argyll

[ii]   Margaret, m Sir Colin Campbell of Glenorchy

[iii]   Marion, m Arthur Campbell of Ottar.

By a daughter of McLaren of Ardveich in Balquhidder, he had a son, born out of wedlock - Dugald, b 1445. Sir John determined to legitimate Dugald (in Scots Law this could be achieved by marrying the mother) so as to make him his heir. In order to secure Macdougall friendship for his son, he made considerable grants of land, including Dunolly Castle, the ancestral stronghold of the Macdougalls, to the Chief, John M'Allan Macdougall, with remainder to his son, John Keir Macdougall. Having done this, he then surrendered Lorn and Innermeath in exchange for a new Charter from King James II in 1452, granting Lorn and Innermeath to Sir John Stewart and his heirs male. This Charter thus excluded the Campbells from the succession to those Lordships, albeit Sir John made generous provision for his daughters from other properties.

In the late 1450s, Lady Lorn died. Sir John was therefore at last free to legitimate his son Dugald, by marrying his son's mother. The marriage was delayed because of the intrigues between John, Lord of the Isles and Earl of Ross, the King of England, and the Earl of Douglas, starting in 1459, and culminating in 1461 with the infamous agreement known as the Treaty of Ardtornish, under which Scotland was to be partitioned into 3 principalities, each of which was to be subject to the English Crown. The agent of the plotters in Argyll was Alan MacCoul, an illegitimate grandson of an earlier Macdougall chieftain. By 1463, the revolt had almost burnt itself out, and the wedding of Sir John Stewart to his McLaren bride was fixed for 20th December 1463. Alan MacCoul - Alan Dubh - was still being paid by the Lord of the Isles to weaken the defences of Argyll, and plotted to undermine and remove the royalist Lord of Lorn. As the wedding party approached Dunstaffnage, Alan Dubh and his band attacked it, and fatally wounded Sir John. Dugald was for setting off in pursuit of Alan Dubh, but Sir John, realising his condition, called him back. A priest was sent for, and the ceremony was hastily conducted with the dying man.

7.   **Dugald Stewart** de jure Lord of Lorn; 1st of Appin. 1445 - 1497[1].

As a result of the murder of his father, Dugald at the age of 18 became de jure Lord of Lorn. But too many other people had an interest in the succession for his rights to be accepted without question - Alan MacCoul (who had seized the Castle of Dunstaffnage), the Campbells, and his own uncle Walter Stewart of Innermeath. Dugald had to contend with all 3 factions, and in the end gained only part of his patrimony - Appin. Colin Campbell, Lord Argyll, and Campbell of Glenorchy, did not wish to use Campbell military force to get rid of Dugald if that could be avoided. So they got their kinsman Duncan MacFarlane, 6th chief of the MacFarlanes, from western Loch Lomond to come to the military aid of Alan MacCoul. Dugald Stewart went back to Balquhidder to get help from the MacLarens. On his return the fierce and bloody battle of Leac-a-dotha near Dalmally took place. There were heavy losses on both sides, and Dugald retreated into Appin, the northern part of Lorn, to prepare to defend that against all comers.

Meanwhile, his uncle Walter Stewart, supported by the Earl of Argyll, reported John Stewart's murder to the Privy Council in Edinburgh, stated that no marriage had taken place, and claimed to be Lord of Lorn. The Privy Council duly reported this to the youthful James III and to the Estates. In 1464 the Privy Council belatedly ordered royal troops to Dunstaffnage to retake the Castle and to punish Alan MacCoul. But none got there; and neither Walter Stewart nor the Campbells took any steps to avenge the murder of Sir John Stewart. Far from that, Walter supplied Alan MacCoul with money and mercenaries to continue war with his "illegitimate nephew". But significantly Walter dared not go anywhere near Lorn where he was detested. Dugald was unanimously accepted in Appin as Chief - the principal families supporting him being the Livingstones, the Carmichaels, and the MacColls.

In 1468, the Campbells and Walter Stewart decided on a major offensive to get rid of Dugald, and supplied Alan MacCoul with money and mercenaries to invade Appin. There in Appin the battle of

Stalc took place. Dugald personally slew Alan MacCoul, and the rest of MacCoul's militia were slaughtered to a man.

Walter Stewart realised that he would never physically succeed to Lorn; and Dugald realised that the might of the Campbells of Argyll and their allies was too great to give him any hope of holding onto any more than Appin. No help lay in Edinburgh, because Argyll was too powerful as Justiciar of Scotland, and James III was still a minor. Reluctantly in the autumn of 1469 Dugald consented to the terms proposed by Argyll and Walter, under which he ceded his rights to the Lordships of Innermeath and of Lorn, save for Appin, to Walter, but he would keep Appin, to be held direct of the Crown. On 28th March 1470, Walter took seisin of Lorn. On 14th April 1470, Walter resigned the title and lands of the Lordship of Lorn to King James III. 3 days later James III granted the Lordship of Lorn to the Earl of Argyll. In this shameful and treacherous way the Earl of Argyll became the most powerful of the Campbells, and Walter Stewart acquired Innermeath. But Dugald Stewart at least was left with most of Appin.

Dugald Stewart married a daughter of John Macdougall of Macdougall, and had 3 sons:

[i]   Duncan, II of Appin,
[ii]   Alan, III of Appin, of whom hereafter
[iii] Robert, who died without legitimate issue. From his natural son, Alan, descend the sept M'Rob or MacRob, "Sliochd Ailein 'ic Rob", renowned as the backbone of the Stewarts of Appin from their ability to muster so many fighting men.

In 1497 Dugald went to the aid of the MacLarens who were facing attack by the MacDonalds of Keppoch. The MacDonalds were routed in a battle in Glenorchy, but Dugald was killed.

8. **Duncan Stewart II** of Appin was recognised by James IV as his kinsman, and appointed the King's Chamberlain of the Isles. James IV could not restore the Lordship of Lorn, for this had been held for 30 years by the Campbells with the consent of his predecessor James III and Parliament. But he bestowed many lands on Duncan extending

from Loch Creran in the south to Inverlochy in the north. Thereby Duncan gained lands of similar value and extent as the Lordship of Lorn. Significantly by a Charter of 1500 James recognised Duncan's hereditary right to Appin. In 1501, Sir Duncan Campbell of Glenorchy restored to Duncan the one third part of Appin which Glenorchy had received in 1470. And on 24th September 1501, the Earl of Argyll and Sir Duncan Campbell bound themselves to recognise Duncan Stewart as the legal possessor of the forty pounds lands of Appin "held in heritage by his deceased father, Dugald Stewart of Appin". James IV visited the west Highlands many times, and it was for him that Duncan rebuilt Castle Stalker for James IV, as a hunting lodge as it had originally been for the Lords of Lorn. The castle sits romantically just off shore, in Loch Linnhe, on the Cormorant's Rock.

The bestowal of lands and powers by James IV on Duncan, caused a simmering resentment in the MacLeans. The last straw was the granting of Lochaber territories in 1512. Not realising this bitterness, Duncan accepted an invitation in 1512 by Lachlan MacLean of Duart to go to Duart Castle, and went accompanied only by his Gille, Sorley MacColl. After 3 days of lavish entertainment, Duncan was savagely murdered and his body was left lying between Duart Castle and the shore. He was buried at Lismore Cathedral. Being unmarried, he was succeeded by his brother Alan.

9. **Alan Stewart III of Appin** led the clan at Flodden on 9th September 1513. He had lands in Lismore from Campbell of Glenorchy, and had them regranted to his grandson John, V of Appin. He fought at Flodden, and is said either to have been killed there, or to have died at an advanced age in 1562. He married a daughter of Cameron of Lochiel and had 5 sons:

[i]   Duncan Stewart, IV of Appin
[ii]   John Stewart, 1st of Strathgarry (first family of that name)
[iii] Dugald Stewart, 1st of Achnacone.

Achnacone is the only Stewart house in Appin still to remain in Stewart hands. In the 1820s, the then Stewart of Achnacone went bankrupt from sheep farming. He sold Achnacone to another Stewart, whose daughter married old Achnacone's oldest son. Thus the estate came back into the original family. Brigadier Ian Stewart, 13th of Achnacone, was the epitome of a gallant, courteous, highlander. He won 2 Military Crosses in the First World War. In the Second World War, he was in command of the Argyll & Sutherland Highlanders during the Japanese Conquest of Malaya and Singapore, and was awarded the DSO.

[iv] James Stewart, 1st of Fasnacloich. One of the Stewarts of Fasnacloich - Charles Stewart - was purse bearer to Prince Charlie.

[v] Alexander Stewart, 1st of Invernahyle.

The family of Invernahyle provide a colourful history. Alexander Stewart, 1st of Invernahyle was treacherously murdered by "Green Colin", brother of Campbell of Dunstaffnage - the cause of a deadly feud between the 2 families for a long time. His son and heir, Donald 2nd of Invernahyle, was a babe in arms. He only escaped being murdered with his father, because his nurse Morag, wife of the smith of Moidart, fled to Moidart with him. So for a number of years, Donald was brought up as though the son of the smith. He achieved great repute for his strength and skill, and could take in each hand one of the great hammers which normally took the strength of a man using both hands to lift - and he could wield them both. Hence his nickname Donald nan Ord - Donald of the Hammers. Alexander 4th of Invernahyle fought under Montrose at Inverlochy. One day he turned up at Church, with his 12 sons - all fully kilted, with belted plaids, and in full armour.

Alexander 8th of Invernahyle was a noted Jacobite. At Prestonpans, he took prisoner a Colonel Whitefoord, with whom he developed a great friendship. After Culloden, Whitefoord strained every limb to obtain a pardon for Invernahyle. Everywhere he met with refusals, so eventually he went to the Duke of Cumberland. The Duke also declined to help. Whitefoord then limited his request to protection for Invernahyle's house, wife, and family. Cumberland refused that too, whereupon Whitefoord laid upon the table his commission, asking to be allowed to retire from the service of a Sovereign who did not know how to spare a vanquished enemy. Cumberland was so affected that he granted the request - though Alexander was not himself pardoned until the Act of Indemnity. In old age, he used to entertain the young (later Sir) Walter Scott at Invernahyle. Scott wrote of him "Alexander Stewart of Invernahyle, a name which I cannot write without the warmest recollections of gratitude to the friend of my childhood, who introduced me to the Highlands, their traditions and their manners... He was a noble specimen of the old Highlander - gallant, courteous, and brave even to chivalry"[3].

10. **Duncan Stewart, IV of Appin** appears to have predeceased his father before the Battle of Pinkie in 1547. He was certainly dead before 1562. He married Jonet Gordon, daughter of Alexander Earl of Huntly. He had one son, John V of Appin, and a daughter who m Rainall MacDhonail 8th of Keppoch.

11. **John Stewart V of Appin** married twice. By his first wife Katharine, daughter of John Gorm Campbell, 1st of Lochnell, & widow of John MacLean 1st of Morvern, he had:

[i]   Duncan, his successor.

By his second wife, a daughter of John Macdonald of Muidart, he had:

[ii]   John, 1st of Ardsheal; of whom hereafter
[iii]   a daughter who married Alan Cameron 16th of Lochiel.

John V of Appin died in or before 1595.

12. **Duncan Stewart, VI of Appin** married a daughter of Archibald Campbell 2nd of Lochnell. He was in possession of lands in Lismore in 1595, and was alive in 1623. He had issue:

[i]   Duncan, his successor
[ii] John   } apparently dsp
[iii] Alan. }
[iv] Dugald, alive in 1634.

13. **Duncan Stewart, VII of Appin** was the chief who was persuaded during a carousal to give up Castle Stalker to Campbell of Airds in exchange for a rotten 8-oared boat. The people of Appin were incensed. Their Chief insisted that honour demanded that he keep to the bargain. They met to consider whether they should depose their Chief. They did not, but they resolved that he should never lead them in war. He married the 3rd daughter of Ewen Cameron of Lochiel, and had issue:

[i]   Duncan, his successor
[ii] Alan, who m Beatrix or Margaret, daughter of Hector Roy MacLean of Coll, and died in 1675[4]. . She married secondly Donald MacLean 7th of Kingairloch. They had issue:

   I.   Robert Stewart IX of Appin.

   II. other sons

[iii] Donald, who was the father of William Stewart, a priest murdered in Rome in 1737.
[iv] Moir, m. Alexander Stewart 4th of Invernahyle in about 1598, and had 12 sons.. There was a John Stewart alive in 1699, described as a "cousin germain to the Laird of Appin" [MacColl magazine Sept 1934] - whether he was one of Moir's descendants is not clear.

14. **Duncan Stewart, VIII of Appin**. His brother Allan Stewart[4] was described in his will as "brother german to the deceased Duncan Stewart younger of Appin". On this basis, he did not outlive his

father, but acted as Chief. Certainly he was the virtual leader of the Clan during his father's lifetime, and led the clan at the battle of Inverlochy on 2nd February 1645. On 7th August 1649, he was forfeited by the Scots Parliament; but his forfeiture was cancelled on the accession of Charles II in 1660. He married Jean, 3rd daughter of Sir Robert Campbell, 9th of Glenorchy; and had an only child Margaret who married Alexander Campbell 6th of Lochnell. He was succeeded by his nephew Robert.

15. **Robert Stewart IX** of Appin, nephew of Duncan VIIIth of Appin, succeeded in 1685[5]. He was a noted Jacobite. As a minor, he fought under the command of John Stewart 3rd of Ardsheal at Killiecrankie, in the campaign of 1689-1690. As a result he was forfeited; but the forfeiture was lifted by Queen Mary II. In 1695, he was appointed Commissioner of Supply for Argyllshire, and his appointment was renewed in 1704. He led the Stewarts of Appin in the '15, was forfeited and went abroad. He again led them in the '19. In 1725, he petitioned General Wade praying for the attainder under which he then lay to be lifted[6]. He married first a daughter of MacLeod of MacLeod by whom he had issue:

[i] Duncan, who died at school
[ii] Mary, who m Lachlan MacLachlan of MacLachlan
[iii] Anne, who m Alexander Macdonald of Glencoe.

His second wife was Anne, daughter of Alexander Campbell 6th of Lochnell, by his wife Margaret daughter of Duncan Stewart VII of Appin. [Sir Duncan Campbell, 7th of Lochnell, was her brother]. The marriage contract was made in 1710[7]. They had issue:

[iv] Dugald, who succeeded him
[v] Isabel, who m Donald Macdonald of Kinloch Muidart (m in or before 1730)[8]. He was executed at Carlisle in 1746.
[vi] Janet, who m (in or before 1730)[8] Alastair Macdonald 18th of Keppoch, who fell at Culloden 1746.

[vii]   Margaret, who m. Rev John Stewart of Inverness (a descendant of Ardsheal, via Glengalmadale). She was still alive in 1802 17.

[viii]   Katharine, who m Alexander Stewart, 8th of Invernahyle on 30 December 1742 [Stewart Lockhart Mss at The Stewart Society]

[ix]   Anne, who d unmarried

[x]   Jean, who died young

Robert Stewart IX of Appin was still alive in 1730, for he is so mentioned in Duncan Stewart's History. Further, he is mentioned in the Argyll Register of Sasines as alive in October 1735. 3 manuscripts make it clear that Robert was involved in the negotiations and decisions which culminated in the command of the Appin Regiment being given to Charles Stewart of Ardsheal in 1739. Probably, these negotiations took place in 1738-1739, for it was in 1738 that seven chieftains swore to gather their vassals to the King's Standard as and when it should be raised [The Duke of Perth, Lord John Drummond, Lord Linton, Cameron of Lochiel, Campbell of Auchinbreck, MacGregor of Balhaldy, and Lord Lovat]. Pressure would then have been put on other Jacobites to commit and prepare themselves.

These 3 manuscripts - a Gaelic Manuscript, the original of which is in the Library of the Faculty of Advocates in Edinburgh; a manuscript among the Dewar Mss at Inveraray; and a manuscript in the Campbell of Stonefield Mss, which are deposited in the General Register Office, Edinburgh - show the role of Robert Stewart in choosing who was to command the Appin Regiment in the '45.. The Gaelic manuscript, translated into English, reads:

".....Robert Stewart was the Chief of the Stewarts and resident in Appin. His son Dougal Stewart was in Edinburgh finishing his education. About this time secret preparations were taking place with the intention of placing (King James) on the Throne. Robert Stewart wrote to his son, Dougal, at Edinburgh, asking him to come home to Appin, so as to command the Appin Stewarts in the imminent endeavour to place (King James) Stuart on the Throne. Dougal Stewart wrote to his father declining absolutely to help in such a movement, and said in his

letter he would much rather waste his substance on the harridans of Edinburgh than support the cause of a dissolute Prince."

The Dewar Mss gives Dougal's reply as

"I would rather spend the inheritance of Appin among the gay women of Edinburgh than risk it being lost striving to recover the Crown for the Prince, that I know cannot be done."

It continues that Robert was so furious at the reply, that he contemplated depriving his son of the inheritance of Appin and giving it to his daughter Mary.

The Gaelic Mss continues that

"Robert then wrote to his daughter Mary, who was married to Lachlan MacLachlan of Strathlachlan, to see if her husband would command the Appin Stewarts. When the Stewarts of Appin heard of this unwelcome arrangement, they notified Robert Stewart that they would on no consideration participate in the impending rising, unless they were commanded by a Stewart. The choice then fell on Charles Stewart of Ardsheal, who consented to command the Stewarts of Appin in support of Prince Charlie."

Dewar adds that Ardsheal at first refused the command, and only agreed when his wife said to him

"If you, Charles, are not willing to become Commander of the Men of Appin, stay at home and take care of the house, and I will go myself and become their Commander."

Probably, therefore, Robert Stewart of Appin was still alive in 1738 - 1739[12]. He must have died in or before 1743, for it was in that year that his son Dugald, 10th of Appin, was created a Jacobite peer as Baron Appin[11]. His widow lived on until 1771 - In the Sheriff Court Book of Argyll at Inveraray there is an entry:

"1771 - May 2nd: Disposition and Assignation by Mrs Ann Campbell, Dowager Lady Appin, widow of Robert Stewart of Appin and mother of the

deceased Dugald Stewart late of Appin, in favour of Alexander Stewart of Invernahyle of certain sums provided to her by contract of marriage in 1710 which she disponed and assigned in 1761 to Sir Duncan Campbell of Lochnell, baronet, now deceased, her brother german, in trust, who made over the same in turn to John Campbell of Cloichcomby, also now deceased. The said Alexander Stewart supplied and maintained her and her daughter, Ann Stewart, to the extent of £695.55 sterling; dated at Glenstockdale 15th December 1767."

Her will is mentioned in the Abstract from the Sheriff Court Books of Argyll at Inveraray, Vol XVII:

"1771 - May 2nd: Latter Will and Testament of Mrs Ann Campbell, Dowager Lady Appin, widow of Robert Stewart of Appin, desiring to be buried beside her deceased children at the Church of Appin, and appointing Alexander Stewart of Invernahyle, whom failing Charles Stewart, his eldest son, with the consent of Major General John Campbell of Barbreck and John Campbell of Ardstignish to manage her funeral. She appoints Katharine Stewart of Invernahyle, to be her sole executor, leaving to Margaret Stewart, also her daughter, her riding clothes & linen etc, and to Anna Stewart, daughter of the deceased Dugald Stewart of Appin, her grandchild and other persons certain articles & goods; dated at Glenstockdale 15th December 1767."

16. **Dugald Stewart 10th of Appin** was the second, but only surviving son of Robert Stewart 9th of Appin. It is probable that he was born around 1715. "The "Stewarts of Appin" [1] set out the traditional view that Dugald was a minor at the time of the '45. Hence the Appin Regiment was commanded by Charles Stewart 5th of Ardsheal. The truth is that Dugald was of age, but refused to fight for the Jacobite cause - as is shown by the 3 manuscripts 10 referred to above, and by the fact that he was of sufficient age in 1735, to witness the Renunciation by his father of certain debts [9].

He was created a Jacobite peer in 1743, as Baron Appin[11] The Warrant reads:

"Dougal Stewart of Appin, Lord Appin

"James the Eight etc., Whereas we are fully satysfied with the duty, loyalty, and affection of our Trusty and Well Beloved Dougal Stewart of Appin, and of the many and good services performed by his family to the Crown upon all occasions, and being also well persuaded that he himself as one of the Chiefs of the Clans wants only a good opportunity to exert himself, as his Predecessors have, at the head of his Clan and following, for the recovery and in the defence of our just Rights, and for the relieving of his native country from the present tyranny and usurpation it groans under, We are resolved to confer on him the Title and Dignity aforementioned, as an encouragement to him and an obligation to his heirs to continue firmly attached to their Rightful and Lawful Sovereigns, and to support upon all occasions to the utmost of their power the interest of the Crown. Our Will and Pleasure etc make and create the said Dougal Stewart a Lord and Peer of Parliamt of our said ancient Kingdom, by the name and title of Lord Appin to have and to hold to him and his lawful heirs male with all the privileges etc.

Given at our court at Albano the 6th day of June 1743, in the 42nd year of our Reign."

Granted that he refused to lead the Appin Regiment, it is curious that he should have been given a Jacobite Peerage. The words of the Warrant "as an encouragement to him" may provide the clue - that it was as much a spur to keep him at least neutral, and not to hinder the calling out of the Clan. Two manuscripts from the Campbell of Stonefield Mss at the General Register Office support the view that Dugald was "neutral", but would not meddle with his Clan's support for the Jacobites. Document 89 includes "Dugal Stewart of Appin" in the "List of Gentlemen of Argyllshire in Rebellion", but it does not state what part he, or the others listed, is supposed to have played. Document 116 "List of Suspected Persons in the West Highlands of Scotland" is rather more relevant. It states:

"Dugall Stewart of Appin at meetings with Ardsheall and Invernahyle when rising the men in his country, and some of them in arms at the time, might have hindered people from joining but said he would not meddle but keep a neutrality, did not send his militia, offered them after the rebells retired north, some

of these he talked of sending to Inveraray went to the Highland Army, and when the ground officer was calling the militia, told a confident, it was to the Highland Camp his master was to send them."

After Culloden, Dugald apparently considered it prudent to get his papers carried to security on the Continent. They were brought back to his daughter Anna, in around 1770. Anna married David Loch of Over Carnbee, Fife, at Blandfield, near Edinburgh, on 2nd August 1770[13].

David Loch was an eminent merchant in Leith, who is said to have established communications between Scotland and the Continent, and to have carried to the Stewarts of Appin the call to Arms in the '45 [14]. If this is true, David Loch must have kept his Jacobite role remarkably secret, for in 1756 he was admitted to the Royal Company of Archers, and he generally achieved a position of great respect in Edinburgh Society.

David Loch is also said to have played a part in helping Charles Stewart of Ardsheal to escape from France. Ardsheal managed to get from Scotland to Holland, but there Hanoverian emissaries were busy tracking down Jacobite leaders. A merchant from Leith recognised Ardsheal at an Inn in Holland; and invited him and his companions to drink. The merchant got all the others drunk, save for himself and Ardsheal, whereupon he disclosed his identity to Ardsheal. Sending for his wife, he got her to disguise Ardsheal as her maid, which she did, although Charles had a "lubberly appearance" in women's clothing. Thus they drove out of town in the merchant's carriage, fortunately not challenged by the guards, and thence into France where Ardsheal reached safety. The Marquis of Lorne (later Duke of Argyll) in his "Adventures in Legend"[15] states that this Merchant was David Loch. If so, the wife cannot have been Anna Stewart[16].

The Appin papers passed after the death of Anna Stewart into the general papers of David Loch, which in their turn fell into the ownership of the Lochs of Drylaw (later Lord Loch). There they formed part of the "Loch Collection of Scottish Documents". This

Collection was brought to England in around 1800, and the papers were rediscovered and described in "Notes and Queries" January to June 1910. Specifically mentioned then was that the Collection included letters from James II and the Old Pretender to the Stewarts of Appin. Many of the papers survive in the family of Lord Loch, but not those of Appin. There is a suggestion in the History of the Loch Family that they and other Jacobite documents were destroyed as being "so full of the disastrous tragedies that concerned the Lochs' allegiance to the House of Stewart".

Dugald continued after the '45 to spend his time between Edinburgh and Appin. When the ruthless Captain Caroline Frederick Scott sacked Ardsheal House on 15th December 1746, he is said to have responded to his appeals where he was to go, by suggesting that he walk along the shores of Loch Linnhe and ask the Laird of Appin for help for "wasn't the feeble boy the father of his clan". Whether much is to be deduced from anything said by this venomous subordinate of "Butcher" Cumberland, is doubtful. A manuscript letter in the Public Record Office, London, filed under "State Papers Domestic Geo II", copied out by Miss D Stewart Linney reads:

"Tower of London, Aug 22 1746. Mr John Murray
(Account of Highland Clans)
Discription of Highlanders. Their Chief is their God etc. Steuart of Appin
is a bashfull man of few words and but ordinary parts, he did not appear in the
Rebellion his clan being commanded by Steuart of Ardsheil from whom it is
reckoned near to a half of the following are descended and will join him without
regard to Appin. This gentleman has no son and his nearest Connection of any
Consequence was with the late McDonald of Keppoch who married his sister. The
late Appin forfeited to the Duke of Argyle in 1715 and the present Duke was so
generous as to give his son a Charter some little time before the Rebellion broke
out. The Stewarts are mostly of the Church of England and esteemed the least
given to theift of any of the Highlands. McDonald of Glencoe has but a Small
following and is vassal to Stewart of Appin."

In 1752, Dugald was involved in trying to find means within the law to stop the evictions of Ardsheal tenants which Colin Campbell of Glenure, the Factor for the forfeited estates, was constrained to make. In the same year, he was summoned as a juror for the trial of James Stewart in Aucharn, for the murder of Colin Campbell of Glenure. He did not attend, giving as his excuse for non attendance that he had to stay in Edinburgh because his daughter was ill.

In 1765, he sold the estate of Appin, probably because of debt, to Seton of Touch. Walter Scott WS was the agent of Appin and Invernahyle. His son, the novelist `Sir Walter Scott, recorded in his preface to "Rob Roy" that

"there were very considerable debts due by Stewart of Appin, chiefly to the author's family, which were likely to be lost to the creditors if they could not be made available out of this same farm of Invernenty..."

The farm at Invernenty appears to have been acquired by Dugald, either outright from, or as security for a loan to, Donald MacLaren of Invernenty, after the '45.

Dugald married Mary Mackenzie, daughter of Alexander Mackenzie, the younger son of Kenneth Mackenzie 4th Earl and 1st Marquess of Seaforth [cr 1690, Jacobite Peerage]. He died in 1769, leaving an only daughter, Anna, who married David Loch of Over Carnbee, Fife, at Blandfield, near Edinburgh, on 2nd August 1770 13. She died in 1772, probably leaving no children surviving her.[17]

Notes & Sources:

1. The best printed history is "The Stewarts of Appin" by John H K & Lt Col Duncan Stewart, Edinburgh 1880.
2. Extracted from "The MacLarens - a History of Clan Labhran" by Margaret MacLaren of MacLaren; Eneas MacKay - Stirling - 1960
3. Sir Walter Scott - Tales of the Canongate
4. The Testament Dative of Allan Stewart, brother german to the deceased Duncan Stewart yr of Appin in favour of Robert of Appin "oldest lawful son" to deceased Allan Stewart" is in Edinburgh (?)

Vol 5, 1705-1710. It is said that this shows that Allan died in 1675. I cannot read that in the photostat, but Robert succeeded to Appin in 1685, so Allan must have been dead by then. "The Stewarts" Vol IX p.173 refers to entries in "The Order Book of the Appin Regiment" under "Others in the Regiment" of Stewart, Robert: natural cousin of Dugald X of Appin, killed at Culloden; and Stewart, Robert, natural cousin of Dugald X of Appin, wounded at Culloden. Whether they descend from this Allan is not known.

5. Robert's succession to Appin in 1685 was confirmed in 1697 - record in General Register Office, Edinburgh.

6. The petition is mentioned in "The Appin Murder" by Sir W MacArthur at p.12

7. The marriage contract between Robert Stewart 9th of Appin and Anne Campbell of Lochnell was made in 1710. This date is given in a Disposition and Assignation by Mrs Ann Campbell, Dowager Lady Appin, of certain sums to Alexander Stewart of Invernahyle; dated 15th December 1767 at Glenstockdale; and entered in the Sheriff Books of Argyll at Inveraray on 2nd May 1771.

8. The marriages of Isabel Stewart of Appin to Donald Macdonald of Kinloch Muidart, and of Janet Stewart to Alastair Macdonald 18th of Keppoch are mentioned in Duncan Stewart's "A Short History & Genealogical Account of the Royal Family of Scotland ... and of the surname of Stewart", written 1730; published 1739. [Duncan was himself an Appin Stewart, being the 2nd son of Donald 5th of Invernahyle, and the first of the family of Strathgarry].

9. Argyll Record of Sasines: Vol VII, fol 194, entered Nov 17, 1735 - a Renunciation by Robert Stewart of Appine in favour of "Donald Stewart now of Achnacoan ... of certain debts due from Achnacoan to Appine ... dated at Letter Shewna, 5th October 1735". Witnesses Dougall Stewart, son of the said Robert Stewart & Alexander Stewart Messenger in Invernahyle.

10. The 3 manuscripts are - a Gaelic Manuscript in the Library of the Faculty of Advocates in Edinburgh; one of the Dewar Mss at

Inveraray; and one of the Campbell of Stonefield Mss, deposited in the General Register Office in Edinburgh. The English translation was by Mr Alexander Rankin, Ballachulish, supplied to me by Miss Dorothy Stewart Linney. Dewar was an employee of the Marquis of Lorne, later Duke of Argyll, and was sent round the Highlands to gather and record tales. Some of these were published in "Adventures in Legend" - see Note 15.

11. Ruvigny's Jacobite Peerage. & Warrant in the Royal Library at Windsor.

12. The authors of "The Stewarts of Appin" give his death as between 1730 and 1739 1, assuming that it must have occurred before the exiled King James VIII & II signed Ardsheal's Commission as Colonel of the Appin Regiment in 1739. The references in the 3 manuscripts show that this assumption is not necessarily right. Clearly, by 1739, Robert would anyway have been too old to lead his Clan in battle. Since he had left College in 1689 to join Dundee's campaign, he would probably have been in his late 60's, if not 70. "The Stewarts of Appin" also infer that Robert did not return from exile after 1716. This is clearly wrong.

13. The Scots Magazine, 1770, Vol XXXII, p.397.

14. "The Family of Loch" by Gordon Loch, 1933.

15. "Adventures in Legend" by the Marquis of Lorne, later Duke of Argyll, based on the Dewar Mss, collected for him.

16. That David Loch had an earlier wife than Anna Stewart, fits in with the known fact that he had a son John, whose daughter Jean married Alexander Murray, printer in Edinburgh, and survived him, dying on 9th April 1808. Not only is this time span too short for the marriage to Anna Stewart of Appin; but none of these Loch descendants is mentioned in correspondence over the service of heirs to Dugald Stewart of Appin in the reversion of the estate of Appin [between Walter Scott WS and Alexander Stewart of Invernahyle, 1783; preserved in the Stewart Society Library]; nor in the Service of Heirs to Dugald Stewart of Appin in Invernenty in 1802 [Note 12]. However, in "The East Neuk of Fife: its History and Antiquities",

Wood, 2nd edition 1887, p.331, David Loch's above child John is said to have been by his wife Anna Stewart of Appin. see also DNB, ed Sidney Lee 1893, Vol XXXIV p.25

17. The Index to Service of Heirs in Scotland 1802 show as Dugald's heirs portioner, in the salmon fishings in Invernenty, Balquhidder, Perthshire, Dugald's sister & nephews, viz Mrs Margaret Stewart in Greenock; Donald MacDonald of Kinlochmoidart, son of Isabel Stewart; Alexander MacDonald, son of Ronald MacDonald of Keppoch & Janet Stewart; and Dugald Stewart of Invernahyle, son of Katherine Stewart. Walter Scott WS writing on 26th March 1783 to Alexander Stewart of Invernahyle, believed that the heirs of Dougal Stewart of Appin, in the Reversion of Appin and in Invernenty, were Mrs Stewart of Invernahyle; Mrs Connachar; Mrs Ann Stewart in Edinburgh; and Mrs Stewart in Greenock. [Mrs Connachar was presumably the name by a second marriage of one of the daughters.] The inference is that there were no descendants of Dugald then alive.

Chapter 5: Stewart of Ardsheal

Part I: Main Line of Ardsheal

Chapter 1: **John Stewart, 1st of Ardsheal**, 2nd son of John 5th Baron of Appin, by his second wife a daughter of MacDonald of Muidart; was a young man at Court in 1601. He was a ward in Chivalry of Ludovic Stuart, 2nd Duke of Lennox. This Duke was the last Stuart of Aubigny to command the "Scots Men at Arms" - a body which whilst remaining under the Scots King, virtually formed a personal guard for the French King for generations. John, 1st of Ardsheal, married Mary daughter of Alistair MacDonald 13th of Keppoch - issue:

[i] Duncan, 2nd of Ardsheal

[ii] Alexander ("Stewarts of Appin" p.130)

[iii] John [not mentioned in "The Stewarts of Appin"]

2. **Duncan Stewart II of Ardsheal**, served in 1644-1645 as an officer of the Appin Regiment under Montrose; m firstly Anne dau of John Stewart of Lettershuna, brother of Duncan Stewart 3rd of Invernahyle; secondly Margaret dau Hector Mcleane 6th of Kingairloch, by Sarah dau Hector MacLean 9th of Lochbuie; & thirdly a dau of MacLean of Coll by whom he had no issue. Duncan Stewart died between 1691 and 1711.

By his first wife, Anne dau of John Stewart of Lettershuna, he had issue:

[i] John Stewart 3rd of Ardsheal - see below

[ii] Alexander Stewart of Acharn - see below

[iii]   dau m McDonald of Killieconat

[iv]   dau m John Stewart 3rd of Ballachulish → issue

[v]   Isabel m James Stewart, 5th of Fasnacloich

[vi]   dau m MacLachlan of Cregan

[vii]   By his 1st wife, Margaret dau Hector Maclean 6th of Kingairloch, he had issue:

[viii] Allan, living in 1691, of Glengalmadale & Stron 1711 [2] - see below

[ix]   [Moir, m John Stewart 6th of Fasnacloich ("Stewarts of Appin" p.155) → issue

[x]   Duncan, killed at Dunkeld 1690 ("Stewarts of Appin")

[xi]   James, alive 1686, d. unm

[xii]   William, had issue now extinct.

3. **John Stewart II of Ardsheal**, Tutor to Robert Stewart 9th of Appin; m Ann dau of Colin Campbell of Lochnell; seized the Castle of Eilean Stalker in 1689; yielded it to Argyll's men in 1690; d 1697 [Argyll Inventories]. He had issue 4 sons and 3 daughters:

[i]   John, IV of Ardsheal

[ii]   Duncan, from Morvern. A witness to a sasine from John Lord Glenorchy to Donald Stewart of Achnagoan: Argyle Sasines Vol VII fol 343. He was killed at Falkirk 1747, leaving issue

     I.   Alexander } all in the Appin Regiment - see Order Book.

     II. William } William was transported

     III. James   }

     IV. Janet, who was in the list of Crown witnesses at the trial of James Stewart for the Appin murder of Colin Campbell of Glenure.

[iii]   Allan

[iv]   James, living in 1720

[v]   Ann, m Lachlan McLachlan of Fasifern

[vi]   Janet, m John Stewart 8th of Glenbuckie

[vii] Isobel, m Duncan, son of James Stewart 5th of Fasnacloich

4. **John Stewart, IV of Ardsheal**, m 1700 Elizabeth dau Charles Steuart 8th of Ballechin in Atholc; d. 1757, leaving issue 2 sons & 5 daughters:

Charles 5th of Ardsheal

John, alive in 1734; went to Australia & left issue (per the annotations by Stewart of Coll in "The Stewarts of Appin").

Ann, m Alexander Stewart 4th of Ballachulish (he d 1744)

Helen m Alan Cameron

Isabel m Alexander MacDonald of Glencoe

Margaret m John Glas Stewart of Benmore [see 2.2.(ii) above]

Janet unmarried

There was also a natural son, *James Stewart in Acharn*, known as *"James of the Glen"*, who was convicted of the "Appin Murder" in 1752. This was the well-known murder of Colin Campbell of Glenure "The Red Fox", on the hills above Appin. His trial and conviction was before an all Campbell Jury presided over by the Duke of Argyll. He was hanged and his body remained in chains above Ballachulish. It has been much written about [5]. It seems clear that James was innocent. But he was only allowed access to a lawyer 1½ days before his trial: the trial took place at Inveraray: the Jury was all Campbell, and the trial was presided over by the Duke of Argyll. James was a half-brother of the exiled Ardsheal. That may have sufficed to make him the scape goat. Who the real murderer was remains a matter of speculation. Tradition has it that the name is passed from father to son in the houses of Ardsheal and Achnacone.

5. **Charles Stewart, V of Ardsheal**, led the Appin Regiment with distinction in the '45. His commission as Colonel was signed by James III in 1739. The Regiment mustered 360 men, of whom 92 were killed and 65 were wounded. The Appin banner was the only one to escape capture by the Hanoverians after Culloden. Charles himself was attainted, and became a hunted man. He was huge, and hid with difficulty in and around Appin after Culloden, barely escaping capture. . Charles escaped to France, and died in Sens in 1757. Ardsheal House

was burnt to the ground, with all its contents, by the Hanoverians on the night of 15th - 16th December 1746. Lady Ardsheal, who was pregnant, gave birth that night on the hillside, to her daughter, Anne. 3 days later, she was forced into exile, and eventually joined her husband in France. The Ardsheal estate was forfeited for high treason. Charles m 1732 Isabel (1712-1782) dau Haldane of Lanrick. and had issue 6 sons & 4 daughters:

[i]   John, d young before 1745

[ii]   Alexander, d. 1769, unmarried

[iii]   Duncan, 6th of Ardsheal

[iv]   John d. unm

[v]   Charles, d in Jamaica 1767, unmarried

[vi]   James d unmarried

[vii] Margaret, born on the hillside above Ardsheal, the night that the house was sacked by the Hanoverians (15-16 December 1746); m. George Johnstone of Cowhill, Dumfries (1736-1817) → Keswick family of Cowhill (also of Jardine Mathieson, Hong Kong)

[viii] Elizabeth d. young

[ix]   Ann m + had issue

[x]   Clementine, no issue

6. **Duncan Stewart, VI of Ardsheal**, emigrated to Bermuda where he was Collector of Customs, and then to USA, where he was appointed Collector of Customs at New London, Connecticut, in 1764; sided with the British in the American War of Independence, and managed to leave in 1777, to sail back to Britain. He reacquired the forfeited estate of Ardsheal, and took up residence there in 1788. He married in 1767 Ann Erving, dau Honble John Erving of Boston Mass. Their portraits painted in America by John Singleton Copley were donated by Mary Stewart Stewart-Lockhart to the Stewart Society, and are currently on semi-permanent loan to the Scottish National Portrait Gallery. They had issue:

[i]   Charles, 7th of Ardsheal

[ii] John, from whom descend the present representatives of Ardsheal

[iii] George, who d young

[iv] James Haldane Stewart, a Clergyman of the Church of England; b 23.12.1776 in Boston, Mass, d. 22.10.1854; who m Mary dau David Dale of Glasgow & New Lanark & had issue [see the Stewarts of Appin pp 148-149].

[v]   William George Erving Stewart, who went to Peru & had issue.

[vi] 5 daughters [see the Stewarts of Appin: pp 149-150]

7. **Charles Stewart VII of Ardsheal**: d 1844; m Rebecca, dau of William Sinclair of the Deer Park, co Armagh, and Strabane, co Tyrone; and had issue:

[i]   Charles, his successor

[ii] *Annette*, m *Major Robert Stewart* of the 91st Highlanders, 7th son by his wife Mary dau Alexander Stewart 8th of Invernahyle, of John Mor Stewart, who was the second son of John Stewart, 7th of Fasnacloich, by his second wife, a daughter of M'Nab of M'Nab. She had issue: [see the Stewarts of Appin p.150]

I.   Anna Rebecca Charlotte, who m Miles Lockhart (of the family of Lockhart of the Lee, Lanarkshire) & had issue:

a. Robert Stewart Lockhart b 1854, m Flo Van Renan, and had issue a son who dsp, Lorna who m Col Arthur Borton VC, DSO, MC dsp, and Guenta who m Colonel E Sandys IMS, & had a daughter Patricia who m twice & had no issue.

b. Charles, buried at Ballachulish aet 10.

c. Sir James Haldane Stewart Lockhart, who was the last Stewart to be born in Ardsheal House, and had issue

• Mary Stewart Stewart-Lockhart b 1894, m David Joel, RN, and had one dau Idina Betty b & d 1923. "Cousin Mary" was one of London's leading furniture retailers and designers in the 1920s and 1930s, as Betty Joel Ltd, with premises at 25 Knightsbridge. Clients included the Savoy Group, Lord Louis Mountbatten, and Winston Churchill. She died 21 January 1985, in Andover.

- Margaret Stewart b 1903, m Eric Baumann. dsp 1936
- Charles Stewart Lockhart RN, 1889=1961; m Eileen Hallimond: issue
  o Christopher b 1922, m Deborah Kermode dau British Ambassador in Indonesia : issue
    ▪ Clive Stewart Lockhart (m + c)
    ▪ Sally Louise

d. Elizabeth m Dr Milward and had issue 3 sons who all dsp

e. Mary, m Coffin (Isle of Man), and had issue Sebright dsp in war of 1914-1918, Gladys dsp, and Audrey dsp

f. Tim m Hartford, went to South Africa and had issue a son and a daughter.

8. **Charles Stewart VIII of Ardsheal** 1803-1882; who sold Ardsheal in the 1860s, and died unmarried in Edinburgh in 1882. The representation of the family then fell on the line of John Stewart, second son of Duncan, 6th of Ardsheal.

Notes & Sources:

1. "The Stewarts of Appin" by John H J Stewart & Lt Col Duncan Stewart, Edinburgh, 1880
2. Article by RMS in The Stewarts Vol XIII page 171
3. Kidnapped by Robert Louis Stevenson. "The Trial of James Stewart" - Notable British Trials Series, Hodge, Edinburgh & Glasgow, 1907.

Part II Cadet Branches of Ardsheal

(Editor's Note: Cadet refers to a younger son)

A: Acharn → Coll:

1. **Alexander Stewart of Acharn**, 2nd son of Duncan 2nd of Ardsheal, killed at Dunkeld August 1690; m firstly, Isabel dau George Campbell of Airds, Appin, 31st March 1667; & secondly a dau of Alexander Stewart of Ballachulish [from Argyll Register] → issue a son & 3 daughters:

    [i]   **John of Acharn**, who m Ann dau Campbell of Dunstaffnage, with issue

    I.   **Alexander of Acharn**, later tacksman of Lagnaha, Appin; alive in 1717 (Register House), who had 2 sons:

    a. James, killed at Culloden 1746
    b. John, Captain in the Appin Regiment, killed at Culloden 1746.

    II.   **John Glas, of Benmore**, Perthshire; a Captain in the Appin Regiment, killed at Culloden; m firstly Margaret [see 4.6 below] dau John Stewart 4th of Ardsheal & had issue:

    a. John, who m Mary dau Duncan Stewart of Glenbuckie dsp
    b. Elizabeth, afterwards of Glenbuckie d unm

    John Glas Stewart m secondly Catherine McNab, & had issue

    c. Duncan, a Captain in the Western Regiment of Fencibles, who acquired **Glenbuckie** from his half sister. By his first wife Susannah dau Captain Campbell of Kilberry, he had no issue; by his second wife, Margaret dau Duncan Stewart VI of Ardsheal, he had issue 2 sons + daughters:

2. **John Lorn Stewart of Coll**, who d 1878 leaving issue by his wife Mary Campbell

    [i]   Duncan went to Lima, Peru and had issue

    I.   Anne

II.   Margaret

III. Janet

[ii]   Archibald, d unm
[iii] John Lorn Stewart of Coll
[iv]   2 daus

B: Glengalmadale & Stron:

Chapter 1: **Allan Stewart 1st of Glengalmadale & Stron**, was the 3rd son of Duncan 2nd of Ardsheal, and the oldest son of Duncan by his second wife, Margaret dau Hector McLeane 6th of Kingairloch, by Sarah dau Hector MacLaine 9th of Lochbuie. Hector McLeane 6th of Kingairloch was killed in a fight with marauding Camerons c 1650. In 1651, Margaret McLeane remarried, this time to Ewen MacLean, son of Allan MacLean, 7th Chief of Ardgour. Because of this marriage, Margaret has sometimes, erroneously, been described as "of Ardgour". On 4th May 1674, Margaret McLeane or Stewart was granted a Charter of Kilmalieu in Kingairloch, by her brother Duncan McLeane, 7th of Kingairloch. She died in or before 1676, and Duncan Stewart 2nd of Ardsheal died between 1691 and 1711. Their issue was:

[v]   Allan, 1st of Glengalmadale & Stron
[vi]   Duncan, killed at Dunkeld in 1689
[vii] James, living in 1686, d unmarried
[viii] William, who had issue, of whom no details are known, save that they are supposedly extinct.
[ix]   Moir, who m her first cousin, John Stewart 6th of Fasnacloich, and had issue ("The Stewarts of Appin p. 155)

In "The Stewarts of Appin" this family of Duncan 2nd of Ardsheal is set out as being the family of his grandson, Duncan, son of Alexander, 2nd son of Duncan 2nd of Ardsheal. That this account is wrong is demonstrated in "The

Stewarts of Appin" when dealing with Fasnacloich; and by an extract form the Argyle Sasine Rolls: fol 307 [1]

"1691 June 18; Sasine on disposition by Duncan Stewart of Ardsheall to Allan eldest lawfull son of the second marriage to Duncan Stewart of Ardsheall lawfully procreat between him and the decd. Margaret McLeane his spouse, of the threepenny halfpenny lands of Glengalmadill and Strone lying in Kingairloch parish of Killmaluig in Lismore and shire of Argyle.

At Ardsheall 15 Feb 1686 John McLeane in Duror and Duncan and James Stewart sons to the said Duncan Stewart are witnesses".

A second sasine on contract of wadset is contained in Vol IV part 5, folio 125:

1711, Aug 8; Sasine on contract of wadset between Donald McLain of Kengerloch on the one part and Allan Stewart eldest lawful son of the second marriage to the deceased Duncan Stewart of Ardsheall, and Duncan Stewart his son of the other part, of 29th June last, inffeffing the said Allan Stewart in liferent and the said Duncan Stewart in fee in the threepenny halfpenny lands of Glengalmadale and Stron etc lying in Kengerloch, parish of Killmaluich and shire of Argyle, at Killearn in Lismore 29 June 1711. John Stewart of Ardsheall, Alexander Stewart writer in Glenery and Murdoch McLean of Lochbuy are witnesses. James Stewart yr of Fasnacloich, Allan Stewart brother to John Stewart of Fasnacloich and others are witnesses to the Sasine on 31 July 1711.

In Folio 126, there is reference to a Sasine of 1711, Aug. 8, of the same lands and Kilmalieu etc on a precept of clare constat.

It is not known who was the wife of Allan Stewart 1st of Glengalmadale. He was still alive in 1719, when he was a witness to a deed. But the names of two of his children are as follows:

I.   Duncan Stewart, 2nd of Glengalmadale

II.   Donald, who with his brother was a witness to a bond in 1718, between their Father Allan Stewart, and E McLean. It would seem reasonable to suppose that both Duncan and Donald were born prior to 1700.

Note 1: The 3 sasines noted above were copied from the Macleod Collection at the Society of Genealogists, sub. nom Stewart of Achnacone; 18.05.1965

3. **Duncan Stewart 2nd of Glengalmadale.** Little is known of this Duncan, though he is mentioned in the sasines set out above from the Argyle Sasine Rolls, of 1711. The issue of Duncan Stewart 2nd of Glengalmadale were probably:

[i] James of Glengalmadale, paymaster of the Appin Regiment in the '45

[ii] Rev John Stewart 1710 - 1770, an Episcopalian Clergyman, & Minister of Tain from 1742, later of Inverness 1746 - of whom hereafter.

4. **James Stewart, 3rd of Glengalmadale.** He was paymaster of the Appin Regiment in the '45. From time to time it has been suggested that this James was a half brother of Ardsheal - for example, in the appendix to an Article in "The Stewarts" [Vol. IX no 2, 1952; p.169] where the Quartermaster of the Appin Regiment is given as "James Stewart of Glengalmadale, natural brother of Ardsheal". It is likely that there is confusion here - and indeed there clearly was confusion as to the roles and identities of individuals in the minds of the Hanoverians who arrested them. It is probable that there were at least two, and possibly three, relevant people by the name of James Stewart:

[i] James, known as James of the Glen, natural brother of Ardsheal; who was ultimately tried, convicted, and hanged in 1752, for the murder of Colin Campbell of Glenure "The Red Fox". The story of the murder & trial was written up in "Notable British Trials" & by Robert Louis Stevenson in "Kidnapped". He was

probably a Captain in the Appin Regiment - see The Stewarts Vol IX no 2, page 168.

[ii]   James, Quartermaster of the Appin Regiment; said in the same Article to be a natural brother of Ardsheal; and said ultimately to have been transported [ibid p.169].

[iii] James, Paymaster of the Appin Regiment. He was clearly James of Glengalmadale.

Whether James the Quartermaster, and James, the Paymaster, are the same person is not clear. It is probable that they were. In "The Stewarts" Vol. IX no. 4, 1954, page 341, there is an Article by Miss D Stewart Linney on "Two Jacobite Prisoners", based on State Papers for 1746-1747. Among the extracts are the following - all of which Miss Stewart Linney clearly thought referred to the same man:

I.   From petitions for pardon, undated and unsigned, there appears:

"James Stewart of Glengalmadell in Kingairloch in the month of May last surrendered himself in terms of the Duke's proclamation to General Campbell who received him and gave him a receipt for his arms. He lived peaceably at home and was serviceable to General Campbell and those under his command. But some malicious information being lodged with the General ag him he was made prisoner his whole Cattle drove and his wife and eight or nine small children left in a miserable condition. He now lyes Prisoner aboard a ship in the River at Tilbury. He is none of those who drew lots for Transportation and as his case is singular and that he never had a Commission any further than being paymaster to the Stewarts of Appin, it would be an act of charity to dismiss him and allow him to go home to assist his poor family's misery. There are severalls discharged from Tilbury more concerned and not such objects of pity".

II. His name appears in a

"List of Prisoners in England Concerning whom no Directions have as yet been given"
as being at Tilbury in 1746. There is a footnote which reads

"N.B. These prisoners were sent up from Scotland and were not admitted either to Lot or Petition".

This refers to the system of selection of persons for trial, other than persons who had taken a prominent part in the Rising, which was by the process of drawing lots and taking one man in twenty to stand his trial, the remainder being pardoned and either banished or transported, some few being released with free pardons.

III. There is a Certificate signed by Major General John Campbell of Mamore (who later succeeded as Duke of Argyll: a humane and thoroughly decent man) undated:

"This is to certifie that James Stewart now prisoner in the New Jail in Southwark did surrender his arms as a Common Man which does appear by a receipt for his arms signed by General Campbell's Aid de Camp. But upon Information sometime thereafter that he was the person who ferryed from his house Lochiell, John Murray and his brother, when his Majesty's forces were in search after them, and of his being a Quarter Master or Paymaster in his brother's regiment in the Rebell Service, I sent a Party of His Majesty's Troops under my command, and apprehended the said James Stewart. But at the same time was informed that he was a man of no Estate, being no head of a Clan, and had a considerable family of small children."

IV. In a "Short Account of Rebels committed to the New Gaol, April 1747 for High Treason", there is the following:

"James Stewart, natural brother of Ardshiels was a quartermaster of Ardshiel's Regiment. Is a man of no consequence nor Fortune. He surrendered his Arms to Gen Campbell after the Battle of Culloden and was thereupon released, but afterwards he was taken upon suspicion of having assisted Mr Murray and Charles Stewart Paymaster of the Rebel Army to make their escape from a place in the Highlands, which is not true. This man was an instrument of saving the life of Capt Campbell of the Argyllshire Militia, who had the misfortune to be taken by the Rebels and in general is said to have acted a very humane part by such of the Kings troops as fell into

the hands of the Rebels. The evidence against this man is not strong & will hardly be sufficient to convict him and if he be tried he must take his trial in Scotland. He will be able to prove that after the Battle of Culloden he surrendered himself pursuant to the Duke of Cumberland's proclamation".

    V.   A list of prisoners in Tilbury Fort in April 1747 has a crossed-out entry "James Stewart, Appine, Argyll, Grazier" with the marking beside it "New Gaol".

    VI. In a memorandum dated 27th April 1747 it was recorded that

"James Steuart a natural brother of Ardshiels lately committed to the New Goal is very ill and in Irons and desires his irons may be taken off. The Goaler of the New Goal has demanded 6 Gns of each of the six Prisoners lately brought up from Tilbury for taking off their irons".

This James Stewart was ultimately transported. Whether extracts [v] and [vi] above in fact refer to the same James Stewart as James of Glengalmadale cannot be said to be certain. However, it is to be noted that in "A Muster Roll of Prince Charles Edward Stuart's Army" ed. Livingstone of Bachuil, the Quartermaster of the Appin Regiment was said to be "James Stewart, Natural Brother of Ardsheal" - who was transported. The question has to be asked whether Ardsheal really had two natural brothers, both named James? Or was the James who was transported, James of Glengalmadale? If it was he, then he left behind him a wife and "eight or nine small children". One person who may well have been turned to for help in those circumstances would have been Rev John Stewart.

5.   **Rev John Stewart** 1710-1770. It is suggested above that he was probably a son of Duncan II of Glengalmadale. The Stewarts of Appin at p. 132 refer to "Allan of whom was the Rev John Stewart of Inverness" (as set out above, this Allan was a son of Duncan II of Ardsheal). If he was not the son of Duncan II of Glengalmadale, he must have been his nephew.

John Stewart was an Episcopalian Clergyman, a comparative rarity for those days. The Episcopalian Church had been disestablished by William III in 1689, and the Protestant Church had been established in its place. In 1746 severe penal laws were introduced against Episcopalians - a move not unconnected, no doubt, with the general atmosphere of vindictive persecution against the Jacobites. The Scottish Clergy were prohibited from conducting services other than in their own houses, and with no more than four persons present. Many Chapels throughout the country were burnt - particularly after Culloden - and many Episcopalian Clergymen were thrown into gaol. "My meeting house (at Tain) was burnt to ashes in the moneth of May 1746" John Stewart wrote to Bishop Forbes on 28th February 1759, "and my dwelling house was plunder'd of all that was not put out of the way before the plundering party came" [Lyon in Mourning, Vol III, p.165]. This was no chance episode, for that plundering party of the Earl of Sutherland's militia was said to be acting under official orders [Lyon in Mourning: ibid; & Bishop Forbes' Journals p.124].

He was a deacon in Edinburgh. The Records of the Dioceses of Argyll & The Isles 1560 - 1860, ed Rev J B Craven - Kirkwall - 1907 record at p. 194

> *Edinburgh, May 2 1734, Rev Alexr Hunter to Rev John Alexander (afterwards Bishop) ... "we have here one Mr Stewart, a Deacon, to be putt in Priest's orders and to serve in Argyllshire with Mr John McLachlan".*

His ministry appears to have been firstly in Lochaber, then from 1742 to 1759 in Tain (where he had meeting houses at Cadboll, and Tain [this being the "best meeting-house" burnt in 1746] and finally from 1757 to 1770 in Inverness. In 1762 he accompanied Bishop Forbes on his major tour of the diocese of Ross, when he was equally at home preaching in Gaelic and in English. Such was the esteem in which he was held, that in 1759 Bishop Alexander of Dunkeld wrote "Stewart of Tain is a sensible and honest man..." one "fit for the Episcopate" [Journals of Bishop Forbes: p.17]. In 1762, he was one of the 4 Presbyters of Ross & Caithness who elected Bishop Forbes as a Bishop ["Journals" p.126].

Few formal records survive about the life and career of Rev John Stewart, but there are many references to him in the" Journals of Bishop Forbes" [London: Skeffington & Son Ltd, 1923, ed Ven J B Craven] & a number in Vol. III of the Lyon in Mourning [edn 1975, Edinburgh, Scottish Academic Press]. From the" Journals" in particular it is possible, however, to get a picture of a dedicated and unassuming man, clearly of considerable charm, who suffered much hardship, both for his Jacobite leanings and for his Episcopalian profession. Rev John MacLauchlan wrote to Bishop Forbes, telling of their experience after Culloden. MacLauchlan had attended the Prince to Derby and back, was at Falkirk and Culloden, and had a commission as Chaplain General to all the Forces. After Culloden he went into hiding in Ross-shire near Lochbroom, and gradually crept back towards Dingwall accompanied by Rev John Stewart "whose agreeable conversation did much to alleviate all along the irksomeness of skulking"... "In the spring of 1747, my dear comrade, Mr Stewart, was kidnapped and laid up in a prison" - this only a year after his meeting house was plundered and destroyed by the Earl of Sutherland's militia. By 1748 such was the sickness and distress in Rev John's family, that he found himself forced to accept a gift of money from Bishop Keith.

On Bishop Forbes' first episcopal journey in 1762 the entry for Friday July 16th reads:

"We took breakfast with the Rev Mr John Stewart and his Family (in Inverness); after qch he conducted me to visit Mrs Hay and Mrs Stewart, and then, returning to his House, I read prayers there at 11 o'clock to an Audience of about 100. We dined in Mr Stewart's upon a Salmon of 16 pd weight at a penny per pd., and likewise drank Tea there..." [p.148]

On Saturday July 17, 1762 [p.150]:

"Mr Stewart and I dined with Mr Fraser of Foppachie at Torbreck, two miles up the River of Ness. In passing along the side of the River by a

charming Road, you see a pretty Island of a good Length in the midst of it, being one continued Thicket of Wood..."

On Sunday July 18th, 1762 [p.150]:

"At Dinner with Mr Stewart, Mrs Mackenzie ... told ye following Narrative: - The Second or third Day after the Battle of Culloden, one Fleming, an Irishman and an Officer came roughly into her House, crying out, "O charming glorious Orders!" Lieutenant Goar, in Lord Sempil's Regiment, an Irishman, asked "What are the Orders?" - "accounts, said Fleming, are just now come to the Duke's Levee, that about 20 Rebels are found in a House or Barn, upon qch he has ordered a Troop of Dragoons to go and set fire to that House, and burn them alive; and, if any one of them should peep out his Head, let him have a bullet". "Oh Lord! what orders are these?" said Goar. Accordingly people in Inverness saw the House on Fire".

On Monday July 19, 1762, Bishop Forbes set out from Inverness, "Mr Stewart [and his son William] in the Chaise with me ... as I did not know the Roads through Ross-shire..." [p 150 ff]. They visited many people and places; and William Stewart left them after they visited Mr Thomas MacKenzie of Highfield, a "pretty new House in View of Castle-Brahan, the seat of the Earl of Seafort". John Stewart clearly had friends between Inverness and Tain, such a John Monroe of Culcairn, who used to make a present of gold to John every time that they met in Ross-shire "though he himself be a Whig and a Presbyterian" [Journals pp 232-233].

Tradition has it that it was he who removed from Appin the old parish registers for safekeeping during the '45. What is clear is that the old registers have disappeared.

John Stewart appears to have been married twice. His first wife was Anne, dau of - Mackenzie (a cousin of Mackenzie of Coul) by Anne, daughter of Alfred Gordon; and sister & eventual heiress of Colin Mackenzie Dhu, merchant of London, who by his will 1798 left £40,000 for the purchase of Newhall, Balblair, Conon Bridge, Ross-shire, which had previously been owned by his Gordon ancestors. They had issue:

[i]   William

[ii] Duncan

[iii] Charlotte; b 15th February 1746; d 19 December 1775 aged 28; and buried in the Chapel Yard, Inverness. She married Captain Alexander Shaw of Tordarroch & had issue.

William and Duncan died, apparently, without issue or at least without descendants surviving to 1842, for the succession to the entailed estate of Newhall passed in 1842 to the grandson of Charlotte - vide Burke's LG sub nom Shaw-Mackenzie of Newhall; &o "Shaw of Tordarroch".

According to the Stewarts of Appin p.124, Rev John Stewart married Margaret, dau Robert Stewart, 9th of Appin. I have found no other Rev John Stewart, than this one. If the book entry is correct, Margaret Stewart of Appin must have been a second wife, for on 19th July 1802, she was served heir portioner special to her brother Dugald Stewart of Appin (who died March 1769) in Invernenty with salmon fishings in the parish of Balquhidder, Perthshire. She was the described as being in Greenock. Her co-heir was her nephew Dugald Stewart of Invernahyle. Where this marriage took place, and whether there were any children of it, is not known. But the fact of the marriage is confirmed by a note from the Records of the Dioceses of Argyll and The Isles:

> "In 1660, Mr Arch McCalman was appointed to repair the kirk in Appin. Mr McCalman became Minister of Lismore and Appin in 1688. Robert Stewart, 9th of Appin, was laird at that time. He died abroad between 1730 and 1739, was twice married and had a large family. His daughter Margaret married Rev John Stewart of Inverness".

Rev John Stewart died in Inverness on 10th April 1770. His papers were sealed up for Bishop Forbes, who removed two bundles of their correspondence and took them to Leith. Bishop Forbes composed a lengthy Latin inscription for John's tomb

H.S.E.

Reverundus Joannes Stewart A.M.

a familia de Appin oriundus
qui
Animam Christo placide exhalavit
Aprilis X   Anno MDCCCLXX
Aetatis suae LX.
In spem beatae resurrectionis.
Presbyter
Ecclesias direptae, gementis, lachrymantis,
Nunquam sine laude nominandus
Filius et subditus fidelissimus
Nihilo lucri emendus,
Nullo periculo deterritus,
Amicus sincerus, firmus
Maritus et parens amantissimus,
ut verbo omnia
Pastor religiosus prudens intaminatus
Christianus vere orthodoxus, pius
Marmor hoc
Maesti posueri amici.
Moriar ego morte justorum et sit finis meus sicut illius -
Num. 23.10
In memoria perpetua est justis - Ps. 112. 6.
Memoria justi est benedicta - Prov. 10. 7.

Rev John Stewart was buried in the Chapel Yard, Inverness. After his death, without consulting anybody, and much to the consternation of Bishop Forbes and others, his widow, Mrs Stewart, sold the chapel which John had erected at his own expense, to the Jurists.

C: Other Ardsheal Stewarts

Apart from those already mentioned, the Order Book of the Appin Regiment lists:

Captain James Stewart	brother to Ardsheal ? James of the Glen?
Lieutenant William Stewart	of Ardsheal's family"
Colour Bearer Dougal Stewart	? of Ardsheal's family
Adjutant William Stewart	"of Ardsheal's family"

Others:

Allan Mor Stewart	in Ardsheal's family (wounded at Culloden)
3 John Stewarts	all killed at Culloden

Chapter 6: Stewart 1828 Onwards

Murdoch Stewart

Born circa 1790; married 1828; died circa 1835-1837.

He is the earliest proven forebear. He was a sawyer or shipbuilder[1], ie a shipwright, in Merkinch, Inverness. In the late 18th and early 19th centuries, there was a fairly considerable ship-building industry in Inverness, building ships both for the Caledonian Canal and for ordinary sea going Merkinch is that part of Inverness, on the west side of the River Ness, where the industry was centred.

He married on 19th August 1828 in Inverness **Ann Ross,** daughter of Robert Ross, of the family of Ross of Morangie, near Tain . They were my great-great grandparents.

They died in a plague of cholera probably in around 1835-1837. Aunt Annie I'ons, née Stewart, said that her father, Robert Stewart, was orphaned when he was 6. Cholera was almost an annual occurrence in the 1820s and early 1830s in Inverness (and in many other places). [2] The

---

[1] Murdoch was described as a sawyer on his marriage certificate; and as a shipbuilder on Robert Stewart's marriage certificate in 1860.

[2] Cholera was particularly prevalent in Inverness in 1832 and 1834. The Cholera Records stored in Nairn include a "Sanitary Enquiry - Scotland - Inverness - G Anderson 1841, "During the prevalence of Cholera in 1832 and 1834, a Board of Health was organised, which applied very stringent means for removing filth and cleaning and ventilating and

practice was to bury all the cholera victims in a common pit, with no gravestones. Certain it is that I have found no record of their deaths. But registration of births, marriages, and deaths was not then compulsory in Scotland.

It was left to **Alexander Ross**, Ann's brother, to bring up my great grandfather, Robert Stewart. Alexander Ross was a tenant farmer at Seafield of Raigmore, Inverness, and did not marry until 1835. That date raises the question Robert Stewart, if orphaned earlier, should have been brought up by his Uncle Alexander Ross, rather than by another, married, Ross relative.

Family Tradition, as handed down to me by my grandmother Freda Stewart, is that our family came from Appin. When, or from which branch of the Appin Stewarts, she did not relate - and since I was under 11 when she died in 1949, I did not have the foresight, or knowledge, to ask. She was a Scot, interested in her family. On that count, tradition handed down from her should be reliable. And some cousins hold the same tradition.

But why, if this is right, did our family adopt the crest of the demi-lion rampant, holding in its dexter paw a cross-crosslet fitchée? This goes back at any rate to my great grandfather, Robert Stewart 1830-1885. It is not a recognised Stewart crest, though the demi lion simpliciter, or holding some object for difference, is. It is almost invariably associated with Stewarts of Royal (now invariably illegitimate) descent.[1]

On evidence of the crest alone, it might be expected that the family was of Royal Stewart descent; with the cross crosslet fitchée denoting a connection such as Mar, through one of the illegitimate sons of the Wolf of Badenoch, Alexander Stewart, 4th son to King Robert II by his first wife, Elizabeth Muir - such as the Stewarts of Kinchardin in Strathspey.

---

whitewashing the dwellings of the poor by which they were much benefitted..." Dr J I Nicol MD reported "When cholera prevailed in Inverness it was more fatal than in almost any other town in Britain...."

[1] Correspondence of 1970 with Sir Iain Moncreiffe of that Ilk, one of the leading experts on Scots Heraldry; & of 1959-1963 with Lyon Office and Others.

According to Duncan Stewart (1739) "most of the Stewarts in Strathspey, Murray, and Inverness are come of Kinchardin". And it is known that there were Kinchardin Stewarts in (the city of) Inverness in the 18th Century.[1] But such descent does not accord with the tradition handed down to me.

Robert Stewart 1830-1885 was described as "armiger" - ie of coat armour - in J Foster's "Alumni Oxoniensis 1715-1886" under the entry for my grandfather, Robert Barton Stewart's degree of BA in 1886. It must, however, be said that the term "armiger" was often used very loosely. I have never been able to trace any registration or matriculation of arms to Robert Stewart. Theoretically, at least, each generation is supposed to matriculate their arms in the Lyon Court, though the requirement is regularly broken. A crest is not immutable or sacrosanct in Scottish heraldry, unlike the shield. For example, Cameron of Lochiel changed his crest, for reasons now not clear, in the 18th century.[2] But it remains odd, if Robert Stewart was an Appin Stewart that he used as a crest something not associated in any known way with the Appin Stewarts [their crest being the Unicorn's head].

Two Stewart cousins said that the family originated from Aberdeen. One was Lucy Beck, daughter of my great aunt Mary Hamilton Beck née Stewart. The other was Margaret Freeman, daughter of my great uncle Percy Lee Stewart. Lucy Beck had little, if anything more, to back up what she said, other than that she had discovered that Aberdeen was one of the last places to be hit by a plague of cholera; and Murdoch and Ann Stewart died of cholera. But it is known that they married and lived in Inverness; and that cholera used to hit Inverness with regularity. It seems to me to be more probable than not that they died in Inverness.

Margaret Freeman's account is altogether of more interest. It is that Robert Stewart 1830-1885 was not buried in the grave at Winkfield Parish Church, Berkshire, where the tombstone bears his name and the names of

---

[1] See Chapter 3, page 26
[2] Correspondence of 1969 with Major John Stewart of Ardvorlich.

his wife and of all their children; but that he was buried in Aberdeen - the inference being that he was buried in the place where his family came from. This is however wholly incorrect. The burial Register for St Mary, Winkfield, records that Robert Stewart was buried there on 25th March 1885. [1]

I have only ever seen one direct piece of evidence of any connection of our Stewart family with Aberdeen. In an obituary in the Port Elizabeth Observer on Robert Stewart in 1885, it was stated that he "entered the banking business after a residence in Aberdeen". Whether this is right, what the residence was, for how long, or with whom, no clue was given. All that can be said is that since he started his banking career in 1847, he cannot have had "a residence in Aberdeen" for long, if at all.

Margaret Freeman (in South Africa) has a Jacobite goblet, which is said to have been handed down through generations of the Stewarts. This may be indicative that our Stewarts were Jacobites, which would not be at all surprising if they were of Appin.

I have never been able to trace for sure who was Murdoch's father, or indeed where he was born. The search of registers has concentrated on Inverness, Dingwall & district, and Aberdeen [see note at end of this section on records searched].

The only entries found that could be relevant were:

> a. Fodderty: 29th Jan 1794, a son to John Stewart,
> Inchrorie, baptised Murdoch
> b. Kiltearn 30th July 1790, Alexander Stewart, tenant in
> Clare, had a son baptised before witnesses name Murdoch.

No further trace of either Murdoch has been found. I incline to think that the Kiltearn Murdoch is unlikely - because there were several other siblings, and I have not heard of anything indicating that my great grandfather Robert Stewart kept in touch with any Stewart, as opposed to Ross, relatives. This makes me suppose that Robert Stewart was an only child of an only, or only surviving, child.

---

[1] Berkshire Record Office letter, 3rd October 1995

It is possible that John Stewart, Inchrorie, Fodderty, was our forebear. Fodderty is in the Dingwall district, and Hugh Ross, brother of Ann Ross or Stewart, lived in Dingwall, where he was a Messenger at Arms. There were a number of Stewart families in the Dingwall district, mostly of Bute descent, some from Galloway (due to intermarriage of the Mackenzies of Seaforth with the Stewarts of Galloway), and a few, I believe, of Appin descent. John Stewart, Inchrorie, does not appear to fit anywhere into the main tree of Stewarts in the Dingwall district (those in and around Dunglust) supplied to me by the late Hector Stewart. It may well be therefore that he was not a member of the Stewarts established there for some time; but that he was, as speculated in the previous chapter, of Ardsheal descent.

At this stage, all that can be said is that Murdoch Stewart may be the son born on 29th January 1794 to John Stewart, Inchrorie; that John Stewart does not fit in with the chart of the main family of Stewarts in the district; that Inchrorie was a farm near to Brahan Castle, the seat of the Mackenzies of Seaforth; and that if a descendant of Ardsheal via Glengalmadale, as speculated in the previous chapter, his presence at Fodderty could be explained by the fact that Rev John Stewart 1710-1770 is said to have been married to Margaret, dau. Robert Stewart 9th of Appin, whose brother Dugald Stewart 10th and last of Appin married Mary Mackenzie of Seaforth. Rev John Stewart was therefore not only a Stewart of Glengalmadale descent, but related to Mackenzie of Seaforth by marriage. Whether this will ever be proved, or disproved, remains for the future.

The only child of Murdoch Stewart & Ann Ross was Robert Stewart, my great grandfather.

Hope and Faith

Note:

Correspondence 1960-1962 with the Scots Ancestry Research Society & Others detailing the following searches:

Registers searched for birth of Murdoch Stewart:

Inverness 1790-1810: & the neighbouring parishes of:

> Petty
> Kirkhill
> Kiltarlity
> Croy and Dalcross
> Daviot and Dunlichty
> Urquhart and Glenmoriston [all 1798 - 1810]

Dingwall 1790-1800, and the neighbouring parishes of:

> Fodderty
> Kiltearn
> Urray
> Urquhart and Logie Wester (for Conon Bridge)

The Black Isle parishes of:

> Urquhart and Logie Wester
> Killearnan
> Avoch
> Knockbain
> Cromarty
> Rosemarkie and Resolis
> Kilmorack for Beauly [all 1790 - 1800]

Aberdeen and Old Machar 1798-1810.

Registers searched for the deaths of Murdoch & Ann Stewart:

> Inverness 1830-1851
> Aberdeen & Old Machar 1830-1839.

Grave Yards searched:

The Chapel Yard
The Old High Church Yard
The Greyfriars Church Yard, all at Inverness

Robert Stewart, 1830 - 1885

The only child of **Murdoch Stewart & Ann Ross**, Robert Stewart was born in Inverness on 6th October 1830, and baptised there on 13th October 1830. He was orphaned at about the age of 6, and was brought up by his mother's brother, Alexander Ross, who kept a hotel in Inverness and farmed 49 acres at Seafield of Raigmore (as a tenant). -see 1851 Census of Inverness. Seafield is an estate about a mile from the centre of Inverness, whose one time owner was Aeneas William Mackintosh, b. 1819, Liberal MP for Inverness 1868-1874. Seafield Farm, where Alexander Ross lived, had 9 rooms with one or more windows [1861 Census of Inverness] - it was a substantial house, the average being 2-3 rooms. The Census shows that Alexander Ross was then farming 73 acres, employing 5 labourers.

Robert was schooled at the Inverness Academy[1], where he was a classmate and became a lifelong friend of Roderick Noble, who himself rose to eminence as a Professor in South Africa. The Port Elizabeth Observer in its Obituary of Robert Stewart in 1885 recorded that after leaving school he resided in Aberdeen If this happened, it cannot have been for long.

In 1847, he joined the Bank of Scotland[2] in Inverness, staying there until 1853. From 1853 to 1856, he was a Clerk in the National Provincial Bank in Manchester. From there he was promoted to Accountant (i.e. second officer) of the National Provincial Bank at Bangor, North Wales. He held that position 1856-1863; and was then promoted to Manager at Cowbridge, 1863-1864. In 1864, Robert joined the Standard Bank of South Africa, as their first General Manager, to which he travelled in 1865. He remained in South Africa until 1876, when ill health forced him to return to England, to the less onerous, but also less remunerative post of London Manager and Secretary.

It is of interest to note the enormous growth in his rate of earnings, as he achieved promotion and success:

Bank of Scotland	1847-1850	£10 pa
	1850-1851	£25 pa
	1851	£40 pa
	1851-1852	£50 pa
National Provincial	1853	£80 pa at Manchester
	1856	£90 pa Second Officer at Bangor
	1857	£100 pa
	1859	£110 pa
	1863	£150 pa
	1863	£200 pa, Manager at Cowbridge
Standard Bank	1864	£1,000 pa; job guaranteed for 3 years; with one free passage, and to be on half pay during the voyage.
	1866	£1,200 pa, retrospective to date of his original employment.
	1866 (end)	£1,500 pa.

Thus in the 3 year period 1863-1866, his salary increased 10 fold; and over the 19 year period since he had started in banking, his salary had risen 150 fold.

While at Bangor, he met and married **Sophia Ann Boyce**. [Her name is spelt Ann in Robert's will; but Anne in the copy of their marriage certificate]. She was a governess to a local family. The Boyce family came from Chertsey, and a number of them were Quakers. They married on 14th August 1860, at Chertsey - one of the witnesses being his uncle Alex M Ross.

Robert & Sophia Ann Stewart went to South Africa, arriving in Cape Town, in February 1865, with their 3 oldest children - Alec aged 3½; Annie aged 2; and my grandfather Robert [Bertie] aged 2 months. It was an unpropitious arrival, for their ship was wrecked off Cape Town. But the Stewart family escaped unharmed; and Robert rapidly set about organising the affairs of the Standard Bank. Their home was in Port Elizabeth.

He was viewed as "a born banker and a consummate organiser and man of business". Lewis Mitchell said "The Bank's foundations were so well and truly laid by Robert Stewart that his successors have only to follow in his footsteps". At the time of their arrival, the economy of the Cape was essentially in wool. But it was an inferior quality wool, ill got up, badly sorted, or half grown. The whole scene was set for a collapse in the price of wool, and for the years of depression (1864-1870). Another part of the background to his appointment was the damaging tendency of branches to operate independently as isolated units, each intent upon making the best possible showing in terms of profits. In the First Hundred Years of the Standard Bank, the passage appears:

> *"The root of the trouble was the autonomy previously enjoyed by local banks whose Directors still remained in charge. The creation of a system of "circles" within each of which a number of smaller branches were controlled by a larger one did little to improve the position. The effective remedy had to be a new esprit de corps, not easy to instil in a staff scattered over vast distances and physically isolated from one another. What could be done to change the frame of mind, for instance, which led the Port Elizabeth office to bank in Cape Town with the Cape of Good Hope Bank, on the grounds that its charges were lower than those of the Standard Bank itself: or which prompted the branch in King William's Town to complain that it could make little headway against competitors, if Cape Town continued to levy such a high rate of interest on its overdraft? Here lay one of the reasons for the appointment in 1864 of the first General Manager, Robert Stewart, 'for the general unity of the Bank, without which it cannot prosper... While the Cape is at issue with the Frontier and each circle of the Frontier is disputing on the privilege and independence of action which they suppose*

*particularly to belong to themselves, it is impossible that this unity of purpose and
action can obtain'."*

At the end of 1867, the Secretary of the Bank, Mr W F Searle, wrote
to Robert asking him to suggest suitable representation so that he could
visit the Directors in London in October 1868.

By 1869, the economic clouds began to clear in the Cape - though the
impending completion of the Suez Canal seemed to threaten the very
existence of the Cape with its traditional position as the half way house to
India. But the long drought in the interior was over by 1869; business
seemed to be taking heart; and the Press was reporting, almost daily, new
finds of diamonds in the interior.

Robert Stewart was personally responsible for the Bank's policy
towards the diamond fields. There were many difficulties. South African
diamonds, with their yellowish tinge, had a lower value than white stones.
The natives would accept nothing for their services other than gold coin.
Criticism was made of the prices obtained for stones sold in Europe.
Matters were not helped by the fact that many of the best stones were
acquired at the fields by experts such as Alfred Beit, who had the
experience and training of Amsterdam to draw on. Nevertheless, for many
years the Standard Bank was the only Bank to be represented on the
diamond fields; and this made a major contribution to the success of the
Bank. Further prestige accrued in 1875, when it was appointed Sole
Bankers to the Cape Government, under arrangements formally
sanctioned by the Cape Parliament.

As the Bank prospered, however, Robert's health suffered. In 1872,
when his salary was increased to £2,000 pa, he was invited by the Board to
go on a visit to England, in the hope that his health might be fully
restored. Furthermore he was to be on full pay during the visit. He was in
London in September 1872, and staying with his Ross cousins in Glasgow
in May 1873. He returned to South Africa later in 1873.

By 1875, his health had broken down, and he applied for and was
appointed London Manager and Secretary - at the reduced salary of
£1,500 pa. He took up this post in 1876, and was shortly after given the

title of Chief General Manager. In South Africa, he was succeeded by his cousin, Hugh Cameron Ross, and by Gilbert Farie, who were appointed Joint General Managers at Port Elizabeth.

On his retirement from South Africa, the staff of the Bank in South Africa subscribed 400 guineas to present him with a service of silver, made by Edward & Son of Glasgow, in the Chinese style, and hallmarked for 1875 - an Epergne, Tea Pot, Cream Jug, Sugar Bowl & tongs, Coffee Pot, and Hot Water Jug. The Tea Pot is inscribed

"Presented as a tribute of respect and esteem by the Officers in South Africa of the Standard Bank to Robert Stewart Esquire on his retirement from the office of General Manager in the South African Colonies 8th June 1876".

After the death of Sophia Ann Stewart in 1925, the silver was disposed of as follows: the Epergne went to the oldest son, Alec; and thence to his oldest son, Robert Ross Stewart, who, to his later regret, sold it. The Tea Pot, Cream Jug, Sugar Bowl & Tongs went to the older daughter, Annie I'ons - who later gave them to Robert Ross Stewart. He in due course gave them to me, as the senior line of the family after him. The

Coffee Pot and Hot Water Jug (along with some Kimberley diamond brooches and rings that Robert had had made up for his wife) went to the second daughter, Mary Hamilton Beck. Her daughter, Lucy Beck, had them until her death in 1968.

On his return to London in 1876, the Directors of the Bank commissioned Sir Daniel MacNee PRSA to paint his portrait, voting 100 guineas for the purpose. It was shipped to Port Elizabeth to hang in the offices there. After Robert's

Picture 1 Joan Pell's copy of Robert Stewart's portrait

death in 1885, Sophia Ann asked to be given it. The Bank refused for some time, but had the portrait brought back to hang in the London Office. Then in 1900, they presented the portrait to her. After her death in 1925, it passed to the third son, Hugh, and from him to his daughter Margaret Alston. In 1953, she gave it back to the Bank, who in 1960 had a scaled down copy painted by a South African painter, Joan Pell, which they presented to me [3]. The original now hangs on the 27th floor of the Standard Bank Centre in Johannesburg [4].

He was a keen Freemason - I have several Certificates recording his admission to different degrees of Freemasonry, between 1856 and 1877. On 11th February 1874, he was elected a Fellow of the Royal Geographical Society. He also served in the Territorial Army. On 7th April 1864, he was appointed Ensign in the 18th Glamorganshire Rifle Volunteers. On 30th September 1864, he was promoted to Lieutenant. On 13th August 1874, he was commissioned as Captain in Prince Alfred's Volunteer Guards in Port Elizabeth - the uniform being of dark green, scarlet facings, with white helmets, and scarlet puggarees. Though there was a Highland Company, it appears that he was not in it [5]. He was also a Magistrate in Port Elizabeth, the commission being dated 2nd November 1870.

There were problems in Prince Alfred's Volunteer Guard, when the junior officers "mutinied" in 1876 against the commanding officer, Colonel Wylde [6] at the Zwartkops Regatta. RS took over Command for a few months. At the monthly parade the following Commanding Officer's Memorandum was read:

> *"The Officer Commanding takes the earliest opportunity of referring in the strongest terms of reprobation, and with feelings of extreme regret, to the disgraceful acts of drunkenness and insubordination committed by several members of the corps, at Zwartkops, on the occasion of her Majesty's Birthday.*
>
> *These acts were of so serious a character as to call for investigation by a Court of Enquiry, composed of officers of the Corps. Before this Court, which sat on 2nd inst, several of the officers pleaded guilty of the disgraceful acts*

charged against them. Discipline being essential not only to the usefulness and popularity, but even to the very existence of the corps, several of the officers have been punished by the infliction of fines, varying in amount in proportion to the gravity of the charges brought against them. In the case of two others, however, no mitigating circumstances could be adduced in extenuation of their disgraceful conduct, and in justice to the respectable members of the corps, and as an example to others, it was deemed necessary to adopt the painful course of purging the corps of their presence, and they have accordingly been dismissed.

Volunteers! Let me beg to remember the obligations you are under, and the duties which you owe to your officers, to the Government, to the community around you, and to yourselves. Never forget that when you put on the uniform of a volunteer, you cease for the time being to be a civilian; you become amenable to those rules and regulations which are essential to the good discipline and control of all large bodies of men. Though the discipline, to which you are expected to submit, may not be of so rigid a character as that which prevails in the Regular Army, there cannot be a doubt that the qualities which best adorn a noble British soldier, are those which deserve to be highly cultivated by every volunteer. When on duty there should be the same steadfastness and sobriety of conduct, the same respect for your officers, the same ready cheerfulness to carry out all their commands.

Assist your officers in every possible way to check the slightest signs of insubordination, and to perfect the discipline of the Corps. Look upon the honour of the Corps as a thing to be jealously guarded, and remember that even one disreputable character, or one disgraceful act, may be sufficient to tarnish the reputation of the body to which you belong, and to throw reproach and suspicion upon the whole volunteer movement.

As the strength of the chain is the strength of the weakest link in it, so the public will judge of the character of the Corps, not by the hundreds of steady respectable men to be found in its ranks, but by the few who through ignorance, carelessness, or vicious propensities expose the Corps to unfavourable comment.

Let what has taken place be a timely warning to this latter class, and let all henceforth in their respective positions, work together with hearty goodwill for the prosperity, discipline, and moral elevation of our Corps."

R. Stewart, Captain Commanding.

In 1879, he was invited to accept the post of Agent General for the Colony in London, which he declined. In 1880, he was active in helping to float a loan for the Colony of £1,023,200. In 1882 he was appointed a Member of the Council of Advisers established in London to assist the Colonial Agency. In 1884, he was appointed a Trustee of the Cape of Good Hope Sinking Fund.

Picture 2: Robert Stewart by Malcolm Stewart

He was an Honorary Member of the London Invernesshire Association and took great interest in its work [Inverness Chronicle 1st April 1885]. At the time of the 1881 Census Robert was not recorded as being with his family, who then were living at Minova Vale, Lordship Lane, Camberwell. He was at the time in South Africa assessing the boom at Kimberley – see p.70 in the Standard Bank.

Apart from the MacNee portrait of Robert Stewart, there is another portrait, by Malcolm Stewart, dated 1883. My great grandmother lived latterly with her son Walter. This portrait was in the possession of the descendants of Walter Stewart (the youngest child) until Sal Stewart (widow of Brigadier Gordon Stewart) gave it to me in 1996. I have never heard of any portrait of Sophia Ann Stewart.

Robert died on 20th March 1885, at his home, Seafield, Blakeney Road, Beckenham, Kent. He was buried at St Mary's Church, Winkfield,

Berkshire, next to his father in law, John Pierce Boyce, and the Revd George Boyce. Sophia Ann Stewart was buried in the same grave after her death on 19th December 1925 (at Denham, Bucks, the home of her oldest son, Alec). Probate of his will was granted on 30th April 1885 to his executors, his widow, Sophia and his eldest son Alec. The estate was sworn at £9,483:13:4.

The Diamond Fields Times, 25th March 1885, reported:

> *"No man wielding such power as he wielded in this Country, ever used that power with greater consideration for the general welfare than he did. He was a most conscientious and upright man in all his dealings. There was excellence in all he did. He, by courteous manner, amenable temper, and generous treatment of his subordinates, won for himself not only their respect, but their sincere affection."*

Robert Stewart & Sophia Ann Boyce had 8 children

[i]   Alexander Boyce Stewart, 1861-1930

[ii]   Annie Ross (Stewart) I'ons, 1862 - 1950

[iii] **Robert Barton Stewart**, my grandfather, 1864-1908

[iv]   Percy Lee Stewart, 1866 - 1943

[v]   Hugh Milton Stewart, 1868 - 1942

[vi]   Mary Hamilton (Stewart) Beck 1870 - 1940

[vii] Gilbert MacDonald Stewart, 1873 - 1900

[viii] Walter Grahame Stewart, 1874 - 1947

Notes:

> Note 1: Letter Inverness Royal Academy 4th May 1965 - no records going back to RS date
>
> Note 2: Letter 17.09.1959 Bank of Scotland to RMS
>
> Note 3: Correspondence of 1959-1960 about the copy of the MacNee portrait
>
> Note 4: Letter Lord Barber, Chairman Standard Chartered Bank to Joan Haw, 25.04.1986
>
> Note 5: Letter Standard Bank 2.05.1960
>
> Note 6: Letter Port Elizabeth City Librarian 20th May 1966

Sources:

> Birth, Marriage, and Death Certificates.
>
> 1851 Census of Inverness
>
> History of the Standard Bank of South Africa, 1862-1913 [Glasgow, 1914]
>
> The First Hundred Years of the Standard Bank, by J A Henry [OUP 1963]
>
> South Africa Illustrated News, 28th March 1885

Documents & Certificates in possession of Robin Stewart:

National Provincial Bank:

1. Appointment as Clerk, Manchester; 20.05.1853; salary £80; + security £1,000
2. Appointment as Accountant, Bangor; 5.02.1856; salary £90; + security £1,000
3. 1.4.1857: Salary increase by £10, to £100 pa, from 1st January 1857
4. 19.04.1859: salary increase to £110 pa, from 1st Jan 1859
5. 29.12.1862; letter acknowledging RS' request for promotion
6. 30.3.1863: salary increase to £150 pa
7. 25.06.1863; appointment as Manager, Cowbridge.
8. 22.12.1864: Nat Prov Bank releases 2 life policies & confirms bonus for1864

Standard Bank of South Africa Ltd:

9. 14.11.1864: RS to Directors, accepting office of General Manager in South Africa @ £1,000 pa; min contract 3 yrs; no sailing before Jan 1865; rent free house in Port Elizabeth.

10. 18.11.1864: Searle (Secretary of Bank) to RS, confirming appointment; half pay during voyage.

11. 7.01.1865: Searle to RS, with Board's Regulations for guidance in general management of Bank's business in South Africa.

12. 9.01.1866: Salary increase to £1,200 pa, retrospective to date of original appointment.

13. 26.02.1866: Bank to RS confirming above increase

14. 9.11.1866: Bank to RS, salary increase to £1,500 pa from 5.12.1866

15. 3.07.1867: Bank to RS - new 3 yr contract at £1,500 pa

16. 3.07.1867: Searle to RS, re RS recommendation that Bank should acquire its own shares, & reference to Counsel's opinion thereon.

17. 4.12.1867: Searle to RS, to ask for suggestion for suitable representative in South Africa, to enable RS to visit Directors in October 1868.

18. 24.1.1868: Searle to RS, re issue of shares by the Bank, wanting opinion & advice

19. 6.01.1872: Searle to RS; salary increase to £1,800

20. 8.03.1872: Bank Chairman to RS re salary increase

21. 9.05.1873: Bank to RS in Glasgow: resolution that house in Port Elizabeth be granted to RS rent free.

22. 14.09.1875: Robert White, Chairman of the week of the Bank, to RS, appointment as London Manager and Secretary @ £1,500 pa; & regretting that ill health was forcing him to take less lucrative and less onerous position. Request to recommend successor in South Africa.

23. 22.01.1884: Power of Attorney, Standard Bank to RS

Appointment as Justice of the Peace:

24. 2.11.1870: Colonial Office, Cape Town - Commission as JP for Port Elizabeth.

25. 14.11.1870: RS to Colonial Office, re issue of Commission in right name

26. 24.11.1870: Colonial Office to RS - issue of new & correct Commission

Miscellaneous Documents re South Africa

27. 8.03.1872: Agent General to RS at 10 Clements Lane, asking for his services on Council of Advice to be appointed to Agency in London.

28. 10.01.1879: Alex Mais, of Standard Bank Cape Town, re wish that RS would accept position of Agent General for the Colony.

29. 13.04.1880: Hampden Willis, Acting Under Colonial Secretary, to RS, thanking him for help in floating loan of £1,023,200

30. 13.04.1880: John Miller, office of Treasurer of Colony, Cape Town, ditto.

31. 3.08.1880: John Hampden to RS, re conferment of borrowing powers on Cape Government, and copies of Cape Acts of Parliament.

32. 19.09.1882: Hampden Willis, Under Colonial Secretary, Cape Town, appointing RS as Member of Council of Advisers in connection with establishment of Colonial Agency in London.+ copy Rules & Regulations for the Department of Agent General in London.

33. 19.09.1882: copy/ Commission Sir Hercules Robinson, Governor & C in C, Cape, to Captain Charles Mills CMG, Agent General for Colony in London; certified true copy by RS. + copy of Commission of Appointment of Captain Charles Mills as Agent General.

34. 21.09.1882: Charles Mills, Agent General, inviting RS to meeting of Council on 27.09.82.

35. 14.08.1884; Government Notice no 714 of 1884, Appointment of RS as Trustee of Sinking Fund.10.09.1884;

36. Instructions for guidance of trustees of Cape of Good Hope Sinking Fund (several copies) + covering letters relating thereto.

Freemasonry:

37. 11.09.1856; Admission to United Grand Lodge in 3rd degree, St David's Lodge, Bangor
38. 23.11.1874; Admission as an "Excellent and Perfect Prince Rose Croix of HRDM"
39. 12.04.1877: Notice of election to 30th degree, conferment to be on 8th May.
40. 8.05.1877: Proclamation as "Grand elected Knight K H"

Royal Geographical Society:

41. 11.02.1874; Fellow of the Royal Geographical Society

Territorial Army:

42. 7.04.1864; Ensign, 18th Glamorganshire Rifle Volunteers
43. 30.09.1864: Lieutenant's Commission, ditto
44. 13.08.1874; Captain, Prince Alfred's Volunteer Guards, Port Elizabeth
    Probate:
45. Probate of Will, on copy of Will, granted to Sophia Anne Stewart, of Seafield, Blakeney Road, Beckenham, Kent & Alexander Boyce Stewart, eldest son, as Executors. Estate of £9,483:13:4

Obituary:

46. Copy Obituary, Inverness Courier, 9th April 1885

Bible:

47. Family Bible recording the marriage, children, and descendants, of Robert Stewart & Sophia Ann Boyce.

Children of Robert Stewart & Sophia Ann Boyce

1. **Alexander Boyce Stewart**: 1861 - 1930. Uncle Alec was born 15th June 1861, at Bangor, North Wales. He was a stockbroker with J & A Scrimgeour, one of the most reputable firms in London. He always declined to join the partnership, because he would then have had to share the commissions from his personal clients (including the Salvation Army). Uncle Alec had a large income, around £5,000 pa in the 1920s; but his standard of living was also high - the norm for lunch was a dozen oysters and a half a bottle of champagne. When he died, he left barely £5,000. He married 5th July 1892 Amy Tolhurst (who died 5th March 1940). They lived at Denham, Bucks. Alec died on 18th March 1930 at Funchal, Madeira, leaving twin sons and a daughter:

   I. *Robert Ross Stewart*: 1893-1988: Captain RN, Justice of the Peace, DL Hampshire. b 25th October 1893. Educated at Royal Naval Colleges at Osborne and Dartmouth. Joined the Royal Navy in 1908. Served through the Great War 1914-1918; Lt Commander 1923; Captain 1935. Served in 2nd World War 1939-1945 as Press Liaison Officer, London Naval Conference, and in command of HMAS President, HMAS Hobart, and HMAS Australia; Commodore commanding Londonderry Escort Force; Chief Staff Officer, Orkney & Shetland Command; & Senior British Naval Officer, Trinidad. ADC 1944. Retired 1945.

   In retirement, he was a County Councillor (1946) & Alderman (1959); a keen cricketer and member of MCC; and (with Aileen) a knowledgeable gardener, and philosopher, and a Member and Trustee of the Findhorn Trust.

   He married 3rd April 1923 Aileen Elizabeth Hastings, daughter of George Hastings of Runcton, Chichester (Solicitor in Hastings & Hastings of Hong Kong). He died aged 94, on 27th February 1988. She died 2 days short of her

99th birthday, on 30th December 1994. They had no children, save an adopted daughter Mary Christian (b. 25.12.1934) who married (October 1960) Major Charles Gilchrist-Fisher, 5th Royal Inniskilling Dragoon Guards (with issue).

II. *George Duncan Stewart:* 1893-1959; b 25th October 1893 (a twin). Duncan was a stockbroker, and a partner in Scrimgeour's - his father's old firm. During the war he was a Lt Colonel. After the war he retired to Jersey. He married (18.01.1926 in London) Lilian Joan Pyman, and died in Jersey on 29th January 1959. She died 1994. They had no children, save an adopted son, Andrew Howard Stewart, b 27.03.1945, who is married & lives in Jersey (with issue).

III. *Barbara Lillian* 1896 - 1935; b 4.04.1896; m 5.04.1930 at Karachi, India, Hugh Lawrence Francis - by whom she had a son, John, b 1.01.1931. All three of them were killed in the Quetta earthquake on 31st May 1935.

Thus the descendants of Alexander Boyce Stewart are now extinct.

2. **Annie Ross (Stewart) I'ons:** 1862-1950. Born 17th December 1862 at Bangor, North Wales; she died 9th November 1950, in her 88th year. She married 24th June 1903, at Sydenham, Algernon I'ons, a commercial artist, who designed posters for companies such as Heinz. He died 12th September 1954. They lived at Hatch End, Middlesex. She had no children. Aunt Annie had, on her mother's death, the Presentation Silver Tea Pot, Cream Jug, Sugar Bowl & Tongs, given to Robert Stewart by the Standard Bank Officers in 1876. She gave these to Robert Ross Stewart; who in turn gave them to me in 1976. She also had the "Kimberley" diamond rings and brooches, made from stones collected by Robert Stewart for his wife. She died intestate, and he husband gave them to Lucy Beck.

3. **Robert Barton Stewart**: 1864-1908. My grandfather - of whom hereafter.

4. **Percy Lee Stewart**: 1866-1943; he was born 26th July 1866 in Port Elizabeth, and died in South Africa on 10th October 1943. After school in England, he returned to South Africa. For a time he worked for the Standard Bank. He had Robert Stewart's library of South African Books. Most of it, apparently, was destroyed by white ants. He also had a collection of early rare and valuable South African stamps formed by my grandfather. And his daughter Margaret Freeman has some crested silver (from Robert Stewart) and an old Jacobite goblet of a rare design, said to have been handed down successive generations of the Stewarts since the '45. He married on 11th December 1901, at Port Elizabeth, Ina Frances Ellen Pettit (who died 26th August 1936 in Cape Town). He died in South Africa on 10th October 1943. They had issue:

[i] Margaret Cuyler: b 28.07.1906; m 14.11.1934 Spencer Algernon Freeman; she died 1998, leaving issue:

I. Glen Robert Freeman, b.2.08.1936; m 3.04.1961 Carolyn -; and has 2 daughters Veronica b 1966, and Patricia b 1968, both married & with children in South Africa.

II. Ian Cuyler Freeman: b 3.03.1938; d 14.05.1938.

III. David Spencer Freeman, b 21.01.1946

[ii] Frances Lee, b 4.12.1907, m 6.07.1940 at Nelspruit, East Transvaal, Herbert Vincent Adcock, & had issue:

a. Robert Vincent Adcock; b 12.12.1947
b. Mary Fairbridge: b 13.09.1911; d in infancy.

5. **Hugh Milton Stewart**: 1868 - 1942; 5th child & 4th son; b in Port Elizabeth on 13.09.1868. Educated at Dulwich College, Christ's College Cambridge, and at Guys Hospital. He became a doctor [MD]; and practised as a general practitioner in Dulwich, where he was much respected for his ability. The name "Milton" comes via the Boyce

family - q.v - Revd George Boyce married Mary Milton, said to be of the family of John Milton, the poet. He married 4th February 1896, at Datchet, Lillian Mabel Shipley, 3rd daughter of Sir Alexander Shipley (she was born 5th August 1871 and died 23 December 1956. Hugh Stewart died on 23 February 1942. They had 2 sons and 3 daughters:

[i]   *Robert Hugh Alexander Stewart* b. 30.04.1899, & died 19.09.1971 "Bob". He married firstly Sybil Gysberta Harvey, who d in childbirth, leaving a daughter

    I.   Sybil Josephine. Josephine was a vet in Tolworth, married in middle age, and went abroad.

Bob m secondly Gladys Mary Symons, and had 2 children:

    II.   *Donald Robert Milton Stewart* - b 26.03.1933, m. 1960, was in Africa for some years; married, no children

    III. Susan Alice, b 10.07.1938 at Minehead, & is married.

[ii]   *Gilbert Reginald Shipley Stewart* b. 16.02.1902, d. 25.07.1986 - "Bill" was a doctor in Lymington; m 27.09.1933 at Weybridge, Margaret Mary Rob (she was b. 19.02.1902, & d.19.02.1978). They had 2 children:

    I.   *John Hugh Shipley Stewart*, b 15.01.1941; a chartered accountant; m 1968 Heather Mary de Pury Orr at St Paul's Cathedral, London. Issue 2 children

       a. Iain Charles Milton b. 17.02.1973; m.
       b. Alice Louise de Pury b.29.11.1971; m. 2002 – Snell

    II. Jennifer Shipley, b 25.01.1937; became a nurse; m 1966 Maurice Wiles, a schoolmaster.

[iii] Margaret Lillian, "Brownie" - b 25.12.1896; m 2.01.1917 at Dulwich, Cedric Rowland Alston (who d 1963). She d. 10.06.1989. They lived in Sevenoaks, and gave back to the

Standard Bank the MacNee portrait of Robert Stewart. She had two children:

I.   Patricia Margery: b 23.08.1919; m 3.04.1948 Peter Graham Mallett

II. Michael Stewart Rowland Alston, a chartered accountant b 13.12.1927, d. 198?; leaving issue

[iv] Honor Kathleen Milton: b 17.031907, d. 13.10.1978; m at Nairobi, Kenya, Sydney Hubert La Fontaine DSO, OBE, MC (he died 1963/64). They lived in Kenya, & had 3 daughters:

I.   Jean Sybil, b 13.11.1931, m 1958 Christopher John Sackur

II. Clare Honor, b 3.10.1933

III. Hilary Dawn: b. 19.10.1937

[v] Elizabeth Mary Grace "Beth": b 30.05.1909, m 18.02.1933 at Dulwich, Kenneth Percival Smith, and d. 5.05.1943, leaving 2 daughters & a son:

I.   Janet Lillian Cooper, b 13.02.1936; m David Dixon, lives in Epping

II. Carol Cooper, b 16.12.1938

III. Graham Kenneth Cooper Smith, b 6.04.1943

[vi] **Mary Hamilton (Stewart) Beck:** b 27.08.1870 in Port Elizabeth; m 13.07.1895 at Beckenham Alfred John Beck (who died 15.02.1940). He was a relative of the famous Joseph Lister, later Lord Lister. She died at Ealing 7.01.1940, having had 4 children:

I.   Dorothy Lister: b 1.05.1897, dsp 15.01.1921.

II. Lucy Hamilton: b 5.11.1898, dsp in Tunbridge Wells 19.11.1968. [she had the Presentation Coffee Pot & Hot Water Jug, given to Robert Stewart in 1876, and some of the "Kimberley" diamonds; also an interesting ashtray made of silver and incorporating an old Austrian coin of the reign of the Empress Maria Theresa, which Gilbert MacDonald Stewart found in his pay packet]

III. Elizabeth Mortimer: b 21.04.1904, d. 09.10.1995 in Tunbridge Wells; m 3.09.1931 Francis David Murley Richards - a one-time clergyman. Issue

   a. Shirley Jane, b 28.06.1933, a doctor
   b. Francis Stephen John Richards ("Stephen") b 22.06.1936, m without children
   c. Charles Austin James Richards b 19.07.1940, m circa 1967 Sheila Baird.

IV. Joseph Lister Beck; b 8.07.1912; a Lloyds Underwriter. Unmarried – d.about1999

[vii] **Gilbert MacDonald Stewart:** b 4th February 1873 at Windsor, Berks. He joined the XX Regiment and served in Quetta, Baluchistan. The XX Regiment was the Lancashire Regiment of Foot. He fought in the Boer War, and was killed in action on 24th January 1900, at Spion Kop, South Africa, dying in the arms of Jack Adam, whose sister Freda Adam was to marry my grandfather Robert Barton Stewart less than 2 weeks later in Bombay. Gilbert was then a Captain in the Manchester Regiment. He must have transferred Regiments, presumably to get into active service in South Africa. He died unmarried - d.s.p.

[viii] **Walter Grahame Stewart:** MBE, MD, b. 4th October 1874 in Port Elizabeth, d. 6th March 1947; qualified at Guy's Hospital; a General Practitioner in Ware, Herts. He m. 6th September 1902 at Detling Rebecca Charlotte Daniell (who died 1933) - issue:

I. *Gordon Walter Francis Stewart*: b 9.07.1903; educated at Malvern and RMA Woolwich. Joined the Royal Artillery, ending as a Brigadier. OBE 1943. m. 27 August 1934 at

Jutogh, India, Alison Wilson ("Sal") dau Major General Maurice Wilson CMG of Yoxford, Suffolk. He died Oct 1983 leaving issue:

a. *Alastair Hugh Graeme Stewart* "Hugh": b 27.02.1936, a Major RA; d.s.p & unmarried 17 May 1986.

b. Alison Jean, b 5.03.1939, m Aug 1963 Simon Spearing [b. 1932; d. 20.04.1996] & has issue:

♦ Simon Mark, b 17.12.1964, m. Lisa ...; m. secondly (06.09.2002) Elnor Allhusen. Professor of Engineering Materials and Pro Vice-Chancellor at the University of Southampton. They have issue:
   • Anna Elnor Margaret, b. 10.07.2005
   • Michael Christian James, b. 09.04.2007
   • Clare Sophie Alison, b. 14.04.2009

♦ Susannah Jean "Susie" b 07.03.1967, married Nicholas Christian James Calvert and have issue:
   • George Simon Henry, b. 29.09.1999
   • Frederick James Samuel, b. 14.01.2002
   • Freya Elizabeth Jean, b. 12.02.2004

c. *Robert James Malcolm Stewart*: b 18 December 1944, Lt. Col. RA (retired), m. 1972 Anne Rowntree; issue

♦ Sarah Margaret b 13.09.1974 in Hanover.
♦ Katherine Elizabeth b 07.09.1982 in Heidelberg.

II. Margaret Mary Rebecca "Peggy": b 2.06.1905; unmarried. d.s.p 7th August 1995

III. Joan Mary Lloyd; b 10th January 1908, m 1962 Basil Haw (he died c 1987) - a childhood friend. Staunch Conservatives - long-time Kensington residents. For many years, Joan was secretary to William Fletcher-Vane MP, later Lord Inglewood. Joan gave to me the silver rose bowl, inscribed that it was presented to her parents "by the Staff and Workers of the Priory V.A.D Hospital in remembrance of work together 1915 - 1918". She died 8th May 2001 aged 93.

Robert Barton Stewart: 1864 - 1908: "Bertie".

2nd son, and 3rd child, of Robert Stewart & Sophia Ann Boyce, my grandfather was born 20th December 1864, in Chertsey, Surrey[1] (where the Boyce family lived). He was taken as a babe in arms to South Africa, and was educated there at Grey Institute, Port Elizabeth. When his parents returned to England in 1876, he was educated at Dulwich. He then went to Trinity College, Oxford, where he got his BA in 1886 - 3rd Class Honours, Jurisprudence. On 10th October 1883, he was admitted a student of the Inner Temple, but was never called to the Bar [2].

Picture 3: Robert Barton Stewart

In 1886, he joined the Indian Civil Service, and left for India. He rose through various grades of the Service, to District Officer, & to the rank of Collector - doing some very useful work in connection with two famines. He also spent time as an extra officer on plague duty during the Bombay riots; and from District Work he went to the Secretariat in 1898, two years before his marriage. Prior to this, he had been a year in the plague-ridden area of Godhra - the worst infected spot in the whole of the Bombay Presidency. He was specially selected for this position, and for his conspicuous services during a period of extreme anxiety, and unremitting toil, he was awarded the Kaisar-I-Hind Gold Medal - one of the highest awards in the Indian Empire below knighthood. I do not know what became of the medal.

He was an enthusiastic golfer - and was one of those principally responsible for founding the Royal West India Golf Club (which went into liquidation some time after Independence of India) at Nasik, some 120 Miles from Bombay [3].

On 6th February 1900, he married at St Stephen's Bandra, Bombay,[4] **Frederica Sybil Adam**, daughter of **Brigadier General Frederick John Stuart Adam**. Less than 2 weeks before, RBS' brother Gilbert died in the arms of Freda's brother Jack Adam, at Spion Kop, South Africa. It was not a love match; nor was it a long marriage for he died at the end of 1908. Freda had wanted to marry a young clergyman in England. Her parents refused, because he had "no money and no prospects". In fact, he went on to become a Bishop. Instead, Freda was sent out to her older sister, Gertrude Gilbert, in India, to come to her senses, and to be introduced to a suitable husband. Hence she met & married my grandfather. Though not a love match, it became a marriage of love and happiness, albeit clouded by my grandfather's ill health, and somewhat mercurial temperament. Early on after his marriage Bertie had to relinquish his post for a while, because of health problems.

In 1904, he was called to Poona on a special duty connected with the reorganisation of the Bombay Presidency Police. In 1905, he was appointed Inspector General of Police - a post which he held to his death in 1908. He was the first civilian to hold the post, and his appointment received the warm commendation of the local press, which had previously been opposed to the selection of a civilian for it. Thorough as ever, he threw his whole strength into the work. Although he possessed a fine constitution, it once more proved unequal to the strain he imposed upon it. But he did not abandon his task until he had placed the force on a basis of efficiency which endured for many years.

During the State Visit to India of the Prince & Princess of Wales (the later King George V & Queen Mary) in 1905-1906, he was presented with a silver ink stand, which I now have. It is inscribed, and the lid has a blue enamel oval with the Prince of Wales' feathers.

In 1907, he was forced to go on sick leave to Scotland, where he settled in Stonehaven, Kincardineshire. He went there to be near a Dr

Anderson, from the IMS, a friend of his. [This Dr Anderson was the father of my godfather, Major General Vass Anderson].

His home was at Lyndhurst, Arduthie Road, Stonehaven. There he died, on 29th December 1908[5]. He was buried at Dunnottar Cemetery, Stonehaven[6], plot 73, Section C.

Clearly he made his mark in India, An obituary written by a friend read:

> *"He had filled many important posts under Government, but his friends will remember him best as a Collector. Broad shouldered, fair haired, and bluff, there are few of those who served with him but have a kindly and respectful memory of one who was almost an ideal District Officer. So great was his knowledge of the vernacular, that the most cultivated found pleasure in conversing with him, and yet he might have been seen often of an evening, in camp, sitting over a fire and fluently chattering in their patois with the wildest of hill tribesmen. At the same time there was hardly a pursuit dear to Englishmen in which he was not proficient. Riding to hounds, following up a wounded panther, shooting a jheel, joining in station games, making a dismal compound into a flower garden, all seemed congenial to him.*
>
> *In the plague hospitals, cholera sheds and famine camps, his commanding figure and gruff voice were always welcome for both Europeans and Natives, who soon grew to know that behind the keen eye and abrupt speech was a master mind to appreciate difficulties, and a kindly heart full of sympathy for suffering.*
>
> *Such was the man, the all round man, who "aequam meminit rebus in arduis servare mentem". The Great Collector is gone. A few there are who will mourn him as the truest of friends. Many natives will regret, both great and humble, that "Istoot Sahib" will never more come among them. Government itself knows too well how great a gap is made in the ranks of its officers. Truly a Burra Sahib is gone. Requiescat in pace".*

After she was widowed, my grandmother stayed on in Stonehaven for a little while, but then she went to Kent. Her parents lived in Dover; and she lived for a while in Dover, and latterly in Ramsgate. She was left with little money, and two children to bring up - the younger being only a month old. She kept in daily touch with her stockbroker (Uncle Alec), and over the years amassed a sufficient sum to warrant taking a cruise to the West Indies. Alas, the Wall Street crash happened whilst she was on the cruise. She was not totally ruined, but she never recovered financially.

I remember her as a little old lady, hard of hearing, for which she had an ear trumpet; and with heart trouble. She was around 5'4" tall, her once brown hair was grey, and she had deep brown eyes, with spectacles down to the tip of her nose. When outside, she always seemed to have a fur coat or stole, and walked slightly hunched over her stick. But she was a fun person, practical and adept at DIY. She was the first to show me how to use a saw to cut wood. Much in advance of her time, she had insisted, when my father was a teenager, that he spend a summer working at a local garage, to learn how car engines worked. She was a great raconteur of stories to children, and must have known several children's books by heart - Little Lord Fauntleroy was one. As children we used to tease her by making sudden noises in her ear trumpet. She started me on golf, showing me how to swing a golf club. She taught me how to play bridge, when I had measles, at the age of 10. She lived in a flat in an imposing Victorian block in Ramsgate - 21 Westcliff Terrace. The block had been built for the ladies in waiting of Queen Victoria when she visited Ramsgate. Not many tourists went to that part of Ramsgate, for rocks were to be seen on the beach and in the sea. But Granny Stewart knew precisely where the sand was, and where children could bathe safely.

She died in Ramsgate, on 26th June 1949, when I was a little under 11.

Issue of Robert Barton Stewart & Freda Adam:

[i] **Guy Milton Stewart** 1900 - 1943 - my father, of whom hereafter.

[ii] **Robert Donald Stewart**: 1908 - 1970; born at Stonehaven, Kincardineshire on 30th November 1908, less than a month before his father died. Educated at St Lawrence College, Ramsgate, and Christ's College, Cambridge, he became a Chartered Accountant. He was in Turquand, Youngs (long since lost into one of the merged Accountancy firms) - articled in

London, and then a partner in their Singapore office. Like his grandfather, and (I think) his father, he was a keen Freemason. He was a prisoner of the Japanese from the fall of Singapore until the end of the war. This undermined his health, and he died aged 61, on 12th April 1970. He married on 9th August 1938, in London, Madeline Weston [1912-1997]. My great Aunt

Picture 4: Donald Stewart and Madeline Weston, 9 August 1938

father had a dairy business in Kent. Her family were dubious of her marrying someone with so little money!

They had twin daughters:

I.   Sally Madeline b 13.06.1939; m 11.08.1962 at Rustington, Sussex, Lt Commander John Jocelyn "Jo" Streatfeild-James RN & has 3 sons:

a. David Stewart Streatfeild-James: b 22.10.1963, m + issue

b. Douglas Charles b 1967

c. Dominic b 1969

II. Patricia Mary b 13.06.1939; m 1966 Commander Michael Wilson RN, in London, and has 3 children:

a. Catriona, b. 29th December 1967 m Stuart Wilkinson and has 3 children:

♦ Harry

♦ Sebastian

♦ Olivia

b. Heather Lucy Donnelly, b. 10th January 1970 who has one child:

♦ Joshua Crawley, b. 27.02.2000

c. James Michael Stewart Wilson, b. 18.12.1971. Issue:

♦ Lucy Elizabeth, b. 22.02.2007

♦ Oliver Michael, b. 02.11.2008

Notes & Sources:

1: Birth Certificate 20th December 1864

2: Letter from Inner Temple, 30th March 1960

3: Letters of 1960 about Royal Western India Golf Club Ltd

4: Marriage Certificate, 6th February 1900.

5: Death Certificate, 29th December 1908

6: Documents re Dunnottar Cemetery, Stonehaven.

Guy Milton Stewart 1900 - 1943:

Guy Stewart, my father, was born 10th November 1900, at Sydenham, Kent - near to where his Stewart grandmother lived. He lived in India until 1907, when because of my grandfather's ill health, the family left India and settled in Stonehaven, Kincardineshire. (They went there, because Dr Anderson, a retired IMS doctor, lived there). Guy's father died on 29th December 1908, and at some time after that, the family moved to Kent.

Guy was a scholar at Haileybury. He wanted to try for a scholarship to Winchester, and was probably clever enough to get it; but his mother could not afford to risk letting that at Haileybury go. This was still the heyday of the somewhat sadistic English public school, with boys being frequently beaten. Curiously, at Haileybury, this regime was tempered by allowing each boy a tankard of beer each day.

Life at school was overshadowed by the Great War. For this reason, and because his mother could not really afford to send him to University whilst she had Donald to bring up, Guy went into the Army. His service record was as follows:

18.12.1919:   commissioned into the Royal Engineers as a 2nd Lieutenant

31.01.1920:   served at Aldershot (R E Mounted Depot)

01.08.1920:   served at Chatham (SME).

18.12.1921:   promoted Lieutenant 18.12.1921;

07.07.1922:   posted to Depot Battalion R E at Chatham.

03.11.1922:   he left Southampton for India

28.11.1922:   joined the QVO (Queen Victoria's Own) Madras Sappers and Miners. .

16.11.1923:   posted to 63 Coy QVO S & M [Queen Victoria's Own Sappers and Miners] A.G.E. Hinaida, in Mesopotamia.

11.01.1926:   returned to Bangalore.

15.07.1926:   on leave ex India, (S.S. Rajputana) until 12.03.1927

10.11.1927:   transferred to Cawnpore as Garrison Engineer, for 10 months.

31.09.1928:   appointed G S O III, at Army Headquarters, Simla /

Delhi.

28.02.1929:   appointed Garrison Engineer at Wana

12.01.1930:   Joined QVO Madras S & M at Bangalore; and appointed Company Commander, 14 Field Company. Permitted to extend his service for a second tour of 5 yrs from 3.11.1927.

29.03.1930:   on leave ex India, for 8 months, disembarking on return at Bombay on 28.11.30.

30.11.1930:   appointed Company Commander 16 Army Troops Company, Bangalore

18.12.1930:   gazetted as Captain RE. Permitted to extend his service in India for a further period of 5 yrs from 3.11.32.

8.09.1932:   on 5 months leave ex India. 26.01.1933

26.01.1933   disembarked on return from leave at Karachi.

28.01.1933:   joined Staff College, Quetta, as student.

31.12.1934:   posted QVO M & S at Bangalore.

5.4.1935:   appointed Superintendent of Instruction at Bangalore.

17.8.1935:   granted 4 months & 29 days leave ex India.

13.011936:   Attached to G S Br, Army HQ, Delhi

2.03.1936:   General Staff Officer, 2nd Grade, AHQ, India, at Delhi.

1.08.1938:   Promoted to Major, RE.

August 1939:   vacated his appointment at AHQ, Simla. (Having already returned to England)

20.07.1939:   Joint Planning Committee C.I.D London.

1.09.1939:   appointed GSO 2nd Grade, War Office (Central War Room) & MO1 (J.P) at the War Office, London.

26.06.1940:	Posted to GHQ, Home Forces.
10.07.1940:	Acting Lt Col, RE; apptd GSO1 (Ops) GHQ Home Forces.
10.10.1940:	Temp Lt Col
25.11.1940:	Officer Commanding 13 Field Squadron RE.
27.5.1941:	apptd GSO1 (MO5) War Office
13.12.1941:	apptd Director of Plans, War Office; granted acting rank of Brigadier;
13.06.1942:	T/Brigadier with substantive rank Lt Col.
29.01.1943:	Killed in an aeroplane accident, while returning from the Casablanca Conference.

Picture 5: Portrait of Guy Stewart

On 26th July 1930, he married **Elaine Oenone Earengey**, at the Temple Church, London. She was the only child of William George Earengey KC. My parents met during the First World War, in Cheltenham. Because of the risk of bombs landing on the English Coast at Dover, my father's maternal grandfather General Adam had been persuaded to go to Cheltenham to live, until the war was over. The Earengey family lived there then (it was not until after the War that my grandfather went to the Bar, and moved to London). One day in 1918 (probably) Guy and Oenone were at a dancing class, and were beckoned by the teacher to come forward to show how the dance should be done.

One day when he was 17 and she was 14, not that long after they met, Guy invited my mother to tea at Park House, Cheltenham, where his mother lived with her father, General Adam. As soon as my grandmother, Freda Stewart, had met my mother, she went to talk to an old family retainer, Mansell, and announced that she had just met the girl that Master Guy would one day marry. Mansell questioned how my grandmother could be so sure; but she was, and was proved right, 12 years later. Guy only ever had eyes for Oenone - and told her

Picture 6: Guy Stewart and Elaine Oenone Earengay, 26 July 1930

when they were both in their teens that he would marry her one day. To her later regret (for it was a short marriage) it took her until 1930, when she was 26, to agree. She had been determined not to marry until she had fully qualified as a doctor - and by 1930 she had her doctorate of medicine from London University, her speciality being in Obstetrics and Gynaecology. My mother actually qualified, and was admitted a member of the BMA (British Medical Association) in January 1926, when she obtained the degrees of MRCS LRCP. She was then still only 21.

He was promoted Captain on 18th December 1930, and took over command of 16th Army Troops Company, QVO Madras Sappers & Miners, on 31st May 1931. This was in Bangalore - where my sister Rosemary was born on 5th August 1931. She and I share the same birthday, 7 years apart. The house that they lived in, in Bangalore, no longer stands. The Madras Sappers & Miners thrive; and their Regimental Museum is impressive. They clearly cherish their roots from the British.

Picture 7: Madras Sappers (courtesy of Madras Sappers Museum, Chennai). Guy is bottom left.

Guy was a highly able and highly rated Army Officer, though he had little tolerance for fools. He passed the Staff College entrance exam at Quetta (now in Pakistan) with very high marks. At the same time as he was studying for the entrance exam for the Staff College, he took his preliminary exams for the Bar. On 15th December 1932, he was admitted to the Middle Temple, of which both his parents-in-law were members.

They lived life to the full in India - golf, riding, playing bridge: it was a happy and fulfilling time, and theirs was a happy marriage. Guy could play any ball game, and was a first class golfer and a good polo player. But good though life was in India, there can be little doubt that if he had had the means, he would have opted for a professional career, perhaps the Bar, rather than the Regular Army. His younger brother, Donald, being then the only child dependent on my grandmother, went to Cambridge, then became a Chartered Accountant, and was in consequence much more affluent.

Picture 8: Madras Sappers - context unknown. Courtesy of Madras Sappers Museum, Chennai. Guy is centre, front row.

It was while Guy was at the Staff College in Quetta, Baluchistan (then India, now Pakistan) that Shirley was born, on 6th November 1934.

After graduating from the Staff College, he was re-posted to Madras Sappers and Miners, as Superintendent of Instruction. On 2nd March 1936, he was appointed to a Staff job, GSO 2, at Army HQ in Delhi; and was promoted Major on 1st August 1938. I was born 4 days later, on 5th August 1938, at Portmore Nursing Home, Simla, Punjab - the summer capital of the Raj: an extraordinary creation of Surrey stockbroker style housing, in the foothills of the Himalayas. In New Delhi, my parents lived in a Government house at 37 Aurungzeb Road. In 1987 we visited the house, now let to a High Court Judge. It still has the acre or so of land around it. The verandah, which went all around the house, has been filled in; and one of the rooms has been turned into a small Hindu place of worship. Apart from that, it is instantly recognisable from photographs taken by my parents.

Picture 9: Madras Sappers (courtesy of Madras Sappers Museum, Chennai)

Even before my birth, Guy foresaw the inevitability of war. Indeed, as is obvious from the registration of my birth, it took weeks for my parents to settle on my names - my mother explained this as being due to worry over the likelihood of war, and to my sister Rosemary being desperately ill with appendicitis. Guy wanted to get back to the hub of events. So the family left India in the Spring of 1939, and returned to England. In July 1939, he was posted to the Joint Planning Staff at the War Office. In 1940, he was supposed to go to Camberley, as an Instructor at the Staff College. Hence my parents rented a house - Wychwood, Pine Avenue, Camberley; which my mother bought after the war, and which remained her home until the mid-1960s. But the posting changed, and in July 1940 he joined GHQ Home Forces as a GSO 1 Operations. From November 1940 to May 1941, he was in command of 13th Field Squadron.

In 1941, he was appointed as MO[5] with the rank of Colonel. Then on 13th November 1941 he became Director of Plans at the War Office, with the temporary rank of Brigadier. His military chief was General Sir Alan Brooke (later Field Marshal Lord Alanbrooke). But his political, and real, chief was the Prime Minister, Winston Churchill. Churchill was a hard taskmaster, not least because of the odd hours he led. Officers, such as my father, were expected to be on duty at 7 am. Churchill would have a siesta every afternoon - no one working around him had that chance - and then he would often work well into the small hours of the morning. When he did so, staff officers such as my father were expected to be available at his beck and call.

Guy accompanied Churchill to Washington DC, 17th - 25th June 1942, to explain to President Roosevelt the plans he was drawing up for "Bolero" - the proposed landings in Northern France. Whilst there, the news came in of the fall of Tobruk, so North Africa as a field of war was also discussed. - see Churchill's "The Second World War" Vol IV - "The Hinge of Fate" @ p.337. The President was so impressed that he gave my father a signed photograph of himself - which I have. An undated cutting from the Daily Telegraph (I think), of probably 1942, reads:

> *"The fact that Mr Churchill made his third war-time crossing of the Atlantic so soon after M. Molotov's visit, and that he brought with him Gen Sir Alan Brooke CIGS, Maj-Gen Sir Hastings Ismay, Secretary of the Chiefs of Staff Committee, and Brigadier G M Stewart, naturally gives rise to the belief that land operations are under consideration."*

The New York Daily News observes that "in Mr Churchill's opinion Brooke, Stewart, and Ismay are the best military brains in the Empire."

He accompanied Churchill to the Casablanca Conference (in Morocco) with President Roosevelt in January 1943. President Roosevelt originally suggested this Conference in late 1942, for a meeting between Roosevelt, Stalin, and Churchill. Stalin could not, or would not, go; but the Conference went ahead between Churchill and Roosevelt, accompanied by their advisers. (see: Churchill's "The Second World War" - Vol IV - "The Hinge of Fate" pp 598 ff). There Guy wrote a paper. In the ordinary course of affairs, there would have been discussion and amendment, before it got to the Prime Minister. On this occasion Lieutenant General "Pug" (Sir Hastings) Ismay acted differently. Guy's manuscript note to Air

Commodore Elliot (which was sent to my mother after the fatal crash) read:

> *"Bill,*
> *I regret to say that Pug has taken my first-born straight to the P.M. Look for trouble.*
> *Yrs G M S"*

It was expected that great things were in store for him. His fellow Directors of Plans were (for the Admiralty) Captain Lambe (later Admiral Sir Charles Lambe, KCB, CVO) and (for the Air Ministry) Air Commodore Elliot (later Air Chief Marshal Sir William Elliot GCVO, KCB, KBE, DFC). But all was dashed when he was killed on active service – an engine on the Liberator plane in which he was returning from Casablanca, via Gibraltar, caught fire, and the plane crash landed near Talbenny, Pembrokshire in South Wales, on 29th January 1943. The plane turned over twice & broke its back. Guy who was towards the front was thrown out, and died. Brigadier Vivian Dykes was also killed in the same crash. The actual Conference had been kept secret, but after it was over, Churchill took a few of those at the Conference, including the President, to Marrakesh, one of his favourite painting haunts "to see the sunset on the snows of the Atlas Mountains" ("The Second World War, ibid, p.621). From Marrakesh, news got to the Germans that Churchill was in Morocco. They targeted all the planes flying back, in the hope of getting Churchill. Guy did not go to Marrakesh, but left via Algiers and then to Gibraltar, where he took the fateful flight. Ironically, he and Brigadier Dykes had been due to go on another plane; but they changed planes to even out the load.

Two accounts of the accident survive. One is from a letter written on 7th June 1943, from Captain (Gerald) Aylmer Garnons Williams DSO, DSC, RN, of Aberclydach, Talybont-on-Usk. [b. 24.01.1893, eldest son of Gerald Garnons-Williams 1859-1942, who was 4th son of The Revd Prebendary Garnons Williams of Abercamlais, Brecon 1829 – 1908. His son Philip b 1919 lives at Dunleys, North Warnborough, Odiham, Hants –

see Burkes LG , 18th edition Vol III pp 953-955] He was Director of Combined Operations in India from 1942; and on the staff of S.A.C.S.E.A (Supreme Allied Commander South East Asia) until the end of the war against Japan. He wrote the letter to (I think) Humphrey Gilbert whose mother was my father's mother's older sister). The letter was sent on to my grandmother by Humphrey Gilbert, and Granny Stewart gave it to my mother

"Dear Gilbert

I got your letter this morning and knew Guy Stewart well. He was extremely competent, as he must have been to be the army member of the Joint Planning Staff – army D. of P very important job.

I spent a good part of the 28th January with him, first of all at a conference with him, Brigadier Dykes, Charles Lambe the naval D of P and the airman D of P at The Mount. We the walked down to the town, he and I together through the Alameda Gardens, and had a lot of trouble extracting the other 3 from the Trafalgar Cemetery. We naturally discussed many matters which cannot be written down here, and of which he had a very wide grasp. Later on in the day we got the news that our Liberator would be taking off at about 3.0 a.m. on the 29th & the rest of the day was spent in work & exercise. I walked up the Rock with another Brigadier (Macleod) who also broke his back the next morning. At about 2.30 am, Stewart, Dykes & MacLeod marched on down from The Mount (the Gibraltar Admiral's House) & we all certified that the conference papers were safe and correct, scrambled into our flying suits, mae-wests and parachute harness and crawled into the plane. Stewart, Dykes & I were in the bomb bay, and had a couple of mattresses each to sleep on. We talked for a bit and then went to sleep.

At about 8.30 a.m. we all woke up gradually and began to scoff about for tea, then as far as I know the starboard … engine was hit by a bullet or cannon shell & the engine caught fire. It tore out of the wing & took the petrol tanks with it. We saw that, & then went back to the bomb bay to make ourselves as comfortable as possible for the inevitable bump. No one was excited or appeared to be unduly alarmed, the general feeling amongst the passengers and crew was that of annoyance & then in taking as many precautions that common sense dictated to lessen the coming emergency. I am sure his mother would like to know that Guy had no fears or horror & that he had no agony of mind but talked in his normal voice with us all and could have felt nothing. I didn't have any interval between complete normal possession of my senses & absolute unconsciousness. In fact the passage in the Litany against sudden death is quite against one's normal wishes.

Of the loss to his country in Guy's death it is probably difficult to understand fully unless one has been bound up with Joint Planning. With all his great knowledge of the war from a position next only to the hub of affairs, the loss of such an officer is a grievous blow and takes time to amend. He was immensely trusted by his opposite numbers in the other two services, & got on very well with the Americans who heartily appreciated his qualities – all this indicates a character much out of the common & army D of P is, as you know, a position several rungs up the ladder.

Will you give his mother my very deepest sympathy in her awful loss, but it may help her to know that Guy had achieved that most difficult of all things, the admiration & affection of his equals & juniors. That of one's seniors is always easier, but the former always means solid worth.

Yours sincerely   G A Garnons Williams"

The second account was from Commander Robert Currie RN

"Dear Mrs Stewart,   11ᵗʰ February

Captain Lambe has asked me if I would let you know something of the events which led to the loss of your husband. May I first of all express my sincere sympathy. Your bereavement is shared in large measure by all of us who knew him.

Brigadier Stewart with Brigadier Dykes & a number of others were in the forward part of the portion occupied by the passengers. I was in the rear portion for the flight although I had been beside him when we took off & had had some conversation with him during the process.

We had been flying for some seven hours & were approaching land when an engine took fire. I have little knowledge of such matters but I understand that it is an occurrence which happens so infrequently as to be just an Act of Providence, Presumably the exact cause will never be ascertained for after a few minutes the supports were burned and the engine fell into the sea.

Such an aeroplane can normally continue on three engines, but the damage done by the fire caused trouble with another & sighting an aerodrome the pilot decided to land. While making for the runway the second damaged engine failed and the pilot was unable to keep the machine in the air. He brought the aircraft down in a grass field & we went through a hedge into plough.

I believe we turned over a couple of times & the aircraft broke its back.

I found myself still in the tail practically uninjured & was able to scramble out. Initially I assisted the others to pull people from out of the wreckage; we feared fire but fortunately no such thing developed. A number of men from the aerodrome & doctors had by this time arrived, namely some 10 minutes after the accident.

I believe that Brigadier Stewart was thrown out of the machine when she broke her back, for the first I saw of him was lying in a field not far from the machine. He was unconscious at the time, and was quickly removed to the ambulance. When I reached the sick bay he was already in bed. I must pay tribute to the hospital staff. Their speed and efficiency gave everyone confidence. I left the aerodrome about 4 in the afternoon to entrain to London, & it was with the greatest regret that I heard next morning that Brigadier Stewart had passed away in the night.

As you know, of the seventeen in the aircraft, two were lost, and some 8 escaped with slight injuries.

I fear that this is a bald statement of facts such as I know them. I wish I could do more to help. I would like to pay tribute to one who rendered such valuable service to his country & his personality was such that although I can only claim acquaintance with him that was a privilege.

With the greatest sympathy and please don't trouble to make reply.

Yours sincerely

Robert Currie"

Guy had, so my mother recounted, been recommended for a decoration - CB - for the Honours' List of New Year 1943. This was vetoed by General Sir Alan Brooke, on the basis that it would "go to the head of such a young officer". No award could be made posthumously. But his co-Directors of Plans were duly awarded their CBs in the January 1944 Honours List.

Even after 50 years, the letters of tribute sent to my mother, from friends, colleagues, subordinates, and superiors, are poignant. Captain W A Finch wrote:

"It has been a week of expectancy as we looked forward to the Brigadier's return and then came the report of the accident. How we had been looking forward to see him and then to resume the big task under his leadership. He was a great leader and the head of a happy team of comrades; so cool and calm with a sort of quiet smile. No matter how long the hours of daily toil, he always had a "thank you" and an expression of gratitude for all that was done. We looked to him for the lead and he seemed to bring out the best in a person without any sign of drive. His singleness of purpose and quietness of outlook was infectious. I can well feel how happy he must have been in his home life."

Captain C E Lambe CVO, RN, wrote:

"Now we have lost one of the pillars of our inter service planning and it is a blow not only personally to us but to the war as a whole. Guy supplied the healthy scepticism and the sound judgement which kept our feet firmly on the ground [on] many many difficult occasions. He was a tower of strength in resisting the ever present attempts to make us rush our work, would always insist on everything being done really thoroughly and properly whatever the labour involved, and his advice and knowledge of how to achieve our ends was our constant guide."

Air Commodore W Elliot wrote this to Air Vice Marshall J C Slessor, who sent it on to my mother:

"I have lost a friend whom I truly loved and deeply admired, for he was indeed a most lovable and admirable man ... we shall miss him terribly in our work. He was so wise and so sound in his judgement. When Charles Lambe and I were in difficulties it was always Guy who rescued us. And with it as my wife said after she first met him he had such a merry twinkle in his eye..."

Sir James Grigg, Secretary of State for War, wrote on 3rd February 1943:

"I have received a message from the Prime Minister through Mr Casey, the Minister of State in Cairo, saying how deeply grieved they are to learn of the death of your husband and asking me to convey to you their sympathy in your bereavement.

As Secretary of State for War I should like to say how much I deplore the loss to the Army of an officer of your husband's gifts. Although his work had perforce to be done behind the scenes, his sound judgement and unfailing common sense were fully recognised by those responsible for the higher direction of the war, and he was held in the greatest regard by his colleagues in the War Office and in the other two Services..."

On 24th June 1943, The Prime Minister, Winston Churchill, sent my mother a signed photograph of himself. I have this and the accompanying letter:

"Though some time has passed since the occurrence of the accident which led to your husband's unforeseen and untimely death, I have not forgotten his association with my work as Minister of Defence and I hope you will accept the enclosed photograph as a token of my esteem of his services and his devotion to duty".

It is a matter of comment that the one person who might have been expected to write, but did not, was his military boss - General Sir Alan Brooke CIGS. My mother met him once after the war, and described him as "a cold fish" with little conversation.

Because of the War, I saw, and knew, little of my father; and I was only 4½ years old when he was killed. The change in my mother was dramatic. Whilst my father was alive, she would always be playing the piano and singing. After his death, she did this only rarely. Fortunately for us, her medical qualifications could be, and were, put to full use to pay for the education of my two older sisters and myself.

My mother waited until she was in her late eighties before she told how she was hurt by the petty mindedness, indeed callousness, of the pay department of the War Office. A matter of a few weeks after my father was killed she received an official request for return of 2 days' full pay for January 1943, because my father had not survived to work those two days.

Sources & Documents:

1. Birth Certificate, 10th November 1900
2. Commission, 2nd Lieutenant Land Forces, Corps of Royal Engineers, 23.12.1919, signed by George V.
3. Certificate of Marks obtained for admission to the Staff College, 16th June 1932.
4. Obituary from the R E Journal, May 1943 [the author, W A M S, was my godfather Billy Stawell, who became a Major General]
5. Cuttings from Various Newspapers at the time of, and recording, his death.
6. Letters of Condolence sent to my mother
7. Signed photograph of President Franklin Delano Roosevelt.
8. Signed photograph of Winston Churchill MP, Prime Minister, and accompanying letter of sympathy sent to my mother
9. Death Certificate, 29th January 1943

My parents had 3 children:

[i]   Rosemary Elspeth, b 5th August 1931
[ii] Shirley Anne, b 6th November 1934
[iii] **Robin Milton Stewart**, b 5th August 1938

Rosemary Elspeth; b 5.08.1931 at Bangalore, India; MA Edinburgh; married 6th August 1954, at RMA Chapel, Sandhurst, Captain, later Colonel, James Gordon Trepess Polley RE. James was born 17th June 1926. They had issue 1 daughter & 2 sons:

I.   Margaret Elspeth; b 16 June 1955 at Aldershot; m 10 Dec 1984 in Hong Kong, Gregory Robert Scott Crichton of Sydney, Australia - issue

        a. Blair Daniel Scott, b 6th August 1985
        b. Chaanah Zoe, b 3rd October 1986

II.   Neil Guy Trepess Polley; b 23.04.1957 at Aldershot. BA (Hons) Durham (1979); MDA Cranfield (1999). He is now a (full) Colonel – his earlier Regimental Service being in the King's Royal Hussars. He m 11 July 1987 at St Michael & All Angels, Pirbright, Surrey, Claire Mousley, and has issue

        a. Lucy Alda Elspeth b 18.07.1991, educated Sherborne School for Girls and Exeter University.
        b. Alicia Charlotte Oenone, b 10.02.1994, educated Sherborne School for Girls.

III. Robert Duncan Stewart Polley; b 21.07.1959 in Singapore. Queen's Commendatoin for Valuable Service, 1996. MA King's College, London; MPhil University of Madras. He is now a (full) Colonel – his earlier Regimental Service being in The Light Dragoons.

Shirley Anne; b 6th November 1934 in Quetta, Baluchistan - then India, now Pakistan; dsp 10th April 1968 in London. She became a physiotherapist; and spent much time in Australia. Her health became undermined due to a virus which she contracted, and which forced her to give up physiotherapy and hospital work. Instead she turned her energies to the law, read for the Bar, and was Called by the Middle Temple. She practised for several years in London until her sudden death. At the time of her death, she was engaged to Guy Cleaver, a Solicitor & Partner in Blyth Dutton & Co of London. He was born 1917, and died in 1994 - he was godfather to Sholto.

Robin Milton Stewart, 1938 - 2011

Born 5th August 1938 in Simla, India; baptised at New Delhi, 19th November 1938. Died in Northallerton, 31st August 2011.

Educated at Abberley Hall, Worcester, Winchester, and New College, Oxford [2nd Class Honours, BA, Jurisprudence 1961; now MA].

On 8th September 1962, I married **Lynda Grace Medhurst** at St Paul's Knightsbridge. Issue:

[i] **Andrew Douglas Lorn Stewart** b 28th May 1964 at the Middlesex Hospital, London W1. Educated at The Royal Grammar School, Newcastle upon Tyne, St Peter's School, York, and Christ's College, Cambridge [BA Engineering 1986]. m. 18th September 1992, in the Chapel of Christ's College, Cambridge, Valerie Jane McQuiston, dau Mr & Mrs Thomas McQuiston of Belfast, Northern Ireland.

Issue:

I. **Callum Robert Ross Stewart** b 20th June 1997 in Laguna Hills, California. Educated at Bury Grammar School.

[ii] **James Milton Stewart** b 15th January 1966 at the Middlesex Hospital. Educated at St Olave's School, and then St Peter's School, York, and Portsmouth Polytechnic [Diploma in Marketing]. m. 27th June 1994, at the Mairie, Nieuil, 16270 France, Jennifer Jane Ferguson, dau Mr & Mrs Kenneth Ferguson of Sherborne, Dorset (subsequently divorced).

Issue

I. **George Robert Milton** b. 13th November 1997 at St George's Hospital, Tooting. Educated at Sexeys School, Dorset.

II. **Thomas Douglas Patrick** b. 6th October 2000 at St George's Hospital, Tooting. Educated at Sexeys School, Dorset.

James married Sian Marks in September 2012.

[iii] **Sholto Robert Douglas Stewart** b 27th February 1969 at St Joseph's Nursing Home, Beaconsfield, Buckinghamshire. Educated at The Royal Grammar School, Newcastle upon Tyne, St Peter's School, York, University of Newcastle-upon-Tyne

[BA Politics] & Mount Vernon College, Washington DC [MA 1995 Interior Design]. He married 1st May 1993 in Washington DC Emma Louise, 2nd daughter of Mr & Mrs Merwyn Carl Blust of Washington DC.

Issue

I. **Carl Robin** b. 5th June 1998 in Washington, DC

II. **Anna Birgitte** b. 3rd October 2000, in Washington, DC.

By way of comment on their names –

"Andrew" is the name of the patron Saint of Scotland; "Douglas" is after my paternal great grandmother's family; and "Lorn" is after Lorn in Appin. [The Stewarts always spelt their Lordship of Lorn without an "e" at the end; the Campbells always spelt it Lorne. They wrongly acquired the Lordship, by murdering the then Stewart Lord of Lorne, before, so they said, he got to Church to marry; and thereby to legitimate his son the first Stewart of Appin].

"James", a name common in the Stewarts, is the patron Saint of the House of Stewart [St James of Compostella]. "Milton" was my middle name, as my father's, and my great uncle Hugh's, before me. My paternal great grandmother, Sophia Ann Stewart, was a Boyce by birth. Her forebear, Revd George Boyce married Mary Milton, who is said to be of the family of John Milton, the poet.

"Sholto" is a name peculiar to the Black Douglases, who were Lords of Douglasdale, Earls and later Dukes of Douglas. "Sholto Douglas" is a phrase which means "Behold the Black Douglas". Our Douglas forebears are Douglases of Queensberry, scions of the Black Douglases." "Robert" is after my grandfather and great grandfather. As it happens, Sholto was born on the bicentenary of the day in 1769, when the House of Lords gave its judgement in the great "Douglas Cause", under which Archibald Steuart, son of Sir John Steuart 3rd Baronet of Grandtully, was adjudged to be the lawful and legitimate nephew and heir of his uncle the Duke of Douglas, one of the richest men in Europe. No particular connection with us, but a cause celèbre in the 18th century. It is through this Steuart -

Douglas heir that the Douglas-Home family, Earls of Home, acquired their Douglas name and wealth.

ARMS: [er Lyon Office, 1963 page 128, Volume 44] –

Shield - Parted per fesse Or and powdered of torteaux Gules, a Fesse Chequy Azure and Argent, between in Chief a gazelle courant Azure, horned of the second, and in base three lions rampant Argent.

Crest - A demi lion rampant proper, holding in its dexter paw a cross crosslet fitchée azure.

Motto - Motto: Spes et Fides

Robin died on 31st August 2011 after a long battle against the ravages of Parkinson's Disease. His funeral was held on 8th September [the 49th anniversary of his marriage to Lynda] at St Oswald's Church, Sowerby, Yorkshire.

Sir Christopher Holland delivered the following tribute.

It was in March 1978 that Robin and I started our professional association. The day was memorable. The occasion was the oath taking of that year's appointees as Queen's Counsel. There were some 30 of us in all, three of whom had practiced on this, the North Eastern Circuit: Robin, Franz Muller and myself. For the lunchtime partying, Robin and I joined forces. Resplendent in our new silk gowns with associated outfits that started with full bottom wigs and stretched down to tights and court shoes, we stare out of the several joint photographs, uncertain whether to look fierce or friendly, but exuding obvious and justified satisfaction at having attained this professional milestone of which we were both proud.

Prior to 1978 our respective professional paths had run parallel without crossing. Respectively called to the Bar in 1963 we had established busy practices as junior barristers, Robin doing so from Newcastle Chambers, I doing so from Leeds Chambers. For junior barristers there was little or no cross fertilisation as between these centres and my then knowledge of Robin was by repute alone, as one markedly competent who would go places.

In and after 1978, now a Q.C., Robin did indeed go places. Physically, he left Newcastle and he joined London Chambers; professionally, he established a well deserved and enviable reputation as a 'must-have' specialist in the field of personal injury litigation, particularly such arising out of Professional Negligence. That reputation centred upon Robin's frequent role as leading counsel for Plaintiffs (as they were then called), Claimants (as they are now called), who had suffered truly devastating injuries with consequent lifelong major disabilities, whether through accident or professional, commonly medical, negligence. Robin believed that this distressing class of litigants had hitherto been poorly served by the courts. Medical negligence was not being proved through a misguided belief that the relevant medical procedures were too specialist to be the subject of litigation at the hands of lawyers; whilst those who did establish liability were being woefully undercompensated through failures to appreciate and evaluate the full dimensions of their respective disabilities and the consequent financial implications. Bringing to bear Wykehamist intellect, hard work and a sense of mission, Robin did indeed do wonders for a multitude of grateful clients, lay and professional, by way of his vision as to a just result and by his consequent case preparation and presentation, forcing courts to re-think and re-appraise - as wincing insurers (occasionally represented by me) would testify. Robin's role in this field led to his participation together with Rupert Jackson Q.C. (now Lord Justice Jackson) in the inception and formation of the still thriving Professional Negligence Bar Association, he being its first Chairman from 1991 to 1993.

Those who would seek a memorial to Robin's professional career need look no further than that which he achieved in bringing a new vision and markedly different standards to this type of litigation. He was not alone, but his role was prominent and inspirational.

As with any common law practitioner, crime has to form part of his practice. As to this, he sat part time as a Recorder and from time to time he undertook criminal cases. One such, I participated in as Prosecuting Counsel. Three men were charged with forgery, it being alleged and readily proved that they had utilised the facilities at their Newcastle Prontoprint shop to produce 50 dollar US bank notes. In memory, three matters stand out: the astonishing quality of the forged notes, the professed inadequacy of the Defendants – too sick to be tried – and Robin's frustration as Defending Counsel with his own client and fury with his Clerk for getting him into the case – or perhaps for not getting him out of it.

In 1992 our respective professional paths diverted. I became a judge. It was and remains a matter of widespread surprise that Robin was not similarly appointed. Whatever his resultant emotions, none such were addressed at me. His support was continuing, warm and practical, extending (with the aid of Lynda) to giving me hospitality in their Temple flat for the duration of my London sittings. My gratitude remains.

One privilege that now accrued to me was having Robin in front of me as an advocate and thereby gaining full on appreciation of his forensic talents. One case comes inevitably to mind. In 1995, then sitting at Leeds, I tried a case that concerned a claim for damages by Mrs June Hancock. She was then terminally ill having contracted mesolthelioma, that is, a form of lung cancer commonly attributed to exposure to asbestos. It was indeed her case that she was so exposed in childhood when living in the immediate vicinity of an asbestos factory that conducted in the centre of Armley, a Leeds suburb. She sued J.W. Roberts, the proprietors of the factory. The case raised novel issues of fact and law and involved much documentary research together with an appreciation of Armley life in the late 30's and the 40's. Mrs Hancock had Robin as her leading counsel; he proved more than equal to the demands of the case. It was my contemporaneous judgment, widely expressed, and not one reflecting current sentimental recollection, that Robin's performance was quite outstanding. Head and shoulders above others in the case (none such being inadequate), his advocacy, preparation and presentation were truly outstanding. I should add that it is fortunate from every point of view that I was able to find for Mrs Hancock, (who against all the odds survived until after the case was concluded) and that Robin was able to uphold my judgment in the Court of Appeal.

Robin's professional life as a Q.C. had other aspects. He was involved with the Bar Mutual Indemnity Fund, and the Professional Conduct Committee of the Bar Council. He was a bencher of The Middle Temple and Master of its Silver.

He sat as a Deputy High Court Judge, trying contested civil cases on Circuit. He undertook the thankless role of Head of his Chambers – though it has to be said that when he retired as such, he was handsomely thanked at a dinner that I was privileged to attend. With all these activities there was, alas, a subtext, his health. From 1993 it had had serious implications for him eventually bringing a memorable professional life to a distressing close.

In conclusion, I turn back to that day in March 1978 when our paths first crossed. Upon taking the oath, we each received our Letters Patent, a magnificent document confirming the appointment as One of Our Counsel learned in the law and doing so using the Royal 'we' and attaching the Royal Seal. Upon checking mine, I am reminded that having confirmed my appointment it then sets about any resultant ego by specifically designating my resultant place in the overall scheme of things. The words chosen are:

"We have also given and granted unto him as one of our Counsel Aforesaid precedence and pre audience next after.... Robin Milton Stewart"

And so it should be.

Andrew Stewart read the following poem by Ralph Waldo Emerson:

To laugh often and much.
To win the respect of intelligent people,
And the affection of children.
To earn the appreciation of honest critics.
To appreciate beauty.
To find the best in others.
To leave the world a bit better, whether by a healthy child,
Or a garden patch.
To know even one life has breathed easier because you have lived.
This is to have succeeded.

Picture 10: Robin & Lynda Stewart, 18 September 1992

Hope and Faith

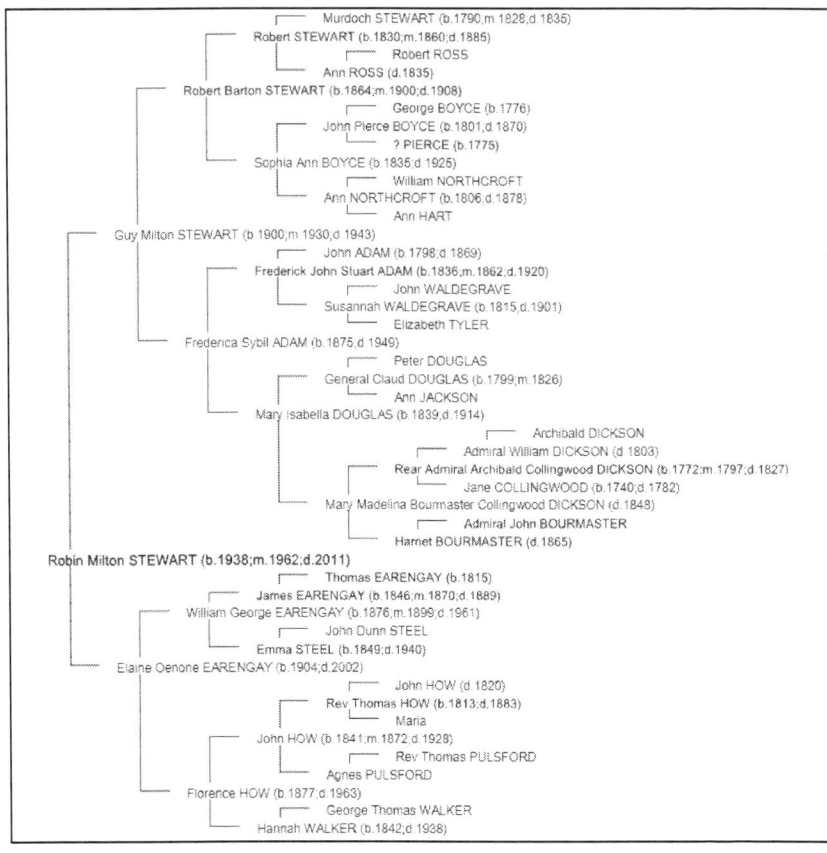

Figure 1: Ancestors of Robin Milton Stewart

Chapter 7: Ross

On 19th August 1828, **Murdoch Stewart** married **Ann Ross** in Inverness. They were my great-great grandparents. She was the daughter of **Robert Ross & Catherine Ross,** his wife.

In the 19th Century our branch of the Ross family claimed to be the rightful heirs of the Earls of Ross; and either presented, or were about to present, a petition to be so recognised, when Queen Victoria let it be known that the earldom had been forfeited many centuries before, and she would not consent to its revival. Their claim must have been based on being the senior male line of the Rosses of Pitcalnie; and thereby heirs male of Ross of Balnagowan - see para 6 below.

The Ross Clan takes its name from the Earldom, which was originally held by the progenitor of the Clan. The first Earl was **Fearcher Mac An Tsagairt** [Farquhar, son of the Priest] who was hereditary representative of the lay Abbots of the Monastery of Applecross. He was created Earl of Ross by Malcolm II and died in 1251.

His great-grandson, **Hugh 4th Earl of Ross,** was killed at the Battle of Halidon Hill on 20th July 1333. He had, by his wife Jean, daughter of Walter, Lord High Stewart of Scotland, 2 sons who survived him:

1. William, 5th Earl of Ross, whose daughter Euphemia succeeded to the Earldom of Ross [most Scottish titles could be inherited by females].

2. **Hugh** of Rarichies & 1st of Balnagowan,

Ross of Balnagowan:

Hugh Ross, of Rarichies & 1st of Balnagowan, was the second son of Hugh 4th Earl of Ross. He was the progenitor of the Ross Clan, & married in 1332 Maud, sister of King Robert the Bruce. In 1351, he was named as one of the hostages for David II's liberty. He received various charters of lands in Ross-shire and in other counties in Scotland. He was father of:

1. **William Ross, 2nd of Balnagowan.** He married Lady Jean Dunbar, daughter of Patrick 13th Earl of March, by his wife Agnes, daughter of Thomas Randolph 5th Earl of Moray; and had 2 sons - Hugh, his successor; and John, who was witness to a deed granted by one of the Lords of the Isles & signed at Kessock. William died before 1380, and was succeeded by his son:

2. **Hugh Ross, 3rd of Balnagowan** who married Margaret Stewart, daughter of Robert 5th Earl of Athole, and had issue:

3. **William Ross, 4th of Balnagowan**, called "Crumbache", who had a precept of the lands of Invercassley 9th May 1384. He m Christian dau Lord Livingstone, and died before 1394, leaving his son:

4. **Walter Ross, 5th of Balnagowan**, called "Cluganach". He married Catherine daughter of Paul McTyre, a notorious brigand chief of Royal Norse descent. Paul McTyre was described in the "Cronicle of the Earls of Ros" as a "very takand man" - takand used not in the sense of being attractive, but in the sense of taking away land and cattle by force. He had made himself master of nearly all of Kincardine or Creich; and endowed Walter Ross with his lands. Walter had 3 children - Hugh, his heir; John; & Katherine who m John Earl of Sutherland & had issue. Walter died c 1420 & was succeeded by his eldest son:

5. **Hugh Ross, 6th of Balnagowan**, m Janet dau William Earl of Sutherland, by whom he had:

   [i]   John, his heir

[ii]   Hugh Ross 1st of Tolly
[iii]   William, killed at the battle of Auldicharish in 1492
[iv]   Thomas
[v]   Alexander Ross, 1st of Little Tarrel.Hugh died in 1447.

6. **John Ross, 7th of Balnagowan**, m Christina dau Torquil McLeod of Lewis, & had issue:

[i]   Alexander, his heir
[ii]   William, killed with his uncle at the Battle of Auldicharish
[iii]   Hugh, one of whose daughters married William Dow Mackay, 2nd of the Clan - Abrach branch of the Mackays
[iv]   Elizabeth who m John Earl of Sutherland
[v]   Jane

7. **Alexander Ross 8th of Balnagowan** who fought at the Battle of Auldicharish - caused by the Mackays invading Balnagowan's lands in Kincardine, in revenge for the Rosses having burnt in the Church of Tarbat, the Chief of the Mackays. The battle was a severe one, & Alexander was killed along with his brother & uncle. He married a daughter of John 10th Earl of Sutherland, and had issue:

[i]   David, his heir
[ii]   Hugh
[iii]   Margaret

8. **Sir David Ross 9th of Balnagowan** played a conspicuous part in the history of Ross-shire, being Sheriff for several years. By his second wife Helen Keith dau Keith of Inverugie, he had:

[i]   Walter, his heir
[ii]   William Ross, 1st of Invercarron
[iii]   Hugh Ross, 1st of Pitkerie
[iv]   [A daughter

Sir David Ross died in 1527.

9. **Walter Ross 10th of Balnagowan** m Marion, dau Grant of Grant, & had:

    [i]   Alexander, his heir

    [ii]   Hugh Ross 1st of Shandwick

    [iii] David

    [iv] Catherine, who m John Denoon 3rd of Cadboll - ancestors of Rt Hon W E Gladstone, Prime Minister.

Walter Ross was killed in 1528 at Tain

10. **Alexander Ross 11th of Balnagowan** who was twice married - first to Janet Sinclair dau George 4th Earl of Caithness, & had issue:

    [i]   George, his heir

    [ii]   Catherine, m Hector Munro of Foulis

    [iii] Agnes m Duncan Campbell of the Cawdor family

His second wife was Catherine MacKenzie, dau Kenneth MacKenzie 10th of Kintail, by whom he had:

    [iv] **Nicholas Ross**, Abbot of Fearn & 1st of Pitcalnie

    [v]   Malcolm Ross of Cambuscurie & Dolles

    [vi] Several daus.

Alexander died in 1592 & was buried in the Abbey of Fearn.

The line descends to

11. **David Ross 15th of Balnagowan**, who died in 1711, when the estate and castle of Balnagowan passed out of the family. The estate was in considerable debt due to the support given to the Royalist cause by David 14th of Balnagowan - who had brought at his own expense a battalion to the Battle of Worcester, who was captured there, and who died a prisoner in the Tower on 29th December 1653. In 1707, the estate was infeft in the name of Lord Ross of Halkhead in Renfrewshire [nothing to do with the Clan Ross]. In 1711, it was conveyed to Lord Ross' half brother General Charles Ross, who redeemed the wadsetts and became laird, though of no kin to the old line of Balnagowan.

The heir as Chief of the Ross Clan was Malcolm Ross, 5th of Pitcalnie, for whom **Robert Ross,** or **"Robert of the Sword"** - our earliest proven ancestor - see below - was factor. In 1778, Munro Ross 7th of Pitcalnie, formally laid claims (a) to the estate of Balnagowan - a claim pursued without success; and (b) to the Earldom of Ross. He based his claim on the ground that he was the lineal male descendant of Hugh Ross of Rarichies and 1st of Balnagowan, brother to William, the last Ross Earl of Ross. His claim was sustained by the Court of Session and by the House of Lords, on the ground that the title was wrongfully assumed by Euphemia Countess of Ross, the title being limited to heirs male. No further decision seems to have been made on the subject [1] - probably because they were financially embarrassed by the litigation over the Balnagowan estate.

The Rosses of Pitcalnie:

Chapter 1: Nicholas Ross 1st of Pitcalnie was the 2nd son of Alexander Ross 11th of Balnagowan. He married 1587 Margaret, 2nd dau Hugh Munro 1st of Assynt & had

[i]   David, his heir

[ii]   Christian who m Donald McLeod, 7th of Assynt, Sutherlandshire.

Margaret Ross died in 1592, and Nicholas died in 1611.

2. **David Ross, 2nd of Pitcalnie**, who was also heir, in 1618, to his uncle Malcolm Ross of Cambuscurry. He m Jean dau Alexander Dunbar of Moyness & had 3 sons:

[i]   David, his heir

[ii]   Nicholas, witness to a sasine 15.12.1640

[iii] Malcolm Ross 1st of Kindeace

David Ross d 14.10.1646 & was buried at Fearn

3. **David Ross 3rd of Pitcalnie**, Tutor of Balnagowan; a Commissioner of War for Ross-shire; and 1661 Commissioner of Excise for Ross, had by Jean dau Alexander MacKenzie 1st of Kilcoy, several daughters and a son:

4. **Alexander Ross 4th of Pitcalnie**, Commissioner of Supply for Ross-shire 1685; m Agnes eldest dau Hugh Ross of Balmuchie & had 4 sons & a dau:

   [i] Malcolm, who succeeded as 5th of Pitcalnie in about 1700, & who died after 1733. It was for him that our forebear **Robert Ross** "Robert of the Sword was factor.

   [ii] George

   [iii] a son

   [iv] William, who went to Antrim; and whose great grandsons James succeeded as 8th of Pitcalnie, and George succeeded as 9th of Pitcalnie. The eventual heir of the estate was George Ross Williamson, son of their sister Sarah who m Donald Williamson.

Our branch of the Ross Clan is said to be that of **Ross of Morangie** near Tain. Apparently in the mid to late 19th Century, one or more of the Ross family (one of my great grandfather, Robert Stewart's, first cousins brought a petition claiming to be the senior line of the Ross Clan, and thus heirs of and entitled to the Earldom of Ross. The claim must have been based on the premise that they were the senior male line or heirs male of the Rosses of Pitcalnie - see above. It is said that Queen Victoria commented that the Earldom of Ross had been forfeited in 1476, and that she was not going to allow it to be revived. Whether there was actually a petition to the House of Lords, I have not checked. But my cousin Colonel Walter Ross told me that there were many papers gathered in support of the claim: he had last seen them prior to his father's death in 1935: and his father then deposited them somewhere for safekeeping. Candidates vary between Solicitors such as MacLay Murray & Spens of Glasgow; and the Register Office, Edinburgh. They have not been traced[2].

I have a blank sheet of crested notepaper, from a letter of 1876, from Hugh Cameron Ross - source, Standard Bank Archives [3].

Since Robert Ross "Robert of the Sword" - see below - was both a tacksman and factor for Malcolm Ross 5th of Pitcalnie, it is quite likely that he was close kin to the Rosses of Pitcalnie. A tacksman was a leaseholder of land. To grant a tack was in the gift of the landowner (Ross of Pitcalnie). The laird's kin would come in for preferential treatment in getting a tack; and at that date, the factor could well have been a close relative of the laird to whom he was factor. Hence the claim to be the (male) representative of the Rosses of Pitcalnie and thus of the (old) Earls of Ross is quite possible.

I have not been able to trace further back than **Ann Ross or Stewart**'s great grandfather-

5. **Robert Ross**: known as Robert of the Sword, or Robb Leathann, a man of great size and strength, lived in Pitcalnie. He was born, presumably, in the latter part of the 17th century. He lived in Pitcalnie & was factor for Callum Og, Malcolm Ross, 5th of Pitcalnie (who succeeded to that property in about 1700, and died in 1733). Malcolm Ross, like most of the Rosses, was anti Jacobite, and pro Hanoverian, during the '15 Rising. He mobilised 500 men and marched off to Alness, the rendez-vous of the Northern Hanoverians, where he joined the Munros and the men of Sutherland.

Robert Ross, Solicitor in Glasgow [IV: i: below] believed that this Robert Ross had his own small estate in the parish of Kincardine. J M Ross wrote in his 1861 letter [4] "Alexander Ross, Ardgay, did not know of an estate. He knew of him as a tacksman".

Robert of the Sword died in 17--, and was buried in Tutim Churchyard, above the River Oykel in Strath Oykel. If any tombstone was erected, none was visible in 1970 when we visited Tutim [5]. He had two sons:

[i]   **David Ross**, of whom hereafter
[ii]   Thomas, Tacksman in Tournaig. He had 4 sons:

I.   John: died at home; his family went to Picton, Canada

II. Hugh: became a Major in the Royal Marines, and died childless in 1828. His grave is still visible, with the inscription "Hugh Ross Esq, second son of Mr Thomas Ross of Turnack & Grace his wife, late Major Royal Marines, died 2nd day of March 1828, aged 48".

III. Malcolm; a Captain in the Army; went to America with his Regiment, where he died.

IV. David; a Lieutenant in Mexico, where he died.

6. **David Ross**: the oldest son of Robert of the Sword, was a tacksman in Invercassley and Invercarron. He was the father of:

7. **Robert Ross:** (per J M Ross "Robert Og") b presumably circa 1765; married Catherine Ross, daughter of David Ross tacksman in Invercassley. Shortly after their marriage, they decided to go to America, and went to Ullapool where they were to take ship. For some reason they did not go to America, but remained in Ullapool. They raised a large family including:

[i]   Hugh Ross, of whom hereafter.

[ii] Alexander Ross; b Creich 1802. Creich is in Sutherland, but the parish is huge, and includes Invercassley in Strath Oykel, the home of his mother's parents. He went to Inverness, where he took a hotel, and farmed 49 acres at Seafield of Raigmore. In 1835, he married Catherine Colvin, of Daviot, near Inverness (who was b in Daviot in 1816). Whether they had any children of their own, I do not know. They brought up **Robert Stewart** after his parents died of cholera in or about 1836; and Alexander was a witness to Robert Stewart's wedding in 1860 to Sophia Ann Boyce.

[iii] Donald Ross; a mason; had 2 sons and a daughter. The sons went to Australia.

[iv] **Ann Ross**. Her date and place of birth I do not know. It is likely to have been in the early 1800s in the parish of Creich or

Kincardine, Sutherland. She married in 1828 **Murdoch Stewart** in Inverness. They were my great-great grandparents.

[v]   Hugh Ross: b 1789; married in Ullapool 29th December 1826, Mary (1800 - 1871) daughter of Alexander MacDonald and Jane Douglas. He settled in Dingwall, where he came under the wing and favour of Hugh Innes Cameron [Provost Cameron, Banker & Fiscal of the County of Ross]. He was a Writer, Messenger at Arms, Auctioneer etc. He died 2 March 1849, and is buried in the parish churchyard at Dingwall, where his tomb is still visible [6]. Mary Ross died in Glasgow in 1871 [7]. They had 6 sons & 2 daughters:

I.   Robert 1828-1881, Writer (or Solicitor) in Glasgow: dsp

II.   Alexander 1829-1897; in Glasgow Corporation; dsp

III.   Kenneth; 1831-1833 dsp

IV.   David 1833-1852, buried next to his father at Dingwall

V.   Hugh Cameron 1836-1902 dsp; entered banking, and was brought into the Standard Bank in South Africa by his first cousin, **Robert Stewart.** He succeeded Robert Stewart in 1876 as Joint General Manager, and eventually became a Director of the Bank [1885-1902] [8]. In 1882, he purchased the estate of Ledgowan, a sporting estate of some 10,000 acres at Achnasheen in Wester Ross. Achnasheen is a bleak spot, the Gaelic name Druim Dubh Achad Na Sine meaning Black Ridge of Storm Field. This estate passed to his nephew Robert Ross, after whose death in 1935, it was sold.

I have a Passport of HCR's issued in 1861, a one page document, for "travel on the Continent", [9] and signed by Lord John Russell, then Foreign Secretary.

VI.   **John MacDonald Ross** 1838-1905, of whom hereafter.

VII. Elizabeth b & d 1835

VIII. Catherine, b 1848; m C W Duncan of Richmond, London.

8. **John MacDonald Ross** 1838-1905; was an engineer and contractor who early in life went to Canada and worked around Hudson's Bay with a fellow Scot, Andrew Carnegie. Carnegie tried to persuade JMR to go to America with him as his partner, but JMR preferred to return to his native Scotland. Carnegie went on to make one of the greatest fortunes in 19th century America, and became famed for his philanthropy. He bought Skibo Castle, and endowed Carnegie Libraries - as public lending libraries throughout Scotland.

John MacDonald Ross was the only one of his generation to marry and have children. His wife's name I do not know, but he was moderately well off when he got married. The marriage contract lists shares worth some £22,575 [10]. He died in 1905, having had 4 sons:

[i]   Robert, of whom hereafter.
[ii]   Hugh, who was killed in the First World War, leaving a posthumous son [his widow married, secondly, James Scrimgeour, of J & A Scrimgeour, Stockbrokers]
[iii]   Hugh, a partner in J & A Scrimgeour, Stockbrokers.
[iv]   John, dsp.
[v]   Charles dsp.

9. **Robert Ross**, a Major; m. Marion Cross (d. 1960) daughter of Walter MacFarlane DL, JP. Robert inherited Ledgowan, which was sold after his death in 1935. He had two children:

[i]   Walter John MacDonald Ross, of whom hereafter
[ii]   Helen, m Leslie Dunn, a stockbroker in Glasgow, & had two children

    I.   Peter, m Val --, and lives in Edinburgh

    II. Patricia

10. **Walter John MacDonald Ross:** b 1914, a Colonel; CB (1958), OBE (1955), MC (1945), TD + 2 Bars (1947); had an estate at Netherhall, Bridge of Dee, Castle Douglas, Kirkcudbrightshire. He used to go to Ledgowan as a child, for the summers from Glasgow. His parents would travel first class by rail, leaving the nanny and children to go second class. His father was a powerful personality, and was once accidentally locked in his first class carriage, which was shunted onto a siding to his rage and indignation. None of the railway staff dared go near: it was left to the young Walter to release his enraged father. Even in the 1930s, Ledgowan was extremely remote: to see one car in a week was a major event.

When Ledgowan was sold, all remaining Ross possessions (save it seems, for the genealogical papers which had been deposited elsewhere for safekeeping) were transferred to Glasgow. Most were destroyed when their Glasgow house was bombed in the war. Walter still had some 19th century glass which had on it arms said to be those of Ross of Morangie, near Tain.

He m 1940 Josephine May, dau of Malcolm Cross of Earlston, Borgue, Kirkcudbrightshire. Issue 3 children:

[i]   Malcolm, a Colonel, Scots Guards; m Susan Gow + issue.

[ii]   Robert

[iii]   Susan, m Patrick Hope-Johnstone.

Notes & Sources:

1. History of The Clan Ross, by A M Ross, printed at the Northern Star Office, Dingwall, 1932; The Clan Ross - W & A K Johnston's Clan History Series, by Donald MacKinnon, 1957.
2. Correspondence with & from Colonel Walter Ross 1963 - 1970
3. Blank page of crested notepaper from Hugh Cameron Ross, 1876
4. Letter to John MacDonald Ross from his brother Robert Ross, Solicitor, Glasgow, 30th January 1861.
5. Ross graves visible at Tutim Churchyard in August 1970:

   - Hugh Ross Esq   second son of Mr Thomas Ross, Turnach, & Grace his wife, late Royal Marines, d 2nd day of March 1828 aged 48
   - Hugh Ross. tenant Linside, d 14 March 1844 in his 44th year; & his wife Catherine Morrison d 17 March 1847 in her 70th year; erected by his son John Ross, Smith Linside, who d 12 Dec 1877 aged 70.
   - Neil Ross, Langwell d 11 Dec 1856 aged 74;\and his wife Mary Ross d 23 June 1858 aged 59; erected by youngest son Angus Ross, Langwell, Waeanakarna, New Zealand.
   - Thomas Ross, Achnagart, parish of Kincardine, d May 1833 aged 75 years; and Ann Ross d 1843 aged 74; erected by son William Ross, Southampton, England.
   - Malcolm Ross   d 2nd Oct 1877 aged 77; & Margaret Ross d April 1st 1854
   - John Ross d at Altass 2 Jan 1873 aged 77 & Catherine MacLeod his wife d Altass Nov 1st 1842 aged 36; also dau Grace d Jan 1845 aged 10 - erected by Alexander & Hugh Ross in memory of their parents & sister.
   - Donald Ross   Altass d June 1828 aged 47 (& Others, barely legible) & his spouse Catherine d 1867, 27th Feb, aged 77

- Hugh Ross Miller Strathoykell, d 1st Feb 1859 aged 42; & Margaret Ross his wife, d 4th July 1891 aged 60; and their son William d 21 Jan 1921 aged 64
- Thomas Ross tenant, Brae, d March 1838 & Christina Mackay his wife d 3 Jan 1861; & William their son & Isabella their daughter both died in childhood 1806-1811; erected by Niel Ross of Maungatua, Otago in memory of his parents, brother & sister.
- Alexander Ross pensioner Oape, d 11 May 1843 aged 63; & his wife Margaret, d 24 Nov 1851, aged 61; erected by their daughters
- Angus Ross tenant Inchnadamph, Strathoykell, d 12 April 1891 aged 82; & his wife Catherine Ross d 24 Sept 1879 aged 61; & Christine d 20 Oct 1917 aged 67; Hugh 3 Oct 1930 aged 75; & Farquhar, 7 April 1935 in his 84th year.
- John Ross Oape; d 11 Nov 1865 aged 74; & his brother Hugh, d 8 July 1878 aged 85; & Mary Ross wife of Hugh d 24 Jan 1894 aged 92; erected by Hugh's sons David, John, Robert, & Donald.
- Henrietta Ross (MacLean) wife of David Ross, Shepherd, Craggan, d 2 Jan 1868 aged 28
- Donald Ross d at Doune, Strathoykell, 18 Jan 1899; & his wife Christina d 29 March 1904; son Alexander d 20 Dec 1949, his wife Christina MacGregor d 22 Jan 1947; erected by Jessie Ross their daughter & sister.
- Robert Ross Gamekeeper, Corriemuille, d 26 July 1871 aged 67.
- There are other Ross tombs of the late 19th & 20th centuries; and tombs of various Grahams (one spelt in Gaelic Greum), MacLeans, & MacLeods; also several stones virtually undecipherable.

6. Copy Will, Hugh Ross, writer, Dingwall, dated 31.05.1849

7. Letter 20.04.1871 from Robert Ross, Solicitor, Glasgow, to his brother Hugh Cameron Ross (in South Africa) describing the death of their mother; & Death Certificate of Mary Ross or MacDonald 1871.

8. For Hugh Cameron Ross see - History of the Standard Bank of South Africa 1862-1913, Glasgow 1913; The First Hundred Years of the Standard Bank, by J A Henry, Oxford University Press, 1963; The Ross-shire Journal.

9. Passport, 1861, for Hugh Cameron Ross (ex Standard Bank)

10. List of Shares for Marriage Contract of Mr & Mrs John MacDonald Ross

11. Death Certificate of John MacDonald Ross 1905.

Second Ross Line

Catherine Ross, wife of Robert Ross [III] above, and mother of **Ann Stewart** was also a Ross by birth. Her ancestry is given in a manuscript written by David Ross, of Dingwall, c. 1887 [1]. An earlier, foreshortened, version was given in a letter written by John MacDonald Ross to his brother John Ross, Solicitor, Glasgow, dated 30th January 1861[2].

1. Ross, tacksman of Tournaig / Thuarnach [3] had one son & 5 daughters:

[i] David Ross of whom hereafter

[ii] a daughter who married Ross of Invercassley[2] or Invercarron

[iii] a daughter who married Ross of Ankerville

[iv] a daughter who married Ross of Shandwick

[v] a daughter who married the first MacKenzie of Ord

[vi] a fifth daughter

(per J M Ross "Mr Alexander Ross, Ardgay, told me that one of the above mentioned daughters married Ross of Invercharron, and another married (David) Ross of Mid Fearn who succeeded to Shandwick, but beyond this he knew nothing. Either this David, or his son William, was killed in a duel in London.").

2. **David Ross,** b presumably in the mid 17th century, succeeded his father as tacksman of Thuarnach & had a son

3. **William Ross**, who had 3 sons:

[i] Malcolm, known as the Catechist of Kincardine Parish; and (according to the manuscript) named after Malcolm Ross "Callum Og" yr of Pitcalnie, the heir apparent to the Earldom of Ross, who joined Prince Charlie in 1745 & had to escape to France. [It cannot be right that he was named after Malcolm Ross yr of Pitcalnie, who was the elder son of Alexander Ross 6th of Pitcalnie; was at College in Aberdeen; joined Prince Charles Edward in 1745, was attainted, and escaped to France. Malcolm the Catechist must, on dates, have been named not after the Jacobite Malcolm yr of Pitcalnie, but after the grandfather, Malcolm 5th of Pitcalnie]. Malcolm the Catechist had a son

I. Malcolm, who farmed at Bogcreuch, Kiltearn, who had a son

a. Alexander, who went to Otago, New Zealand + issue there]

Note: Whether this paragraph is accurate is not clear. J M Ross put Hugh, tacksman of Thuarnach, no ii below, as the eldest son of David Ross, no 2 above)

[ii] Hugh, tacksman in Tournaig [3] & [4], presumably circa 1710, of whom hereafter

[iii] William in Lobcroy [5], who m Margaret Graham & had 3 sons

I. David in Lobcroy, later of Bratolly, Ardross, who had 4 sons:

> a. William, in Ardross, who had a dau
> b. John, dsp
> c. Alexander, went to USA + issue
> d. David, in New Zealand & Dingwall, who had a dau. [the author of the 1887 manuscript]

> II. George

> III. Thomas

4. **Hugh Ross**, second son of William Ross, was a tacksman in Tournag [3 & 4]; and had three sons and a daughter:

   [i] David Ross Tacksman of Invercassley, of whom hereafter

   [ii] a dau who married John Ross, the Giant of Fearn or Midfearn, dsp

   [iii] Thomas, tacksman in Tournag who had 4 sons & 2 daughters [1]

   > I. Major Hugh

   > II. Captain Malcolm, who went to Canada

   > III. John who went to Canada

   > IV. David who went to Canada

   > V. dau who m Munro

   > VI. Catherine who m Duncan Cameron from Lochaber

(J M Ross has Hugh, no 4, having but one son, David Ross, tacksman of Invercassley).

5. **David Ross tacksman of Invercassley** [2] son of Hugh Ross tacksman of Tournag, had 4 sons & 5 daughters:

   [i] Hugh Ross, who d in India

   [ii] Donald, dsp joined the army & d in South America (d in the West Indies per John MacDonald Ross to his brother Robert 30.01.1861)

   [iii] Alexander, Lieutenant, 60th Regiment, dsp (in the West Indies per J M Ross ibid)

[iv]   Malcolm, planter in St Vincent dsp. (he was drowned there, per J M Ross ibid). "He left money, not very much, all that was recovered of it our father got" (per J M Ross ibid).

[v]   **Catherine Ross**, who married **Robert Ross** ("Robert Og" per J M Ross ibid).. They were the parents of **Ann Stewart**

[vi]   Elizabeth who m William McGregor, brother to Inchnadamph

[vii]   Marion, m George Ross, tacksman in Gruinard, Strathcarron + issue there

[viii]   Isabella, m Duncan McMillan (& went to America per J M Ross ibid)

[ix]   Anne, m McGregor of Inchnadamph

Notes:

1.   There seems to be a certain confusion here between Thomas, given earlier as second son of Robert Ross, "Robert of the Sword", and Thomas given here as the second son of Hugh Ross tacksman in Tournag. They have virtually identical families.

Their descent from Robert of the Sword comes from a letter written by John MacDonald Ross to his brother Robert Ross, Solicitor in Glasgow, in 1861 - in which he gave the genealogy referred to and said that he had visited the graveyard of Tutim and seen the graves of Robert of the Sword and of his grandson the Major. In that letter, J M Ross gives the descent as set out above, but:

(a):   Has David Ross, tacksman of Thuarnach (no 2 above) as the father of Hugh (no 4 above) who succeeded his father as tacksman of Thuarnach.

(b):   Hugh (no 4) had an only son, David (no 5) who became tacksman of Invercassley.

Thus on the J M Ross version, this confusion does not exist. The descent set out on this page from Hugh Ross, was given in the manuscript of 1887 by David Ross, who had returned from New Zealand to Dingwall.

This illustrates the difficulty in sorting out Highland families, where the same names occur in different branches of the same family.

2. Invercassley is where Glen Cassley meets Strath Oykel in Ross-shire.

3. Tournaig is probably Thurnaig. There is a Loch Thurnaig on the River Oykel, just below Oykel Bridge

4. Lobcroy is probably the same as Lubcroy, higher still up Strath Oykel, on the Oykel River, about 16 miles from Inchnadamph.

5. Manuscript Notes on the Rosses of Balnagowan, Pitcalnie, & Kindeace compiled by RMS

6. On the Highland Clearances - see "The Highland Clearances" by John Prebble, Secker & Warburg & Penguin Books, 1963; The Massacre of the Rosses of Strathcarron, Ross-shire, by Donald Ross 1886, Inverness

Chapter 8: Boyce

1. **Sophia Ann Stewart**, wife of **Robert Stewart 1830-1885** was the daughter of John Pierce Boyce, of Chertsey, Surrey. The furthest back that I have proved is Revd John Boyce, her great great grandfather. Whether the family is connected with that of Dr William Boyce 1710-1779, the celebrated composer, is not known.

   Dr William Boyce 1710-1779, the composer, came from a family closely connected with the Joiners Company. John Boyce (his father) was Stewart of the Joiners Company 1696, Beadle 1722 - 1752, and died 1752/53, leaving 3 children:

   [i]   John Boyce, apprenticed Joiners Company 1711, Freeman 1739, Beadle 1753 (succeeding his father) & died 1755.

   [ii] Dr William Boyce 1710-1779, m Hannah -- & had issue

       I.   Elizabeth; m -

       II. William b 1764 d 1824, a double bass player

   [iii] Elizabeth, m Francis Wyndham, a tailor of Salisbury Court, Fleet Street.

   [Source: Groves Dictionary of Music & Musicians]

2. **Rev John Boyce:** - whose parentage I do not know, was Master of the Lord Ranelagh Charity School, Winkfield, from 1750 - 1772. He was a man of property of some substance, but how he acquired it is not known. He died in 1772, and was succeeded in the Mastership by his son George. He had 2 children, at any rate:

[i]   George,

[ii]   Mary, who married John Milton (if the reading of Rev John's will is correct).

3.   **Revd George Boyce:** - b 1744, d 27 Jan 1824 aged 80; was for 49

years Curate of St Mary's, Winkfield, Berkshire. The fact that he never got a living in his own right, but remained always a Curate, might have suggested that he had little means, and no connections to call on for the gift of a living. But he apparently inherited both the Mastership of the Lord Ranelagh Charity School in Winkfield on the death of his father, and substantial property. In 1817 he was awarded

Picture 11: Rev George Boyce   property under the Enclosure Acts.

I have an oil painting presumed to be of Rev George Boyce with 2 dogs jumping up at him, with Windsor Castle dimly in the background. This was cleaned and reframed in 1996; when the remains of a signature and date were observed. The signature is not readable, but underneath appears "Windsor" and a date, which looks like 1798 or possibly 1793. There is also a drawing of him by Sir George Hayter, with an etching of the drawing, dated 1815. Hayter was said to have been Rev George Boyce's son-in-law. I am doubtful of the accuracy of this, but clearly there was some connection, possibly on his wife's side. I have also a miniature of a man on that side of the family, assumed to be a Boyce, damaged, in costume which would suggest a date of around 1710 - 1730.

He married on 23rd August 1773 at Windsor Parish Church **Mary Milton**. She was born 1749/1750, and died 11th May 1811, aged 61. They had issue:

[i] John Boyce b 1774, who was left the malt mill. The 1841 census records a John Boyce b 1776 , publican, in North Street, Windsor (?)

[ii] **George**, of whom hereafter, b 1776

[iii] William, b 1781

[iv] Thomas b 1784

[v] James b 1786

[vi] Mary, b 1779

[vii] ??? a daughter who m. Sir George Hayter [b.1792] the Court Painter to Queen Victoria[6] (I do not know whether this was Mary or some other daughter).

Note: On a number of items that emanated from Ione Burt, she had written that we descend from John, rather than the second son, George. Having corresponded with Peter Boyce of Bristol, I am satisfied that we descend from the second son, George. I presume that wherever Ione Burt wrote that a portrait was of John, it should be corrected to George.

4. **George Boyce 1776** - was born at Windsor 4th April 1776. He married a Miss Pierce, who was born 3rd April 1775. I have a pair of miniatures of George Boyce & his wife, by Sir George Hayter. These descended to Ethel Boyce, dau George Boyce (see below). From her they went to the Peters family. Ione Burt inherited them and sold them. I had photographs, and saw the originals for sale in a junky antique shop in Cecil Court off Leicester Square, during my pupillage at the Bar. I had the greatest difficulty in persuading the ancient dealer to get them down for me to look at. The price was a princely £5 for the pair. Inside the frames, was Ione Burt's writing as to who the subjects were. The miniatures had originally been rectangular, and someone along the line had cut them down to fit oval frames.

Picture 12: George Boyce

Picture 13: Mrs Boyce (née Pierce)

Picture 14: Uncle John Pierce

I also have (a): a miniature labelled "believed to be Uncle John Pierce", in the handwriting (I think) of Sophia Ann Stewart. This must date to c 1740-1750. It was given to me, unframed, by Lucy Beck. (b): a rather fine silhouette of John Boyce, together with several unlabelled silhouettes of the Boyce family. They had issue:

5. **John Pierce Boyce 1801-1870:** born at Egham - a Chemist (pharmacist) in Guildford Street, Chertsey. He married **Ann Northcroft 1806 - 1878**, daughter of William Northcroft, an Architect in London, by his wife Ann Hart (both of whom originated from Chalfont St Peter, Bucks). By this stage some of the Boyce family, including, I think, John Pierce Boyce, were Quakers. They had issue:

[i] John Pierce Boyce jr, of whom hereafter

[ii] George Boyce b 1832; married Anne Ogden, and had issue Ethel Mary Boyce (a Quaker) who was b 1863 & dsp.

[iii] Martha b 1829; m John Scurr Barton, a cabinet maker & upholsterer in (?) Windsor, by whom she had 4 children:

I. Arthur Scurr Barton, b 1856, who went to South Africa

II. Edith Ellen b 1854, dsp

III. Amy Hart b 1860 dsp

IV. Frances Stewart b 1862 dsp.

It is presumably from this connection that my grandfather was named Robert Barton Stewart

[iv] **Sophia Ann 1835-1925**, who married Robert Stewart 1830 - 1885; my great grandparents

[v] Mary Cecilia 1837 - ; m Samuel Gee & had issue:

   I.   Ernest Alfred Gee b 1863; a missionary abroad; dsp

   II. Annie Louisa b 1864, dsp

   III. Bertha Henrietta b 1866, dsp

6. **John Pierce Boyce (jr)** 1829-1911; m Jane Anne Hills 1828-1902. I have a water colour portrait of John Pierce Boyce on horseback; and a pair of small oil portraits of Jane Anne Hills and her sister Caroline, as young girls, wearing coral necklaces (which we also have); some samplers by the Hills' girls; and silhouettes of the two girls and their mother "taken at Ryde" in 1849. The portraits were painted in, probably 1840 - Caroline's has on the back her age of 8 yrs 10 months; and her sampler dated October 1st 1839 gives her age as 8 then. Thus at the date of the portraits, Caroline was approaching 9, and Jane Anne was probably just 12.

Picture 15: Jane Anne Hills   Picture 16: Caroline Hills

They had 2 daughters:

[i]   Jane Anne 1855 - 1936; she m 1878 Sir George Henry Peters b 1853, whose family came from Bletchingley, Surrey. They lived at Ouseley Lodge, Windsor, Berkshire, which was the dower house to Beaumont, part of the Nation's gift to Warren Hastings. George Peters built a considerable fortune in dealing in coal. He was Honorary Treasurer to Princess Christian, and he endowed the Nursing Home in Windsor named after Princess Christian. He was Mayor of Windsor, was knighted in 1918, and died in 1931. They had 2 sons:

I.   George Henry Boyce Peters 1878 (?) - 1956, a Solicitor in Chichester. His wife was a Miss Hare who died in 1960. They had 2 children:

a. George Charles Boyce Peters, b 1913, killed in the Battle of Britain 1940, as an RAF Pilot, aged 27. dsp.
b. Marion Ione 1911-1976, who m as his second wife Engineer Rear Admiral G G P Burt (he died 1969). dsp.

II.   Captain Reginald Herbert Peters 1879-1970; commissioned into the 1st Royal Berkshire Regiment by King Edward VII, and lived latterly in London. He spent considerable time and effort restoring Ouseley Lodge to its Georgian grandeur - it was hit by a flying bomb in the War. He gave Ouseley Lodge & its entire contents (including pictures, Aubusson carpets, and table silver) to Beaumont, the Roman Catholic School, because of its historic connection as the Dower House. Shortly after Reggie died, Beaumont sold the house and its contents.

Andrew has the oil portraits of Sir George & Lady Peters by Robert Bower (Picture 17& Picture 18 below). We have the oil portraits of Reggie (in the uniform of the 1st Royal Berkshire Regiment) and of young George in the uniform of the 4th Royal West Sussex Regiment (Territorial Army), painted at age 18, in about 1931; also by Robert Bower. There is also a watercolour portrait of young George in his RAF uniform, shortly before the Battle of Britain.

Picture 17: Sir George Henry Peters

Picture 18: Lady Peters (Jane Hills)

Picture 19: Young George Peters

Picture 20: Sir George Peters

Picture 21: Lady Peters

Picture 22: Reggie Peters

III. Ada Caroline 1859 - --; she married Frank Rainford, a Jew, whose original surname was Tibbett, which he changed because he did not like it. Frank was a stockbroker, became very rich, and lived in great style. He purchased the entire dining room, panelling, furniture & all, of the Empress Eugenie, and installed it in his house at Hove. He purchased much of her jewellery as well. They had an only child

a. Gladys Rainford, b circa 1900 and dsp in Hove c 1960

Notes:

1. Many of the Boyces are buried at Winkfield, including Revd George Boyce, John Pierce Boyce sr & jr, and their wives; Robert Stewart & his wife Sophia Ann Boyce.

2. There is also a William Boyce, d 1878 (?); and what appears to be an Edward Boyce d 1783.

3. Winkfield Parish Church records give some Boyce marriages - whether related to us, I do not know:

    - 7.09.1771:   John Milton of Winkfield, bac, to Mary Boyce of Winkfield, spinster
    - 11.06.1774: George Boyce of Winkfield. bac, to Eleanor King of Warfield, spinster
    - 3.01.1804:   George Boyce of Winkfield, bac, to Anne Maria Gibbins of Winkfield [married by Revd George Boyce]

4. Arms (from a signet ring in the possession of Reginald Peters):
    Arms: Argent on a bend sable 3 cinquefoils or
    Crest: A star of 6 points or, within a crescent argent
    see: Burke's General Armoury

5. One of the small engravings that came to me, with other Boyce silhouettes, from Ione Burt, was of Archbishop Howley, Archbishop of Canterbury. He was connected with the family of Kingsmill of Sydmonton (a few miles south of Newbury). Around the turn of the century, there was a Boyce Vicar of Ecchinswell & Sydmonton 1884-1917. He had a son Innes Douglas Boyce, who was in the Royal Berkshire Regiment in the 1914-1918 War. I have not followed this up, beyond a letter in 1974 from the last of the Victorian generation of Kingsmills.

    - Sir George Hayter was b at St James' Street, London 17 Dec 1792. He was a portrait & historical painter. Studied at the

Royal Academy Schools. 1808 joined the Royal Navy as a Midshipman.

- 1809-1815: exhibited several miniatures & portraits in chalk & crayons.
- 1815: appointed painter of miniatures & portraits to Princess Charlotte & Prince Leopold of Saxe-Coburg.
- 1816-1819: went to Rome, & then back to London.
- 1841: Appointed Principal Painter in Ordinary to the Queen.
- 1842: Knighted
- d. 238 Marylebone Road, London 18 January 1871 & buried in the St Marylebone Cemetery at Finchley.
- [ref: The Times 23.Jan 1871]
- He was the son of Charles Hayter 1761-1835; a miniature painter (son of another Charles Hayter, an architect & builder in Hampshire). Charles Hayter developed a talent for small pencil portraits & devoted himself to miniature painting. He m Martha Stevenson of Charing Cross, 1788; and d 1 Dec 1835. He was the father of [i] Sir George Hayter, above; and [ii]: John Hayter, at one time a fashionable portrait draughtsman in crayons, b 1800 d June 1895. [DNB]

The Boyce Family - Portraits etc

1. Small, damaged, miniature of a mid 18th century Boyce, quite possibly the father of Rev George Boyce.
2. Drawing of Rev George Boyce, by his son in law Sir George Hayter. An engraving of the drawing in London is in the cloakroom, dated 1815.
3. Oil Portrait of Rev George Boyce, with 2 dogs and Windsor Castle in the background. (signature virtually illegible).
4. Pair of miniatures of George Boyce and his wife née Pierce.
5. Silhouette of George Boyce.
6. Miniature probably of George Boyce. 3 unidentified silhouettes.
7. Miniature of "Uncle John Pierce" c.1740 - 1750.

8. Photographs of John Pierce Boyce & his wife Ann Northcroft, (with ADLS).
9. Miniature of Ann Northcroft as a child.
10. Water colour portrait of John Pierce Boyce jr.
11. A drawing of a Miss Boyce done at The Cedars, Chertsey, in December 1889, probably a child of one of this generation.
12. Portrait of Robert Stewart (copy of the original in the possession of the Standard Bank at Port Elizabeth); & 2nd portrait by Malcolm Stewart.
13. Oil portraits of Jane Anne Hills and her sister Caroline, both wearing coral necklaces [which we have]; also silhouettes of these two girls and their mother.
14. Oil portraits of Sir George & Lady Peters by Robert Bower with ADLS. Robert Bower so disliked her dress, that he took down a curtain, draped her in it, & painted the portrait as if it was her dress. Bower was a friend of Reggie Peters', and came from a well to do family in Kent / Sussex.
15. Pair of miniatures of Sir George & Lady Peters. His medals are in Thirsk.
16. Oil portrait of Reginald Peters by Robert Bower.
17. Miniature of Reggie Peters.
18. Oil Portrait of George Peters in uniform of Sussex Yeomanry.
19. Water Colour portrait of George Peters in RAF uniform.
20. Medals of G G P Burt.

The Milton Family Link

Mary Boyce, wife of Revd George Boyce, was born Mary Milton. By tradition, her family was connected with that of the poet, John Milton. She is, I consider, unlikely to have been descended from John Milton himself. But she could be a descendant of his brother Sir Christopher Milton.

The MILTON FAMILY were a Catholic Family from Oxfordshire [see Notes & Queries, Vol XI no vii (1913) p 21]

Hope and Faith

1. *Henry Milton* of Stanton St John, Oxfordshire, d. 1559, m Agnes -- who d 1561; leaving issue:

   [i]   Richard, of whom hereafter
   [ii] Isabel
   [iii] Rowland
   [iv] Alice

2. *Richard Milton* of Stanton St John or Holton, perhaps a husbandman or an under-ranger of Shotover Forest, m Elizabeth Haughton, previously wife of John Jeffrey, and had issue

   [i]   John, of whom hereafter
   [ii] Henry (?)

3. *John Milton* 1563 (?) - 1647, was cut off by his father for changing his religion from Catholic to Protestant, and settled in London as a Scrivener. He married Sarah Jeffrey (who d 3.04.1637). By 1632, he had retired to Horton near Windsor; and in 1641 he moved to Reading. He had issue:

   [i]   a child, b & d 1601
   [ii] Anne b between 1602 & 1607, m (i) Edward Phillips of the Crown Office in Chancery, who d 1631, issue 2 sons; & (ii) Thomas Agar
   [iii] *John Milton* the poet 1608 - 1674, who had, by his first wife Mary, dau Richard Powell of Forest Hill, nr Oxford, surviving issue only 3 daughters, viz Anne b 1646; Mary b 1647 & did not marry; a son b & d 1651; Deborah b 1652, who m Mr Clarke a weaver in Spitalfields & had 10 children.

   By his 2nd wife, Catherine, dau Captain Woodcock of Hackney, he had one child who died shortly after his wife in 1655. By his 3rd wife, Elizabeth dau Randle Minshull of Wistason, Cheshire, he had no children

   [Source: English Literature by Henry Morley]

   [iv] Sarah b & d 1612

[v] Tabitha 1614-1615

[vi] *Sir Christopher Milton* 1615-1692

4. *Sir Christopher Milton* 1615 - 1692, m Thomasin Webber, daughter of John Webber "Taylor" of St Clement Danes; lived with his father at Horton. Called to the Bar 1640, Settled in Reading 1641; in Exeter 1643; in London by 1646; and finally in Ipswich before 1656. He was buried at St Nicholas' Church, Ipswich, on 22.03.1692. No will or administration is extant.

A royalist, he became a High Court Judge under James II, but was subsequently dismissed. Issue:

[i] Infant son, b at Horton 26.03.1639

[ii] Sarah bapt at Horton 11.08.1640

[iii] Anne, bapt at St Lawrence Reading, 27.08.1641

[iv] Christopher, buried St Nicholas Ipswich, 12.03.1667

[v] Thomas. bapt St Clement Danes, London, 2 Feb 1646/47; of the Crown Office, Chancery; buried St Dunstan in the West, 17.10.1694; admin to relict Martha, dau Charles Fleetwood of Northampton

[vi] (?) "John Melton Gent" buried at St Nicholas, Ipswich, 29.12.1669

[vii] Richard

[viii] Thomasin, buried St Nicholas Ipswich 6.07.1675

[ix] Mary, baptised St Nicholas Ipswich 29.03.1656, dsp

[x] Anne, m Rev Pendlebury 1682/83, dsp

[xi] Catherine.

Descendants include

I. John Milton, fl 1770, a marine painter, who worked in the neighbourhood of London, first at Charlton, then at Peckham; and was the father of:

II. Thomas Milton 1743-1827, an engraver, practised in London, probably a pupil of Woollett; went to Dublin

1783-1786, and then returned to London. A governor of the short lived Society of Engravers founded 1803. d in Bristol 27 Feb 1827 [Gentlemen's Magazine 1827 Vol I p 379]

[Source: DNB]

Northcroft

Ann Northcroft 1806-1878, wife of **John Pierce Boyce** of Chertsey was the mother of **Sophia Ann Stewart,** my great grandmother. I have a miniature said to be of her as a young girl. The Northcroft family come from Chalfont St Peter in Buckinghamshire, though their progenitor is said to have come from Scotland.

1. **William Northcroft** who must have been born early in the 18th century, was by tradition a foundling, being found in a field in Scotland whilst an infant. Why and when he left Scotland is not known. Some Jacobite Scots came south after the '45, and changed their surnames. But William may have come south earlier. He settled in Chalfont St Peter, and was the father of

   [i]   William Northcroft, of whom hereafter
   [ii] Andrew John Northcroft 1747-1815, who married Sarah, and had issue:

   I.   Andrew

   II.   Thomas 1773-1828

   III. a daughter

   IV.   Lucy 1783-1815

   V.   Sarah

   VI.   Hannah 1794-1815

   VII. Mary Ann 1796-1812

2. **William Northcroft:** 1742-1799, of Chalfont St Peter; d 13 Feb 1799, aged 57 [gravestone at Chalfont St Peter] married Rebecca Roper 1746-1828, and had issue 4 sons and 2 daughters:

[i]   William, of whom hereafter

[ii] Daniel 1783-1840 (d. 27 Oct 1840 aged 57; gravestone at Chalfont St Peter);, m Sarah -- & had 2 sons

    I.   William b 1813, who had a son also William who lived in Chelsea

    II. Thomas 1820-1897 who had 3 children

        a. Alfred 1843-1844

        b. William, of Wimbledon, who had a son Ernest

        c. a dau

[iii] Thomas 1786-1811 [26 Feb 1811, aged 24]

[iv] John 17-- - 18--; of Gerrards Cross

[v]   a dau who live at Goldhill, Chalfont St Peter; and later of Chancery Lane, London

[vi] a dau who married Mr Goodridge.

3. **William Northcroft:** 1780-1853; left Chalfont St Peter for London, where he was an Architect. He married Anne daughter of Thomas Hart, of Mopes, Chalfont St Peter. William is said to be buried at Egham, Surrey. They had a large family of 6 sons & 5 daughters:

[i]   *William* 1807-1888, who sailed for New Zealand in the Cresswell from Gravesend, on 15.11.1850. He married Martha Mary Young & had 8 children. His descendants are in New Zealand - see "Northcrofts in New Zealand". The most distinguished this century was Sir Erima Northcroft, a High Court Judge in N Z.

[ii] Henry Thomas 1814-1903, who m Mary Corderoy & had 9 children - see separate details

[iii] John 1818- --- dsp

[iv] Andrew 1820 - --- dsp - he was drowned in the Hoogli

[v]   Edward 1824 - --- m Elizabeth -- & had 5 children:

    I.   Adeline 1857

    II. Arthur Beaumont 1859-

    III. Constance E 1862-

    IV. Edward W 1867-

    V.   Henry Cecil 1868-

    Some of this family were tailors in Queen's Road, London

[vi]   George 1825-1898: who had 4 children by his first wife Elizabeth Wade

    I.   George 1868-1947 who had

       a. Lionel George 1900 - + issue

          ♦ John Christopher 1932 -
          ♦ David 1939 -
       b. Dorothy
       c. Annie

    II. Andrew b & d 1871

    III. Susan 1866-1948

    IV. Annie Wade 1870-1944 + issue

   By his second wife Lilias Surenne, he had:

    V.   John b & d 1875

    VI. William 1878-1880

    VII. Arthur Gabriel 1879 - (in Queensland) & had a son William 1899 dsp

    VIII. Lilias Robertson 1877 -

[vii] **Ann Northcroft** 1806-1878 who married *John Pierce Boyce*. Their daughter was *Sophia Ann Stewart* 1835-1925

[viii] Rebecca 1808-1897 dsp

[ix] Cicely 1812-1877 m Edmund Neighbour & had seven children

I. Albert Edmund 1840-

II. Henry William 1842-1896

III. William Francis 1845-

IV. James Lovell 1847-

V. Ernest Medbury 1850-

VI. Cecilia Ann 1839-1860 dsp

VII. Alice Maud Mary 1856-1858 dsp

[x] Martha, b 1816 m James Wolton & had a dau Martha
[xi] Mary 1821-1904 m John Hamilton Gavin & had 3 children

I. Hamilton Gavin 1849-

II. Maud 1861 -

III. Ida 1864- m Revd E Stukeley & had 2 sons, Alastair & Gavin

Northcroft Family in New Zealand:

1. William Northcroft [3.i. above] 1806-1888; went to New Zealand 1850; married Martha Mary Young, and had 4 sons & 4 daughters:

[i] Henry William 1844-1923, m Margaret Henderson & had issue

I. James Fraser Suther 1883-

II. Henry Cuthbert 1889-1915, killed at Gallipoli

III. Agnes Mary 1881- m James Wynyard

IV. Hilda Margaret 1882-1951

V. Ruth Gladys 1885-1916

[ii] George Andrew 1849 - -- ; m Mary Drennan & had 3 children

I. George Ernest m Phyllis Parsons

II. Nancy

III. Leslie

[iii] Leonard 1852-1923 m Louisa James & had issue

I. Stanley St Leonards

II. Ernest

III. Cyril 1882-1926 m F Ellmer & had

a. Walter b 1918
b. Joyce b 1913
c. Dorothy b 1915
d. Mary Louie b 1924

IV. Sir Erima Harvey Northcroft 1884 - ; a High Court Judge; m Violet Mitchell & had 2 daughters:

a. Joan 1909 m + issue
b. Nancy 1913 - [x]

V. George Roberts 1886 -, m (1) Annie Gunn & had 3 daus, Annie Gunn; Florence; & Nancy; he m (2) Dorothy Bogie & had 2 sons

a. Gilbert
b. Stanley

VI. Mary 1883 - m

VII. Erica 1893 - m

[iv] Ernest 1854 - m Olivia Payne & had 2 children

I. Earl 1897 -

II. Muriel 1895 -

[v] Ruth 1841-1930 m David Scannell + issue
[vi] Annie 1853-1914 m Arthur G Smith + issue
[vii] Jessie 1845 - 1924 m Charles Brown + issue
[viii] Martha 1847 -

Note ^x Nancy, dau Sir Erima Northcroft compiled the Northcroft Family Tree

Descendants of Henry Thomas Northcroft

Henry Thomas Northcroft [3.ii above] 1814-1903 married Mary Corderoy and had 3 sons & 6 daughters:

Henry 1855 - ; m Ada Mary Perry & had issue

    I. Alfred G C 1894-

    II. Rosemary 1896 - m Denis Sprague & had issue

        a. Jeremy Sprague b 1933, m Suzette -- + has several daughters

    III. Percival E.W.C. 1898-1917, killed in First World War

    IV. Henry Thomas 1904 -, m B.E.P Fitzgerald

    V. Campbell 1904 -

[ii] William 1863- ; m Margaret Hoyle & had issue

    I. Percy Wilfred 1886 - ; in Dakota + son

    II. Jessie 1884 -

[iii] George 1869-1943, a Dentist in Harley Street, London; m Baroness Eva Von Schloztein & had issue

    I. George Bernhard 1911- ; m Mary Skey + 2 daus Joanna & Melinda

    II. William Kersten 1919- m Joan; + son William George

    III. Evelyn Marian b 1919 d 198?, of London

[iv] Mary 1857-
[v] Fanny 1859-
[vi] Jessie 1861-1877 dsp

[vii] [vii]: inf 1864

[viii] [viii]: Katie m Charles Gibbs + issue

[ix] [ix]: Nellie b.1867

Chapter 9: Adam

My grandmother, **Frederica Sybil Stewart** 1875-1949 - "Freda" - was the daughter of Brigadier General Frederick John Stuart Adam, by his wife Mary Isabella daughter of General Claud Douglas. The Adam family come from Forfar, in Fife. Their pedigree was drawn up by Robert Adam, the famous Architect, and was "certified by the Provost and Bailies of Forfar" in 1766 ["The Blair Adam Pedigree]. Our version is almost identical, and derives from a Family Tree going back to 1240, given to me some years ago by Mrs Vere Whyte, an Adam cousin.

The Adam pedigree can be traced back to the early part of the 13th century. The earliest mention of the name is by Bishop Keith, of an Adam, Abbot of Melrose 1213, who was consecrated Bishop of Caithness 1214 by William Malvoisine, Bishop of St Andrews. When Abbot, this Adam was sent as Ambassador to England, to the Court of King John. In 1218, he went to get absolution from Pope Honorius III, together with the Bishops of Glasgow and Moray. They returned in 1219, and Bishop Adam was barbarously murdered by the Earl of Caithness in 1222.

1. **?John? Adam**: The first name is uncertain, but Robert Adam the Architect referred to him as John. He was a military man, and died in 1240, leaving 2 sons:

   [i]   Henry, of whom hereafter

   [ii] Duncan

2. **Henry Adam**: m Margaret Fraser, and died in 1270, leaving 3 sons:

   [i]   Alexander, of whom hereafter

[ii] [Walter, from whom the Adam family of Glenlay, Ayrshire

[iii] William, who was killed in battle

3. **Alexander Adam:** m Elizabeth daughter of William Bissel, chief of that name, and died leaving a son:

4. **Magnus Adam:** who m Isabella Scott, and died in 1325, leaving 3 sons and 2 daughters. Nothing is known of the daughters. The sons were:

[i] Sir Duncan Adam: d.1330; He accompanied the "Good Sir James of Douglas" on his expedition bound for the Holy Land in 1330, carrying with them the heart of Robert the Bruce for burial there. They stopped off in Spain to assist Alfonso XI of Castile in a battle against the Saracen King of Granada, during the course of which both Sir James of Douglas and Sir Duncan Adam were killed (25th August 1330). Sir Duncan Adam was one of the "Seven Trusty Knights" so famous in The Bruce's time, as well as the "trusty" friend of Sir James of Douglas. Sir Duncan assumed the crest of a cross crosslet fitchée surmounted of a sword in saltire, with the motto *"Crux mihi grata quies"* - which has ever since been borne by the Adam family. The cross crosslet fitchée was an emblem particularly borne by Crusaders. It is of note that from the same expedition to take the heart of The Bruce to the Holy Land, the Douglases assumed into their arms and crest the human heart, later imperially crowned.

[ii] Reginald, of whom hereafter

[iii] Magnus, Bishop of Brechin from about 1321. He was a witness to David II's confirmation of the monastery of Arbroath 1342. After David II was taken prisoner at the Battle of Neville's Cross 1346, Magnus was sent as Ambassador to England, where King Edward treated him better than any other Ambassador, paying all his expenses. He died in 1348.

5. **Reginald Adam:** m Anna, dau David Wemyss, co Fife; and d in 1360 leaving:

[i] Reginald, of whom hereafter

[ii] Robert, ancestor of the Adam families of Tankeson & Arnfinlay, Perthshire

[iii] Margaret, who d young, as did another daughter.

6. **Reginald Adam:** d 1390; accompanied Sir John de Vienne, Admiral of France, and James, 2nd Earl of Douglas, on a successful border raid into Northumberland, during the reign of Robert II in 1385. As part of his booty, Reginald captured and brought back "a lady named Katherine Mowbray, who being of uncommon beauty, he soon after married her". She was the daughter of a Northumberland Knight. At about the same date as Reginald, there was another Adam Bishop of Brechin (not the same as Reginald's uncle Magnus) whose character was stained by his having been an agent of the degenerate David II with Edward II. He was Chancellor between 1358 and 1360.

By Katherine Mowbray, Reginald Adam had a daughter Bettina, and a son:

7. **Reginald Adam**: m --- , and d 1425 leaving 4 sons and 2 daughters, of whom nothing is known save the oldest son, William.

8. **William Adam:** d. 1458; m -- Douglas, by whom he had 3 sons and 3 daughters:

[i] James, dsp 1490

[ii] a son whose name is not known

[iii] name is not known

[iv] name is not known

[v] name is not known

[vi] name is not known

9. **-- Adam:** the second son of William; his first name is not known. He had two sons

[i] John, of whom hereafter

[ii] Charles - given on the Whyte tree as the first of Fanno. However, the Blair Adam tree puts the nephew Charles as first of Fanno; on dates this is the more likely.

10. **John Adam**: a hero of Flodden Field, where he was killed, 1513. He had 2 sons:

[i] James, who succeeded him and died in 1532, leaving 3 sons and a daughter. Their names are not known; but they died unmarried & sp, and were succeeded by their uncle, Charles.

[ii] Charles, who eventually succeeded to the representation of the family, of whom hereafter.

11. **Charles Adam 1st of Fanno**, who succeeded his nephews, and was seated there by 1549. Fanno is in the parish of Roscobie and Shire of Forfar. He married Margaret Ferguson, who d 1555, and had 2 sons & 2 daughters:

[i] Archibald, 2nd of Fanno

[ii] Charles, from whom the Adam family of Kingsbarns, co Forfar

[iii] Elizabeth, who married Alexander Murray

[iv] Cecil, who took the veil

12. **Archibald Adam, 2nd of Fanno**: d. 1590; m Flavella Bisset of the ancient family of that name, and had one son:

13. **Robert Adam, 3rd of Fanno** d.1625; m Isabella Hunter, dau James Hunter of Restenet, and had a son:

14. **Archibald Adam, 4th & last of Fanno** - which he sold during the reign of King Charles I. He purchased in lieu Queen's Manor, co Forfar; a part of Malcolm Kenmore's demesne, who resided in the castle with his wife. He married Cecil, dau of John Hay, and d. 1662, leaving issue 4 sons & 2 daughters:

[i] Charles, 2nd of Queen's Manor; m Elizabeth dau of Charles Wishart of Logie; and had an only son:

I. James 3rd of Queen's Manor, who being a bad economist, was forced to sell Queen's Manor. He dsp, whereupon the representation of the family fell on the heirs of Archibald's second son, John.

[ii]   John Adam: d 1695; an Architect and builder in Kirkcaldy, Fife. He m. Helen Cranstoun, one of Lord Cranstoun's family. Only one of his numerous children survived:

I.   *William Adam* 1689-1748; a celebrated Architect, who designed many buildings, including The Drum, Hopetoun House, Lawers, Dun House etc. He became very prosperous and purchased the estate of Maryburgh, Kinross, which was renamed "Blair Adam". He m Mary, dau Robertson of Gladney, by whom he had:

a. John 2nd of Blair Adam + heirs
b. Robert Adam 1728-1792, the celebrated Architect in London
c. James Adam 1732-1794, who went into partnership with his brother in London
d. William
e. 6 daughters.

In succeeding generations, the family of Adam of Blair Adam continued to achieve prominence. John, 2nd of Blair Adam's son, William (3rd of Blair Adam) 1751-1822 took a prominent part in the impeachment of Warren Hastings; was appointed a Privy Councillor, & Lord Commissioner of Jury Court, Scotland. He m. Eleanor dau of Charles 5th Lord Elphinstone. William had 2 famous sons - Admiral Sir Charles Adam KCB (4th of Blair Adam; whose son William Patrick succeeded as 5th of Blair Adam); and General Sir Frederick Adam KCB, KMI, who fought as a general at Waterloo. Sir Charles' son, William Patrick Adam, 5th of Blair Adam, 1823 - 1881, was Whip of the Liberal Party, & Governor General of Madras.

[iii]   Alexander Adam; became famous in Scotland for his knowledge of Architecture. He had a son

I.   John, who had a son

    a. Alexander, who m a dau of John Sturroch of Pitruchie, co Forfar. Their son

- ◆ John, m Margaret dau John Ure Esq. co Forfar; and had 5 sons:
  - John, d 1830; Surgeon HEIC & Secretary to the Medical Board HEIC Bengal
  - Alexander, Col 44th Madras N I; m (i) Matilda Willis; (ii) Mary dau of William Erskine of Kinedden, Lord Kinedden
  - George, d. 1849 m Eliza dau Alex Read Esq, and had a son George Read Adam, and 3 other sons, + 2 daus who died in infancy
  - James
  - Charles, who had 6 daughters

[iv]   **Patrick Adam** of whom hereafter

[v]   Phillis, who m Andrew Wood, of a knightly family in Co Forfar

[vi]   Mary, d in infancy

15. **Patrick Adam:** 4th son of Archibald (4th & last of Fanno, and 1st of Queen's Manor) d 1715, leaving a son:

16. **Peter Adam:** 1675 - 1730: of Shieldhill, co Forfar. He was an active Jacobite, and in consequence of his support for the Stuarts during the Rising of 1715, lost his property. He m. ---; and had issue a dau whose name is not known and a son David

17. **David Adam:** 1723-1816: had, despite his father's forfeiture, a large fortune, though his third son William cleared him of £40,000. He m. Helen, dau Charles Webster Esq. She was b. 1740 and d. 1813. He had 4 sons and 2 daus:

    [i]   Charles, of whom hereafter

    [ii]   John, in the Royal Navy, drowned 1781

    [iii]   William, who cleared his father of £40,000; m. Eliza Watt of Multi

[iv] James, who d. 1843

[v] Agnes, who m John Mackney Esq

[vi] Ann, who m C. Stirling Esq

18. **Charles Adam** 1767 - 1806; a Writer & Merchant in Dundee; m. Ann dau John Ure Esq co Forfar; and had 4 sons & one daughter:

[i] Charles 1796-1802

[ii] John 1798 - 1869, of whom hereafter

[iii] William, b 1800

[iv] George Ure b 1804; m Clementina dau Col Charles Elphinstone & had issue:

I. George Robert 1837-

II. Charles James Elphinstone

III. William

IV. John Elphinstone

V. Emily

VI. Charlotte, m Robert Whyte Esq, JP co Forfar + issue

VII. Anne Ure, b & d 1849

[v] Margaret, m William Whyte + issue

19. **John Adam** 1798 - 1869, the second, but oldest surviving, son, was a Surgeon in the HEIC [Honourable East India Company]; born 4th September, baptised 10th September 1798 in Dundee - the witness at his baptism [1] being his grandfather John Ure. I have a silver snuff box [hallmarked Birmingham 1795] with his initials on – it may have been a Christening present? After becoming a Surgeon, he joined the Madras Army; being Assistant Surgeon at the Fort St George Establishment 1st March 1820; Surgeon 13 October 1831; & retired 20 July 1836[2]. Evidently, he was not on the pension fund, but drew retired pay[3]. On retirement, he went to live in Boulogne, France. This was cheaper than living in England or Scotland, and there was a

considerable colony of Scots there. He lived at 34 Route de Calais, certainly from 1862 when his son was married [4], to his death on 3rd December 1869[5]. He married Susannah Waldegrave (dau John Waldegrave & Elizabeth Tyler or Syler).[6] She was b at Oxford 1815. She died at her home, 58 Grande Rue, Boulogne, on 4th February 1901, aged 85½[7]. In their death certificates[5] & [7] John Adam and Susannah Adam were respectively referred to as "Rentier" and "Rentière" - this means a person of independent means.

I have been unable to trace Susannah Waldegrave's birth record[9], though wide searches have been made. If she was connected with Lord Waldegrave's family, this could explain the 3rd name given to my great grandfather, General Adam, of "Stuart" - the Waldegrave progenitor having married an illegitimate daughter of King James II by Arabella Churchill (sister of the Great Duke of Marlborough).

John & Susannah Adam were buried in the Cimetière de l'Est, Culte Protestant, at Boulogne - plot 78[8]. They had 3, possibly 4, children:

[i] **Frederick John Stuart Adam** 1836-1920, my great grandfather, of whom hereafter.

[ii] Ellen Anne Catherine, baptised 2 Nov 1845[10] [referred to in the Dénombrement in Boulogne as Helène [7]]. She was supposed to be getting married to a man whose name I do not know; but ran away at the altar, and married instead on 14th February 1867, Windham George Conway Carmichael-Anstruther, 2nd son of Sir Windham Carmichael Anstruther Bt. The Anstruthers have ranked as Barons of Scotland for upwards of 700 years. Their original seat was at Elie House, Anstruther, Fife - which was lost to pay gaming debts in the late 18th century. In 1817, they inherited the Carmichael Estates in Lanarkshire, as heirs to the Carmichael Earls of Hyndford. She had issue:

I.   Gerald Yorke Anstruther 1871-1910; who m Ellen Caroline dau of J Milne of Cradock, Cape Colony. Their only child was:

a. Sir Windham Eric Francis Carmichael-Anstruther, 11th Bt of Nova Scotia, and 8th Bt of GB; b 29th May 1900, d. 8th April 1980. He & my father used to push General Adam in his wheel chair at Dover, in the early days of the First World War. The General would wave his stick in fury towards the Germans in France. Windham was twice married (i) to Fay Rechnitzer; and (ii) to Joanne Coates. Both marriages ended in divorce. dsp with no heir to the baronetcies.

II. Eric George Basil 1874 - dsp

III. Hugh John Elphinstone 1875 - --; m Ada Clarke 1906, and had an only child Averil Nina b 1907 who m. Hugh Thompson Dickinson "Boozy Dickinson" of Styford Hall, Stocksfield, Northumberland. No issue.

IV. Maud Ellen Constance, b 1868 d --; m 1888 Major General John Christopher Swann CB, Indian Army. This marriage ended in divorce. 2 children:

a. Aileen Yvonne Marian who m. – Edward Thomas Newton-Clare. Before the First World War, she was engaged to Humphrey Gilbert [see below]. Because her parents were divorced General Adam & the Gilbert parents forbad the marriage. The War intervened anyway and ended it. She had 2 daus - Peggy who m Robert Skelson; and Elizabeth, a doctor, who m Professor John Leonard Burbidge [their son Richard, inherited Carmichael from Windham Anstruther; and has assumed the name and arms of CARMICHAEL of CARMICHAEL]
b. Kathleen Mona who d. circa 1990

V. Mildred Helen Mary, b 1872, m. John Christopher Nevile & had 2 daughters - Barbara Cycely 1896-1971 dsp; and Joyce Audrey Anstruther b 1905 m. -- Coates.

VI. Muriel Vere 1881-1969; m Harold Adam Whyte (a descendant, I think, of Charles Adam, no 18 above). She gave me the Adam Family Tree. dsp

[iii] Emma b circa 1854; never married; lived on in Boulogne after her parents died; and was there when the British landed in 1914 - thrilled with the sight of the Highlanders and pipers. She died somewhere around 1929. She apparently had some Adam miniatures & silver, which she left to her oldest nephew Charles Adam, in Tasmania. The silver was mostly sold, rather than pay to ship it out. The miniatures went to Australia, where they were all subsequently lost.

[iv] There was said to be another son - whose name I do not know. Humphrey Gilbert was the source for this; and said that this son was a parson, & that he had a son, Clement, who had a half share in a Grand National winner named something like "Galtee More" in about 1894. These Adam relatives may be Rev George Robert Adam, Vicar of Shoulden, Deal; who had a son Clement George Montague Adam, b London 13 April 1871. This Clement was educated at Radley & New College, Oxford: Major Royal Glos Hussars in South African War 1900; m. Violet Ethel dau Col T Stock. He was alive in 1923 & then living at 46 Ridgemount Gardens, London WC1.

Notes & Sources:

1. Certificate of Baptism of John Adam at Dundee
2. Letter National Army Museum 20.04.1960
3. Letter National Army Museum 19.05.1960
4. Marriage Certificate of Frederick John Stuart Adam
5. Death Certificate, Boulogne, of John Adam, 3rd December 1869
6. The place & date of the marriage has not been found - letters from General Register Office, Somerset House 30.11.1971; and Guildhall Library 8.12.1971
7. There is some confusion about the date of her birth. On John Adam's death in 1869, her age was recorded as 60 (which would give a date of

birth of 1809). That is unlikely having regard to the dates of birth of her children. All other documentary source indicates that her birth was in July or August 1815 - see

- Her death Certificate, Boulogne, 4th February 1901; giving her date of death as 3rd February; and age at the time as 85½.
- The dénombrement de population de Boulogne, 1 ère section. for 34 Rue de Calais, in 1866, gives her age as 50; and John Adam's as 67
- The dénombrement of 1896, for 2 ème section, Canton-sud, 58 Grande-Rue, gives her age as 80.

The conclusion must be that her age was wrongly stated on the death certificate for John Adam; but rightly stated elsewhere.

8. Concessions Perpetuelles, Cimetière de l'Est, 1869.
9. Correspondence with Mrs Elaine Newbold, 1987 - 1988.
10. Baptism Certificate of Ellen Anne Catherine Adam 1845, Boulogne

20. **Frederick John Stuart Adam**: 1836-1920 - my great grandfather.

He was born 22nd September 1836, and baptised at the British Episcopal Church in Boulogne on 6th November 1836[1].

He served in the Crimea, where he was recommended for a commission by the famous Captain Nolan, who was wrongly blamed for the Charge of the Light Brigade, but in fact died to stop the pompous and stupid Lord Cardigan from making his disastrous mistake.

He was a cadet 1856, Bombay Infantry; Ensign 20 Dec 1856; Ensign 14th NI (shortly transferred to 22nd NI, 21 Dec 1856; Lieutenant 1859; Captain 20 Dec 1868; Major 20 Dec 1876; Lt Colonel 20 Dec 1882; Bt Colonel 20 Dec 1886; Brigadier General 1894.

He also served in the Indian Mutiny. At one night at Dinner in 1857, the Adjutant walked in and called for silence, and read the despatch about the massacre at Cawnpore. This was met with "a growl of rage".

He must have gone to India straight from the Crimea, about which he told many stories in later life: of the huge bearded Russians coming out of the fog at Inkerman; and of how, because he was able to speak French, he made friends with a French Captain of a merchant vessel who gave him a barrel of eggs "which saved my life during that awful winter".

In 1873, he went to serve on the staff in Bombay. He served in the Afghan War of 1879 - 1880; and took part in the defence of Kandahar, including the sortie of Deb Khojah, for which he was mentioned twice in despatches and got a medal. It was he who got the remnants of the British forces into Kandahar after the disaster at Maiwand, and sent the last despatch through, signed Adam. Everyone wanted to know who this Adam was.

After Maiwand, Lord Roberts - whom Fred disliked and considered unfair - stamped upon the Bombay Army, and would give its officers no preferment. Despite this, Fred got as far as Brigadier General and he ended as AQMG [Assistant Quarter Master General] to the Duke of Connaught, with whom he was on intimate terms.

He was put on the retired list in 1894. After his retirement he lived at Park House, Dover, and pursued his past-time as a Military Historian[2]. He remained in Dover during the early stages of the First World War, and was "outraged" at the "impudence" of the Germans who dared to fire a shell at Dover, that landed near him. After that, he was prevailed upon to move to Cheltenham for the duration of the War. It is because of this, that my parents met, as teenagers, in Cheltenham. He died at Eton Lodge, Cheltenham, on 7th March 1920, aged 83.

On 20th January 1862, he married, at the Upper Town Church, Boulogne, **Mary Isabella Douglas**. Her residence at the time was described as "Chateau St Joseph, Route de Calais" [3]. She was the daughter of General Claud Douglas, by his first wife Mary Madelina Bourmaster Collingwood Dickson, daughter of Admiral Sir Archibald

Collingwood Dickson. The witnesses were "Wm Adam" & "Maud Douglas". I do not know who they were. William Adam may, if Humphrey Gilbert was right that Fred had a brother, be the brother; Maud Douglas may be a clerical misreading for the signature of Claud Douglas. I know of no "Maud" Douglas, & General Douglas' second wife was "Eliza".

Shortly after their wedding, Fred & Mary Adam visited her mother's brother Vice Admiral Sir William Collingwood Dickson 3rd Bt, at (I think) Hardingham Hall, Norfolk, which they rented. The Dicksons were wealthy - Fred and Mary were not, and Mary had but one best dress. She was highly embarrassed when her well intentioned aunt, Lady Collingwood Dickson, asked her what dress she was proposing to change into for dinner: she had to admit that she only had one best dress, which she was already wearing.

Mary Isabella Adam was not given to cossetting, spoiling, or molly coddling children. She was strict almost to the point of lack of care. It is to this that my grandmother attributed the death from pneumonia of the youngest child of the family, Guy Anstruther Adam - my grandmother's favourite brother, after whom my father was named.

Mary Adam died in 1914.

I have never sorted out why Fred's third name was "Stuart". A clue may be the Waldegrave connection, through his mother [the first Lord Waldegrave married an illegitimate daughter of James II, by Arabella Churchill]. Vere Whyte told me that the Adam family were very friendly with the Steuarts of Ballechin, Perthshire, and thought they were related. That would not explain the spelling. The mystery remains.

Fred and Mary Adam had 3 sons & 4 daughters:

[i]   Charles Frederick Douglas Adam 1865 - 1933. He went into a smart cavalry regiment, where he kept getting into debt, and relying on his father to bale him out. The General, who had none too much money of his own, got exasperated, and when his warnings were not heeded, packed him off to Tasmania. His

Australian descendants have it that it was deafness that caused Charles to leave the army.

When he got to Tasmania, Charles made good. He had taken his share of the family inheritance with him, and bought land - which proved to have a gold mine on it. Some years later, his partner was killed in a mining accident; which so upset Charles that he immediately packed his family off from Tasmania, and left for Melbourne. He left most of his possessions behind in Tasmania. He had a collection of miniatures of the Adam family - whether directly from his father, or via his father's sister Emma - and these were left behind. Either they were in his house, which was broken into and everything worthwhile was stolen, or they were entrusted to a Solicitor, who had some papers for safeguarding. But when the Solicitor died, some time after Charles, no papers or possessions of the Adam family were to be found.

He married Charlotte Saltmarsh in 1895, and had seven children:

I.   Elizabeth

II. Guy

III. Mary [Mollie, who m. Jim Humphreys, and died circa 1967, leaving an only son Jim, who was at one time Australian Ambassador to Paris]

IV. Freda [who m -- Barker; and had a son Reg & a daughter. Reg married Jessie and had 2 daughters, one of whom, Jenny has been to England several times]. Freda used to send us food parcels, particularly rich fruit cakes, after, and I think during, the War. This continued until rationing ended in the early 1950s.

V.   Frederick John, in the Victoria State Police "Bluey Adam".

VI. Robert

VII. Eileen (who m -- Brooks)

Charles Adam d aged 68 in January 1933. His widow died in June 1946 aged 72.

[ii]   Jack Adam - was in the Army. He fought in the Boer War. At Spion Kop, Natal, Captain Gilbert MacDonald Stewart died in his arms on 24th January 1900. Neither knew at the time that they were almost brothers in law - for on 6th February 1900 Jack's sister Freda married my grandfather in Bombay. In the First War, Jack fought in German East Africa. Apparently he, like his elder brother Charles, had also got into debt. He was sent to South Africa. dsp?

[iii] Guy Anstruther Adam - the third son, but youngest child, so born later than 1875. He was my grandmother's favourite brother. He contracted pneumonia at the age of 18. His mother would not hear of any special care being given to him, and he died of it. My father was named Guy after him.

[iv]   Gertrude Mary Claudine - the oldest of the family, was born in 1861. At the time of her birth, her parents were crossing from Bombay to Poona on a bullock wagon, and Gertie was born on it. There were only her father and a bearer to help. She married Reginald Gilbert, of the family of Gilbert of Chedgrave Manor, Norfolk. He was a Solicitor in Bombay. He owned land in Australia, with a gold mine on it. In the early part of this century, he turned down an offer of £1 million for his gold mine. Within a year or two the gold ran out.

The Gilberts lived in various houses around Builth Wells, and finally bought Bishopstone, at Bridge Sollars, Herefordshire - where my family were housed for the first ten months or so of the War, until they settled in Camberley.

She had an only son:

I.   Humphrey Adam Gilbert 1886-1960, of Bishopstone. He was called to the Bar, but never practised, preferring, and being able to afford, the life of a country gentleman. His passion was fishing, about which he wrote a book "The Tale of a Wye Fisherman".

He was engaged briefly to Aileen Newton-Clare [née Swann], the grand-daughter of his great aunt Ellen Carmichael Anstruther. - see above. The family refused consent, because her parents had been divorced. Anyway the First World War came along. He later married Margaret Money-Kyrle. They had 4 children:

a. John - killed in the Second World War
b. Ernle Reginald Forester Gilbert, Major RA, who inherited Bishopstone. He died 198-. By his Austrian wife Hely, he had an only daughter Sybella.
c. Eleanor, who m. Major Tony English, who was killed in a mountain climbing accident. + issue
d. Olyffe, who m Angus J A Stewart, son of Angus Matheson Stewart of Ardpatrick, Argyll. + issue. [Angus' brother Dugald was eventually recognised by the Lord Lyon as Stewart of Invernahyle; one of the Appin branches].

[v] Kate - who died in childhood.
[vi] Emma Florence, who died unmarried 24th April 1940. In her latter years, at least, she lived with my grandmother, Freda Stewart, at 5 Granville Gardens, Ramsgate, Kent. She converted to Roman Catholicism - but, I think, to no great satisfaction.

In her will, she left a (crested) snuff box of John Adam's & a "daguerreotype" - actually a silhouette- of Charles Adam, to her nephew Humphrey Adam Gilbert. She left a miniature of her grandmother Mary Madelina Douglas née Dickson and a pencil and wash oval portrait of her Uncle William Douglas to my father. And she left a small oil portrait of her Uncle William Douglas and a miniature of her Douglas Uncles as Children, to my Uncle Donald.

[vii] Dorothy; who died in childhood, in, I think, Boulogne. An old acquaintance in the early 1960s, Edward Philip, had been brought up in Boulogne. He could remember John Adam's widow - and the funerals of children with all decked out in white: white horses: white clothes.

[viii] **Frederica Sybil** - my grandmother - see below

Notes & Sources:

1. Baptism Certificate for F J S Adam, 6th November 1836. He was brought up in France, spoke French as his first language, and had to work hard at English when he joined the Army.
2. FJSA's Manuscript about Kandahar
3. Marriage Certificate of Fred Adam & Mary Douglas, Boulogne, 20.01.1862
4. Will of Emma Adam, 1940.

21. **Frederica Sybil Adam**, 1875-1949; my grandmother.

She was born 28th January 1875 at Kurrachee, India[1] [now Karachi, Pakistan]. When she fell in love in the 1890s with a young penniless clergyman and wanted to marry him, her parents refused: he had "no prospects" - actually he ended a bishop. So my grandmother was packed off to India, to stay with her older sister Gertie Gilbert, and to be introduced to a suitable match. Thus she met, and married my grandfather, **Robert Barton Stewart** 1864-1908 at St Stephen's Bandra, Bombay, on 6th February 1900. She died at Ramsgate, Kent, on 26th June 1949, aged 74.

Christmas 1919

From Jean Burbidge, we received an interesting letter, written by Elizabeth Nicholls who was a domestic servant to the Adam family at Eton Lodge, The Park, Cheltenham. She wrote to her parents – the letter is not dated, but simply says 'Friday night'. The calendar for 1919 shows

Hope and Faith

Christmas day was a Thursday, so it is probable that this letter was written on Boxing Day 1919. Elizabeth was 22.

My Dear Mother and Father

Thank you very much for your most lovely gift. I was very delighted with them indeed now I shall be able to go swanking about with the muff and furs and shoes. The nuts were very exceptable.

Mansell and I had the mince pies for our supper and we had to go to bed because they made us feel so queer (it was bed time). We enjoyed them very much only there was not enough. We were very quiet and we also had a good dinner. We had turkey, potatoes, sausages, brussell sprouts, bread source and gravy. Then there was the Christmas pudding I had to carry that in while it was all alight we stuck a piece of holly in the middle of the pudding. Mansell found sixpence in her piece of pudding but I did not have any in my piece. It was very rich and then we had mince pies so we did not do bad at all. I told Mansell I expected you were all enjoying yourself while we were just sitting by the fire reading we were in bed at 9.30.

I had some very nice presents, what do you think Mrs Stewart gave me, why a new pair of boots they are lovely. I never expected such a present. Then the General gave me 5/-, Miss Emma a set of collars and cuffs, Master Phil and Master Donald gave me a lovely box of stationery one each. Miss Marjorie a little scented handkerchief cushion. Mansell gave me a pendant and chain which belonged to her dead sister she said she knows that I shall take great care of it and prize it as it belonged to her sister, then I had a fancy handkerchief from Mrs Davies that is the person that comes to work here and I had a photo frame from Marion and a pair of gloves from Bertha which I was most thankful for and Hilda a matchbox case. I had a card from Aunt Edie, I had several cards. Oh, and I had some toffee and a card from Mr and Mrs Mussett, so I did very well this year. Mansell is also giving me a shimese she bought the stuff some time ago it's a lovely piece of calico it is one of those patterns that you do all the fancy work round the neck with silks she tried to get it done in time for Christmas but she did not manage it we have been so busy.

Master Phil and Miss Marjorie are going away for a weeks holiday in January. Master Donald goes back to school on the 16th of January. I do not think we are coming back to Dover at Easter. We shall be coming in July as far as I know.

Well dear Mother and Father I am still keeping well and I have to still continue to go to the hospital every Tuesday and I have to still keep gargling my throat. We are having very bad weather it is pouring with rain tonight.

I hope Jack enjoyed his bone give him my love and tell him to keep smiling. Our turkey is all gone, it was a very small on. Has Dorothy got a place yet? Thank Alice very much for her letter tell her she [has] no business to stay out till that our. Our chickens have all stop[ped] laying we have got 8 chickens hanging up in the larder that we had killed on Tuesday. How are all of you getting on is your mouth better? I was very pleased with Willie's letters. I could not make out who ever the letter was from as the address was written so nicely and such a nice letter. Tell Willie to try and work hard. Tell him we wil have a good time when I come home again we will have a piano and a tin can so as to make a grand noise. I wonder how Winnie is getting on, having a good time I expect. Has Bertha got a young man yet? I never hear anything. How is Mr and Mrs Clifford and family are they still keeping well? Give Mrs Clifford my love when you see her and tell Bertha I shall write to her and Hilda on Sunday or perhaps tomorrow. I am not certain when I shall write but I expect it will be Sunday.

Oh and I must tell you Mrs Stewart asked me which I liked best out of all my presents, well I did not know what to say as they were all very nice so I said the boots but Mrs Stewart said the muff and furs was the best present she thought but I said they were all very nice and useful.

Well dear Mother and Father I don't think I have any more news at present so give my love to them all at home and Mansell sends her love to you all and thanks you very much for the card. So now I close with heaps of love to you all.

From your loving daughter
Lizzie xxxx
PS Mansell said she wishes you all a happy new year.

Hope and Faith

We presume that Master Donald is Donald Stewart and Miss Emma is Freda Stewart's unmarried sister. We assume that 'The General' is Frederick Adam. Mrs Stewart is Freda Stewart. The members of Elizabeth's family mentioned are her sisters Bertha, Dorothy and Alice and her brother William (Willie).

Elizabeth Nicholls

Eton Lodge, The Park, Cheltenham

Notes & Sources:

1. Birth Certificate 28th January 1875
2. Marriage Certificate (in Stewart Documents).

```
                              ┌──────  Charles ADAM (b.1767;d.1806)
                    ┌─────  John ADAM (b.1798;d.1869)
                    │         └──────  Ann URE
          ┌─── Brig Gen Frederick John Stuart ADAM (b.1836;m.1862;d.1920)
          │         │         ┌──────  John WALDEGRAVE
          │         └─────  Susannah WALDEGRAVE (b.1815;d.1901)
          │                   └──────  Elizabeth TYLER
Frederica Sybil ADAM (b.1875;d.1949)
          │                   ┌──────  Peter DOUGLAS
          │         ┌─────  General Claud DOUGLAS (b.1799;m.1826)
          │         │         └──────  Ann JACKSON
          └─── Mary Isabella DOUGLAS (b.1839;d.1914)
                    │                           ┌──────  Archibald DICKSON
                    │                 ┌─────  Admiral William DICKSON (d.1803)
                    │         ┌─────  Rear Admiral Archibald Collingwood DICKSON (b.1772;m.1797;d.1827)
                    │         │                 ┌──────  Alexander COLLINGWOOD
                    │         │       └─────  Jane COLLINGWOOD (b.1740;d.1782)
                    └─── Mary Madelina Bourmaster Collingwood DICKSON (d.1848)
                              │       ┌──────  Admiral John BOURMASTER
                              └─────  Harriet BOURMASTER (d.1865)
```

196

Chapter 10: Douglas and Garden

My great grandmother, **Mary Isabella Adam**, wife of Brigadier General Frederick Adam, was the daughter of **General Claud Douglas**.

Picture 23: Gen Claud Douglas, 1799 - 1883

Historically, the House of Douglas was one of the most powerful in Scotland. They had vast landholdings throughout the Lowlands, but particularly in South West Scotland. They rivalled the Stewart Monarchs in lands and in power. Periodically, because they got too powerful, the Head of the Family was murdered - eg James 2nd Earl of Douglas and his brother.

The history of the Douglases [1] is thus intricately bound up with the history of Scotland, and the various struggles for power - not only between the King and his Vassals, but also between the branches of the Douglases themselves. There were 3 main branches of the Douglases

1. The Black Douglases - the Earls of Douglas - based on their Castles of Douglas and Threave

2. The Red Douglases - the Earls of Angus - based on Tantallon Castle, &

3. The Earls of Morton - based on Dalkeith.

Inter Douglas feuding was constant between the Black Douglases and the Red Douglases.

Family tradition ascribes our descent as being from the Black Douglases., via their scions the Queensberry Douglases - Barons of Drumlanrig, and later Earls, Marquesses, and Dukes of Queensberry. Precisely how and when our branch comes off, is not clear, although a cousin claims that we descend from a younger son of the 1st Earl of Queensberry.

A romantic tale is told of the origin of the Douglases, by Master David Hume of Godscroft. There was a battle in 746 between Solvatius, rightful King of Scots, and Donald Bane, a pretender. The victory was nearly Donald Bane's, when "a certain noble man, disdaining to see so bad a cause have so good successe" struck in for the King, and turned the fortunes of the day. When the King inquired who the Knight was who had done such valuable service, somebody exclaimed "Sholto dhu glasse", which Hume interpreted "Behold the black grey man".

If there is any truth in the tale, it is more likely that the battle was that of Mamgarvey in 1187, when William the Lion defeated Donald Bane. It is around this time that mention is first made of any Douglas - **Sir William de Douglas**, who acquired the lands of Douglas in Lanarkshire around 1160. Their landholdings expanded rapidly, and their chief castles were Douglas in Lanarkshire, and Threave in Kirkcudbrightshire.

1. **William de Douglas** 1st Lord of Douglas, died in about 1214, leaving issue:

   [i]   Sir Archibald Douglas, his heir
   [ii] 4 other sons, all clerics
   [iii] Brice de Douglas, Bishop of Moray, who d 1222.

2. **Sir Archibald de Douglas**, 2nd Lord of Douglas died 1240, leaving a son:

   [i]   William, who succeeded him

[ii]   Andrew, from whom descend the Douglases of Dalkeith, Earls of Morton.

3. **Sir William Douglas**, 3rd Lord of Douglas who died 1274 had 2 sons:

[i]   Hugh, who died before 1274

[ii]   William who succeeded him.

4. **Sir William Douglas, 4th Lord of Douglas** "Le Hardi" died in the Tower in 1298. He was twice married. By his first wife Elizabeth Stewart, daughter of Alexander, High Stewart, he had:

[i]   James, 5th Lord of Douglas - "The Good Sir James of Douglas" b circa 1290, died 1330. "The Douchty Lord Douglas" was one of the most ardent supporters of Robert the Bruce. Bruce wished to go on an expedition to the Holy Land, but it was never safe enough for him to leave his Kingdom. On his death in 1329, a party of knights was led by Sir James of Douglas, to fulfil the Bruce's vow, by taking his heart for burial in the Holy Land. One of these knights was Sir Duncan Adam - qv Chapter 9 on the ADAM family. On the way, they stopped off in Spain, to assist Alfonso XI of Castile in a battle against the Saracen King of Granada. Both the Good Sir James of Douglas and Sir Duncan Adam were killed. Sir James' body was brought back to Scotland, and buried at St Bride's Church of Douglas. The heart of the Bruce was brought back, and buried in Melrose Abbey. From this expedition, the human heart, later imperially crowned, came into the Douglas Arms.

James had 2 legitimate sons:

I.   William, 6th Lord of Douglas, who died 1333, a minor

II.   Archibald, who presumably died young

He also had an illegitimate son

III. **Archibald "The Grim"**, who succeeded as **3rd Earl of Douglas**, when his cousin the 2nd Earl of Douglas was murdered.

Sir William Douglas "Le Hardi" married (2) Eleanor de Ferrers, whom he abducted 1288. By her he had issue:

[ii] Hugh "The Dull", 7th Lord of Douglas, c 1294-1342

[iii] Sir Archibald Douglas "The Tineman", Regent of Scotland 1333.

5. **Sir Archibald Douglas** "The Tineman" had 3 children:

[i] John

[ii] William who succeeded him, and succeeded as 8th Lord of Douglas.

[iii] Eleanor

6. **William Douglas, 8th Lord of Douglas** c 1327 - 1384, was **1st Earl of Douglas.** He married Margaret Countess of Mar. This united, for the time being, the Earldoms of Douglas and of Mar, each with their vast lands, and thus power. He had issue

7. **James 2nd Earl of Douglas**. He led the border raid into Northumberland, accompanied by Sir John de Vienne, Admiral of France, in which **Reginald Adam** captured and brought back "lady named Katherine Mowbray, who being of uncommon beauty, he soon after married her" [see Adam, Chapter 9, para 6]. James 2nd Earl of Douglas was murdered, with his brother by the Stewart King, because he was getting too powerful. His cousin Archibald "The Grim" then took over as 3rd Earl of Douglas. James, 2nd Earl, also had 2 illegitimate sons:

[i] William, of whom hereafter

[ii] Archibald, from whom descend the Douglases of Cavers

8. **Sir William Douglas,** who was killed in 1427, was the **1st of Drumlanrig**. The Barony of Drumlanrig was an outlying part of the

ancient Earldom of Mar, and was conferred on him by his father the 2nd Earl of Douglas. Sir William Douglas, 1st Baron of Drumlanrig, was knighted by James I in 1424, & died in 1427. He was the original builder of Drumlanrig Castle. [It was destroyed by the English, and replaced by the second castle, built by Sir James, 7th Lord of Drumlanrig 1498-1578. This in its turn was very badly damaged in the Civil War, after which it was pulled down. It was then rebuilt by the 1st Duke of Queensberry]. He was succeeded by his son

9. **Sir William Douglas, 2nd of Drumlanrig** who d c 1458, and was succeeded by his son

10. **Sir William Douglas 3rd of Drumlanrig** who died 1464. He married Margaret, dau Sir William Carlyle of Torthorwald, and left a son:

11. **William, 4th of Drumlanrig**, who was killed 1484, fighting for the King against the rebellious last Earl of Douglas. His son was:

12. **Sir James Douglas, 5th of Drumlanrig.** He m Janet Scott dau of Sir David Scott of Branxholm, and had issue

13. **Sir William Douglas, 6th of Drumlanrig**, who was killed 1513 [at Flodden, as was John Adam - see Adam, Chapter 7, para 10]. He married Elizabeth dau of Sir John Gordon of Lochinvar, and had issue:

[i]   James who succeeded him
[ii]   Robert c 1505-1590, Provost of Lincluden

14. **Sir James Douglas, 7th of Drumlanrig** 1498 - 1578. He m (1) Margaret, daughter of George Master of Angus, by whom he had 3 daughters; and (2) Christian, sister of the 2nd Earl of Eglinton, by whom he had:

15. **Sir William Douglas of Hawick** who m Margaret dau Robert Gordon of Lochinvar & had issue:

16. **Sir James Douglas 8th of Drumlanrig**, who m Mary, dau John 5th Lord Fleming, and died 16 October 1615, leaving issue:

   [i]   William, who succeeded him
   [ii]   James Douglas of Mouswald
   [iii] David Douglas of Ardoch
   [iv]   George Douglas of Penzerie, a Priest executed for holding a Mass

17. **Sir William Douglas, 9th of Drumlanrig** was created **1st Earl of Queensberry** 1640. He married Isabel, dau Mark Ker, 1st Earl of Lothian, and had issue:

   [i]   James who succeeded him
   [ii]   Sir William Douglas of Kelhead. His son was

      I. Sir James Douglas 1st Bt of Kelhead. From Sir Charles Douglas 5th Bt of Kelhead, descend the later (and present) Marquesses of Queensberry.

   [iii] Archibald Douglas of Dornoch
   [iv]   George who d unmarried.

18. **James 2nd Earl of Queensberry** m. Margaret Stewart dau of Earl of Traquair, & d 1671, leaving issue

19. **William 3rd Earl & 1st Duke of Queensberry** (cr 1683) 1637-1695. m Isabel, dau Marquess of Douglas, & had issue:

   [i]   James, 2nd Duke 1662-1711. He was Secretary of State under Queen Anne and virtual ruler of Scotland for 10 years. He was jointly responsible for the Union of the English and Scottish Parliaments in 1707, and hence was known as "The Union Duke". He resigned his Dukedom, and was given a regrant, to enable the children of his daughter to succeed, if, as happened, his son left no heirs. When the 4th Duke died in 1810, the Dukedom of Queensberry and the lands of Drumlanrig went to the Duke of Buccleuch, whilst the Marquessate of Queensberry went to the descendants of the first Earl's 2nd son, Sir William

Douglas of Kelhead. The 2nd Duke d 1711, leaving a son & a daughter:

I.   Charles, 3rd Duke b 1698 who dsp 1778. He married Lady Kitty Hyde, who was famous for her beauty, spirit, and wits, as well as for flouting decorum. On one occasion, she arrived at a ball dressed as a Scottish peasant. On another, she sent her husband to a Royal Fancy Dress Ball dressed in the kilt, though that form of dress had been proscribed after the '45.

II. Jane, who married Francis 2nd Duke of Buccleuch. Their grandson, the 3rd Duke of Buccleuch, succeeded under the regrant of the title as 5th Duke of Queensberry.

[ii] William, 1st Earl of March, whose son was

I.   William, 2nd Earl of March, whose son was

a. William 3rd Earl of March, who succeeded as 4th Duke of Queensberry, and dsp 1810. "Old Q" - the 4th Duke - was a celebrated, and somewhat dissolute, figure in London Society. He made an immense fortune in London, mainly by gambling; and became one of the richest men in Europe. He destroyed many of the old oak forests at Drumlanrig, to provide for an illegitimate daughter (who married the Marquess of Hertford). Upon his death, in 1810, the Dukedom of Queensberry, with the lands of Drumlanrig, reverted to the Duke of Buccleuch; whilst the Marquessate of Queensberry reverted to Sir Charles Douglas, 5th Baronet of Kelhead.

****

Precisely where our ancestors fit into this, I do not know. My distant cousin Mrs Douglas-Bate, claimed that the descent was from where the main Queensberry line split from the Kelhead (later Queensberry) line - ie from a son of Sir William Douglas, 9th Baron of Drumlanrig, 1st Earl of Queensberry. I have been neither able to prove, nor disprove, this. I have not traced further back than **Peter Douglas 1739-1801**, my great-great-great grandfather. In 1879, William Henry Douglas wrote to his nephew Archibald Garden, Colonel IMS as follows:

> *"My grandfather, whose Christian name I never knew, was born in the town of Dalkeith near Edinburgh about the beginning of the 18th century: in which town there are monuments in the church of many of the name of Douglas..."* [2]

Muriel Scaife - a cousin on the Jackson side - told me that Peter Douglas' father was a Writer in Edinburgh. This was also related by Edith Carpenter, who was maid to Ila Douglas (daughter of William Henry Douglas) - letter 4th January 1960. He could be the same as:

> *William Douglas, writer in South Kirk Parish, who married Mary Robertson, daughter of the late William Robertson, writer, on 27th October 1734* [3].

The connection with Dalkeith does not help in tracing the line. Dalkeith used to belong to the Earls of Morton as feudal Lords of Dalkeith. In the 16th Century this Earldom was held by members of the Angus family. Later, King Charles II created his son Duke of Monmouth & Earl of Dalkeith - his descendant the Duke of Buccleuch still owns Dalkeith Palace. In the Churchyard at Dalkeith there is a monument to

John Douglas, of Dalkeith & Elizabeth his wife (d 1648/49); their children

[i] William Douglas, Merchant of Dalkeith 1648-1722 & Isabel his wife & their children: Isobel; Christian; James; Isobel; Agnes; & William.

[ii] Monica Marion 1698-1694

This John Douglas is described as of the stock of Douglas of Spittlehaugh. According to Buchan's History of Peebles-shire Vol III p.170, Spittlehaugh was the property of the Morton family, and during the 16th century it was occupied by cadets of that family. It remained in their possession until 1631, when it was sold to the Earl of Traquair. This makes it unlikely, in my view, that the Douglases on this monument are in any way related to us. By tradition we are of Queensberry descent; and the Chinese armorial plate (the last of the service, brought back by Peter Douglas from China) has on it the Queensberry crest of the human heart imperially crowned, with the motto "Forward". There is, however, a complication. Spittalhaugh is near West Linton in Peebles. In West Linton Churchyard there is an interesting gravestone bearing the Queensberry Douglas arms - viz "A human heart ensigned with an imperial crown, with 3 mullets in chief"[4] of

> *William Douglas of Garwallfoot died 28th June 1705 & his wife Lilias Russell*

So there may be a connection after all, and Buchan's History of Peebles-shire may be wrong that the Spittlehaugh Douglases were of Morton stock. Is it coincidence that Peter Douglas' oldest (natural) son was called Henry Russell Douglas?

Douglas, born at Dalkeith at around the beginning of the 18th Century, and a writer in Edinburgh [may be the same as William Douglas, writer in South Kirk Parish, who married Mary Robertson, daughter of the late William Robertson, writer, on 27th October 1734 [3]] had issue 2 children[2]:

Peter, b 1739 or 1740, of whom hereafter

A daughter, who married a celebrated tragedian actor known as Fearon, whom she had met in a smack going from Edinburgh to London. They had 8 children, whom Peter Douglas brought up after their father's death. One daughter became Lady Garrett; another Anne m 10.12.1805 General James Achmuty HEIC 1775-1864 of the family of Achmuty of Brianstown, co Longford. One of the grandsons, Peter S Fearon married Claudine, daughter of General Claud Douglas.

20. **Peter Douglas:**

He was born in 1739 or 1740[5]; and died in 1801. William Henry Douglas' letter continues:

> *"My father was born in the year 1740. He had no brother & only one sister. His Christian name was "Peter" & early in life he made the sea service his profession, and rose to eminence as a Captain of one of the East India Company's trading vessels. About the year 1790, he married "Miss Ann Jackson" being then her senior by 30 years. At his death in 1801, he left my mother with a family of one daughter and four sons, and another son who was born 3 months after his Father's death. I may mention that as my Father had only 1 sister - so my Mother had an only brother. After having made an ample fortune by the sea service, my Father died insolvent in 1801, in consequence of having lost his money in rash speculations - leaving my mother with her own pension of £250 a year, and each of her children had a pension granted them of £60 per annum..."* [2]

He did not die insolvent; but intestate. Administration was granted to his widow Ann Douglas, & the estate was valued at £10,000.

He had already made two voyages to India before 1765, when he joined the Plassey as Third Mate, sailing during the season of 1765 - 1766 to St Helena and China. In 1768-1769, he again sailed as Third Mate on the Plassey to the Coast and China.

Just before the voyage of 1768, he met William Hickey, whose Memoirs in several volumes are among the most interesting and entertaining books in the English language - they provide a vivid picture of the life of Hickey himself, as well as a panoramic picture of the England of George III, and of what life was like travelling overseas to India and China. A shortened version was published this century[6]. Hickey was taken in November 1768 by Peter Douglas to visit a relative of Peter's who was Master Builder at Chatham, and had a sumptuous house there [Vol I: p.121]. Hickey then went on the voyage to the East, as a Cadet. He described Peter's cabin:

> *"The ship was certainly in a sad and dirty plight, but Mr Douglas' cabin was an exception to the general filth, being neatness itself, and most elegantly fitted*

up. It was painted of a light pea green, with gold beading, the bed and curtains of the richest Madras chintz, one of the most complete dressing tables I ever saw, having every useful article in it; a beautiful bureau and book case, stored with the best books, and three neat mahogany chairs formed the furniture. In all my subsequent voyages I never saw so handsome an apartment in a ship" [1913 edition: Vol 1, p. 121]

Later, Hickey went on to describe some of the officers on the ship, including Peter:

"Douglas, whom I have already mentioned as third officer, was remarkably dressy, so much so, as to be distinguished in the service by the title of "Count Douglas", but although he laid out more money upon his person than was usual with men in his station, no one kept a stricter look out after the main chance than he did, well knowing how to make the best of every shilling, and let pass no opportunity of doing so. His cabin, as I before observed, was elegance itself. His person was pretty good, but his features hideous, so ugly it would have been no easy matter to caricature it. In fact it was more the face of a baboon than a human creature, notwithstanding which, so unacquainted was he with his own countenance, or so eat up with vanity, that he thought every woman that beheld him must unavoidably fall in love with him. His address was certainly that of a gentleman and man of the world. He was from the first very attentive and civil to me, desiring whenever I wanted to write, or wished to be alone, that I would make use of his cabin; and he also gave me the key of his bookcase that I might supply myself with any books I pleased. He likewise was a Scotchman..." [Vol I: p.144]

Just before this voyage of 1768-1769, Peter was passed over for position of Second Mate of the Plassey - much to the disgust of the Plassey's Captain, Waddell. He was due to be sworn in as second mate at the India house. Only a day or two ahead, the managing owner or "Ship's husband" - Mr John Durand - nominated Mr Chisholme as second officer. The Directors adjourned the swearing in, but were prevailed upon to support the managing owner, so that Chisholme got the position, although Peter had been acting as second mate, and had actually refused a second mate's berth on another ship, from attachment to the Plassey. Captain Waddell made up for it by allotting to Douglas a much larger cabin than was his due; by putting his officers upon three watches instead of two, as was usual, giving the command of the third watch to Douglas; and by giving him a seat at his table. [Vol.I: p. 146-149]

It was the custom for officers to invest money in goods, which they would carry in the ship each way: hoping to sell English goods in India and China; and Chinese and Indian goods in England. Those who were adept at this, and whose ship arrived first in port, made a substantial profit. Ultimately, many officers made substantial fortunes in this way. Hickey described the difficulties when the Plassey reached Madras:

> *"Within the space of ten days after the Plassey reached Madras, the whole of the fleet that left the Downs with her, bound to the same place, came in. This brought so great and sudden a supply of European articles as to overstock the market, and in consequence, there were no purchasers for many of the investments. The Commanders and officers were therefore under the disagreeable necessity of disposing of what they had at a loss of 40% under the prime cost of the goods in England, and several at a still greater discount. Glassware in particular, of which there was an immense quantity from that article having been much wanted the year before, sold at a loss of 60%. My acquaintance Mr Douglas had upwards of £1,000 sterling in different sorts of glass, yet by a conduct and management peculiar, I believe, to himself, instead, like his brother officers, of sustaining so calamitous and ruinous a loss, he actually made a profit of 25%, and he effected it thus. He was, as I have already mentioned, a very gay and dressy man, had at least a half dozen suits of rich laced clothes, with bag, solitaire, and sword, his hair dressed in the latest Parisian fashion with three tiers of curls. He was perfectly au fait with small talk, would, if necessary, or through a paucity of men, dance four or five minuets of an evening, and was in every respect what was called "a woman's man". Douglas, though in the midst of dissipation, or going down a country dance with a lively girl for his partner, never lost sight of the main chance, and constantly had an eye to business. He would by the most fulsome and bare faced flattery first talk his partner into high good humour, and having effected that much, he then pulled from his pocket and presented to her "the terms of a raffle" or "scheme of a lottery for a quantity of 'beautiful glassware' ", sometimes with both, saying that*

she must not only fix her own signature, but also procure the names of her friends, and this conduct, mean and contemptible as it was, fully answered his purpose to the extent above mentioned." [Vol 1: p.179-180]

In the season of 1771-1772, Peter was the Third Mate on the Royal Henry on its voyage to the Coast and China. By 1777, he had joined the Queen as Commander; and of this ship he ultimately became part owner, as well as sailing on her at the same time as Captain. In 1777-1778, he sailed on her to St Helena and Bencoolen; and in 1780-1781, to the Coast and China. Then in 1785 - 86 to Bombay and Bengal, and in 1789-90 again to Bengal.

It was during this second trip to Bengal, in 1790, that Peter fell into a certain amount of trouble. Hickey himself was in Calcutta, and in poor health, so Douglas "in the kindest manner told me that he was shortly going to Bombay, and if I would accompany him, the round house would be entirely at my service, and by accepting it I should make him extremely happy." About a week later, Hickey was talking to Captain Larkins, who was shortly going to leave for Madras on his ship the *Warren Hastings*. [Vol 4: pp. 1-2]:

"Captain Larkins replied confidentially that Captain Douglas had got into a serious scrap with the Government of Bengal by the intemperate language he had recently held wherever he went, denying the Governor-General's power over the Indiamen, and declaring that if his ship had been fixed upon as one to be employed in transporting troops he would have resisted the order and positively refused to act upon such service. "Now" added Captain Larkins, "the consequence of such monstrous folly will be that the Queen instead of being despatched to Bombay, as was intended, and which voyage would have been highly advantageous to him, will now, as you will soon find, be employed in a different and to her commander a very disagreeable manner; with me, therefore, you must go, and from this moment I consider you my passenger"."

He continued [Vol 4: p.5]

"Early in December .. (1790) .. Captain Larkins informed me that in consequence of Captain Larkins impertinently and foolishly attempting to oppose the orders of Government, he had the very unpleasant change of bullocks made instead of men. He was directed to receive 300 head of cattle, and given to understand that if the slightest demur was made, or any want of attention shown towards the animals in transporting them to Madras, the command of the Queen would be taken from him, and he sent a prisoner to England. So much for kicking against authority."

In 1791, the Calcutta monthly recorded the arrival on 10th April of the Honourable Company's Ship "The Queen". Presumably, Peter had satisfactorily carried out his orders.

(He resigned his captaincy of The Queen on 16th October 1793. During the seasons of 1793-94, and 1795-96, he was managing owner of the Queen [then under the captaincy of Captain Milliken Craig 7]. The resignation of the captaincy followed on his marriage in 1792.

By about 1791-1792, Peter was becoming a "Bond Street lounger": a man of fashion and fortune [Hickey: Vol 4: p.272]. On 22nd August 1792, he married at St Marylebone Church **Ann Jackson** 1765-1838. She was the daughter of Robert Jackson, a family originating from Derbyshire. Her brother, Richard Jackson, made a fortune as an importer of brandy during the Napoleonic Wars; but was overstocked when the Wars ended, and became ruined [qv Chapter 9: Jackson].

Ann Douglas, née Jackson, was a great beauty at the Court of George III and of the Prince Regent. Reference has been made above to the pensions of £250 pa which she received, and of £60 pa for each son [2]. Implicit in what William Henry Douglas said is that the pensions came from the Hon East India Company. Muriel Scaife told a different tale, altogether more racy, that these were pensions granted by the Prince Regent. If so, the services which warranted the pension, are all too obvious.

After their marriage, Peter and Ann Douglas lived at 8 Fitzroy Square, London - a house on the East side of the Square. Initially they lived in great affluence. But because of speculative investments, Peter lost nearly his entire fortune - including, so Muriel Scaife said, some £100,000 in flax mills in Hounslow. William Henry Douglas says that his father died insolvent [2]. Muriel Scaife said that a fortune well in excess of £100,000 had been reduced to some £10,000; - see para 27 (a) above.

At about the time of their marriage - in 1792 or 1793 - Peter and Ann Douglas' portraits were painted in miniatures, by Samuel Shelley. They are set in oval gold lockets, with half pearls set around the edge, and mother of pearl backs. I now have these. After the death of Ann Douglas, they passed to her daughter, Mary Ann Garden 1794-1892. She lived the last years of her life at Ribsden, Windlesham, the home of her daughter Madelina Douglas Garden, wife of Henry Cadogan Rothery. There they were on a shield shaped frame, with many other miniatures of the Douglas and Garden families. When Mary Ann Garden died in 1892 (having outlived all her children) all the miniatures were rapidly taken by her grand-daughter, Clara Madelina Garden, daughter of Archibald MacDonald Garden. The miniatures by Shelley of Peter and Ann Douglas, eventually passed to Clara's sister-in-law, Grace Garden, wife of Huntly Charles Garden. She sold them in the 1950s to a London collector, a Mrs Ferrier. They were then bought by a London dealer, Arthur G Tite, on behalf of a Canadian collector, one Thomson. I happened to advertise one day in the Times in 1960, for their whereabouts. Arthur Tite replied. The Canadian collector volunteered to let me have then as a descendant of the sitters, at the price that he paid for them - £150; and Arthur Tite charged nominal commission [8]. It only remains to add that the Canadian collector was a newspaper magnate, who shortly after extended his newspaper empire to England, and bought the Times. He became Lord Thomson of Fleet.

Hope and Faith

Picture 24: Peter Douglas

Picture 25: Ann Douglas

Peter Douglas died suddenly at his home on 5th December 1801. Hickey wrote [Vol 4, p.272]:

> *"My letters this season (1803) informed me of the death of the last of the officers of the Plassey at the time I sailed in her, Captain Peter Douglas, her third mate, who subsequently got command of the ship "Queen", by which he acquired a handsome fortune, after being for some years a Bond Street Lounger, was one morning found dead in his bed, having been carried off, very quietly in a fit of apoplexy".*

His widow, Ann, subsequently remarried in 1806 or 1809 - to James (or ?John?) Champain HEIC. He was appointed Judge & Magistrate in 1769 of the 24th Purgunnahs, and came home in 1778. He died 1837 "through the button of his nightshirt pressing on his windpipe, while under the effects of a stroke". She died 28th June 1838, aged 73, at Fareham, Southampton. I have a copy of her will [9]. It reads:

> *"This is the last will and testament of me Ann Champain of no 27 ?Hans? Place, Chelsea in the County of Middlesex, Widow. I desire to be buried in the*

New Cemetery at ?Kensal? Green in the Harrow Road in as plain and simple a manner as possible. I bequeath all my jewels unto my granddaughter Mary Ann Ellen Garden, the eldest daughter of Dr Alexander Garden of Calcutta. I have made a list of the, and I desire them to be sealed up and left in charge of my bankers, Messrs Coutts & Co, until my said grand-daughter is eighteen (?) years of age, or until the arrival or her father or her mother in England. I desire that my plate be divided equally between my sons Claud Douglas and Archibald Douglas, and I give unto my son William Henry Douglas all my books and china and painted glass which was his father's. I give my plaid shawl unto my granddaughter Madelina Douglas Garden, and my scarlet shawl and pianoforte unto my granddaughter Helen Maria Douglas. I give unto Mary Madelina Bourmaster Douglas the wife of my son Claud my set of Mosiacs (sic). I give unto my daughter Mary Ann Garden all my late clothes, linen, trinkets etc etc, in short all such matters as my executors may think worthy of being put by for her. The two paintings in the parlour belong to her. My furniture etc I desire to be sold and I give the money to arise therefrom and all the rest and residue of my estate and effects after payment of my debts and funeral and testamentary expenses, to be equally divided between my three grandsons Claud, Archibald, and William Henry, the children of my son Claud Douglas. And I appoint my son William Henry Douglas of Wickham in the county of Hants, Barrister at Law, and my friend Mr Hugh Garden, of Piccadilly, executors of this my will..... (etc)."

I have an oil portrait of Ann Douglas, 30" x 25". It is probably an (unfinished) portrait by Sir Thomas Lawrence. I also have a miniature of Ann at an earlier date, copied from the original, which was in the possession of Violet Garden up to her death in 1960.

Apart from taking over the responsibility for bringing up his sister's 8 children (her actor husband Mr Fearon) having died without making any provision for them, Peter had a number of children himself. Prior to his marriage to Ann Jackson, he had two sons. Muriel Scaife was adamant that they were illegitimate children, but brought up by Peter in his house as his own. My cousin Mrs Douglas-Bate claims that there was a first wife, Frances Gower [10]. These 2 sons were:

[i]   Sholto b 1787, who was killed by Dacoits in Madras. dsp

[ii] Henry Russell Douglas 1791-1885, Commander RN. He m
      Anne Harfield and had a son:

> I.   Sholto 1833-1913, who became an Admiral. He m Maria
>   Louisa Bickford & had issue 3 sons & 4 daughters
>   [Gertrude Marion; Helen Mary dsp; Ann Mabel; &
>   Margaret]. The sons were:
>
> a. Sholto Grant Douglas 1867-1956 who had by his wife
> Elizabeth Forun
>
> - Helen Mary dsp
> - Marguerita 1905-1952 m Eric Walker, issue an only
>   son, Douglas Walker
> - Peter Sholto 1908-1966, m Gladys Appleby & had an
>   only daughter Gillian Elizabeth, b. 1940. Peter lived in
>   Northampton & had a rather splendid portrait of the 2
>   "illegitimate" sons of Peter Douglas.
>
> b. Vice Admiral Sir Henry Percy Douglas RN 1876-1939
> whose only child was Mrs Kathleen Douglas-Bate, of
> Donnington nr Newbury (she died in her 101st year, in
> 2001)

By his wife, **Ann Jackson**, Peter had 5 sons and one daughter:

[i]   Townley Ward Douglas 1793-1813. William Henry Douglas, his
      brother, wrote [2]:

> *"Townley Ward Douglas, the oldest son, was in His Majesty's Navy,
> and was killed in action against the Danes in the command of the boats of his
> ship in 1813. He was an acting Lieutenant".*

An obituary in the London Courier of 11th December 1813
read [11]:

> *"We are sincerely sorry to announce the death of one of the most
> promising young officers of the Royal Navy, Townley Ward Douglas, acting
> Lieutenant in his Majesty's Ship Ulysses - on 27th October last. This brave*

youth volunteered his services to command one of the boats of his ship against a Danish privateer infesting the harbour of Mystad. On the night preceding (to the admiration of those who witnessed his exertions) he succeeded in making one capture, and was on the point of making a second, when a musket ball in a few seconds deprived the country of a most gallant officer and his afflicted relatives of a deservedly dear and most admirable friend. He was interred with the honours of war on a small island off Gotteburgh and attended by all the Captains and Officers on that station. We can now only lament his loss and revere his memory. He was the eldest son of the late Peter Douglas Esqre of Fitzroy Square, many years a Commander in the Honourable East India Company's Service, and of his inconsolable mother, now Mrs Champain of Gloucester Place."

I have a fine oil portrait of Townley Ward Douglas 30" x 25". I have not identified the artist. It and the oil portrait of Ann Douglas descended to William Henry Douglas, and then to his daughter, Ila. She gave them to her nephew, Major Sholto Douglas. Sholto Douglas gave them to Major Douglas Talbot, his cousin. In 1972, Douglas Talbot gave them to me.

Townley Ward Douglas was engaged to his first cousin, Anna Margaretta Jackson, the daughter of Ann Douglas' brother, Richard Jackson. Anna Margaretta was the grandmother of Muriel Scaife [12].

[ii]   Mary Ann 1794-1892. She m Dr Alexander Garden, Presidency Surgeon, Calcutta. Violet Garden had an engraved portrait of Dr Alexander Garden; a pastel of Mary Ann Garden, and pastel portraits of her father and his sisters. These went to Alexander Garden of Troup after her death. They had issue of whom the descendants are now all extinct, as follows:

I.   John dsp

II.   William Alexander, Colonel Indian Army. 182- - 1884; m Louisa Gee 1857, & had issue:

a. Huntly b & d 1858

b. Mary Mina 1861-195-, m Charles Soltau dsp

c. Eva 1863-1866 dsp

d. Sholto Douglas 1867 - -- dsp

e. Henry Alexander 1868-1897 dsp

f. Violet Helen Catherine 1871/2 - 1962 (lived in Dolphin Road, Slough, nearly all her adult life; & for much of it with her sister Mina. A near neighbour was Ila Douglas, daughter of William Henry Douglas).dsp. I remember visiting her on many occasions in Slough. She had a zest for life, and would sit up in her chair, white cap on her head, adoring every minute of her "pow-wows" about the Douglas and Garden families. She gave me the pair of silver salt dishes with gadrooned edges, William IV, with on one side the initials "M.M"; and on the other side the initial "E". "M.M" stands for Mary MacLean [13], an aunt of her mother's, who was a lady in waiting to Princess Elizabeth, daughter of George III - "E" standing for Elizabeth. These were given to Mary MacLean after the death of, and to commemorate, Princess Elizabeth. Violet used to tell of her parents using the salt dishes every day in India, and of how they used to gleam in the light of the camp fires. Violet also gave me a small crayon and wash portrait of a lady of the Douglas / Garden family, whose identity she did not know. The artist is the same as the artist of our crayon and wash portrait of William Douglas (my great grandmother's brother) killed at Sebastopol. It had belonged to Ila Douglas, who intended it for Douglas Garden, but he died before her. After Violet's death, her executors gave to me the oval portrait of Madelina Douglas Rothery; and a pastel/chalk portrait of a lady who is probably Mrs Gee, her grandmother, and the sister of Mary MacLean to whom our salt dishes were presented.

g. Henrietta Scott 1873-1876 dsp

III. Archibald MacDonald 18-- - 1887. Colonel IMS. m Clara Jane Harris & had issue:

    a. Clara Madelina dsp 1939

    b. Huntly Charles dsp 1901. His widow Grace, died c. 1960.

    c. Archibald Ross Hervey dsp

IV. Henry Campbell 18-- - 1879; Colonel, m Augusta dau General Claud Douglas, & had issue

    a. Henry Douglas Garden 1871-1936. He m Rebecca Jacobs of the Irish biscuit family. He was badly gassed in the First World War, serving in the Buffs (East Kent Regiment). After the War he went to the USA, where he lived in New York & California. He was an actor (his stage name being Henry Douglas) and a fruit farmer. I have the medals of Henry Campbell Garden & his son Douglas Garden.

V. Madelina Douglas 1828-1891 who m Henry Cadogan Rothery of Ribsden, Bagshot, Surrey. They had no children. They built Ribsden, a large Victorian house, where they provided a home for all their nephews and nieces whose parents were away serving in India. They maintained the house and gardens in great style, their next-door neighbour being the famous Joseph Hooker & his family. Ribsden was pulled down and rebuilt in the early 20th century. Henry Rothery was a Barrister and Wrecks Commissioner. He was a cousin of his wife - both being descended from Robert Hartshorne 1717-1779 - see Jackson: Chapter 11. I have a small oval portrait of Madelina Douglas Garden.

VI. Huntly Rothery 1826-1872, m Henrietta Maria Thornhill (who d 1929). Colonel, Indian Army. dsp

VII. Mary Ann Ellen 1827-1870 dsp. She was prominent in working in the soup kitchens, set up to relieve famine & hunger due to poverty.

[iii]   William Henry Douglas: 1797 - 18--. He wrote about himself[2] that he "never distinguished himself in any particular way - went to Rugby School, where he did not learn much." He was gazetted in 1812 to an Ensigncy in the 99th Regiment, and subsequently became a Barrister at Law, being called by the Middle Temple, 3rd July 1829. He became Commissioner of Bankrupts for the County of Hants. On 11th April 1837, he married Helen Sarah Gould; in Fareham Church. They had issue:

I.   Sholto Gould Douglas dsp

II.   Major George Malcolm Douglas, 33rd Regiment (Duke of Wellington's Regiment). On 21st December 1869, he married, at 6 Park Gardens, Glasgow, Jemima, daughter of the late James Jamieson. They had a son

a. Major Sholto William Douglas, CBE, DSO, 1870-1959. He served in the Royal Artillery in South Africa, was twice mentioned in dispatches, and was awarded the DSO in 1900. He was Chief Constable of the Metropolitan Police 1910-1914; and Chief Constable of the Lothians & Peebles-shire from 1914. He married Grace Catherine, 2nd daughter of Colonel Wolfe-Murray RA, of Cringletie, Perthshire (Murray Bt cr. 1628 colls). The marriage broke down, and he dsp. Douglas Talbot said that he had a complete set of table silver with the Douglas crest on, & a lot of crested china [14].

III.   Florentine, m on 12th June 1866 at Tunbridge, Frederick Worsley Bertie Worsley-Roberts, only surviving son of he late Lieutenant-General H Tuffnell Roberts CB, of the Bengal Cavalry. She died at the age of 83, at her residence at Woodleigh, Thenville, Havana. They had issue

a. Frederick Bertie, b.12th July 1867 at Cheltenham; married on 28th January 1889 at St Katharine's Church, Uitenhage,

Algoa Bay, Ellinor Lavinia Philadelphia Nixon-Nixon, daughter of General John P Nixon of Balmoral Estate, Port Elizabeth, South Africa. They inherited the Balmoral Estate, having had issue:

♦ a son, born at King Lear Villa, Uitenhage, on 14th October 1890 Frederick Bertie died 14th June 1899 at Bournemouth, aged 31.

b. Henry Douglas, who died 25th February 1891 at Uitenhage, aged 22.

c. Bertie Worsley, who died on July 9th 1902, aged 30, of tuberculosis of the bowels, at Agnew's State Hospital, Agnew, California.

d. Daisy Eleanor, who m -- Talbot & had 2 sons:

♦ Valentine Douglas Lynch Talbot ["Douglas"] - who gave me the 2 oil portraits, of Ann & Townley Ward Douglas. dsp 1986

♦ Basil Lynch 1904-1962 dsp

IV. Donnaquilla ["Ila"] - dsp 24th January 1940.

The line of William Henry Douglas is now extinct.

[iv] **Patrick John Douglas**. He entered the 66th Regiment in about 1814; and was sent after the Battle of Waterloo to St Helena as a guard for the Emperor Napoleon. I have no knowledge of any descendants of his; and infer from the fact that he was not mentioned in his mother's will, that he dsp before 1838.

[v] **Claud** 1799-1883, of whom hereafter.

[vi] Archibald Douglas. He was born posthumously, in March 1802. Sometime prior to 1820, he entered the East India Company's Military Service. I think that he was the father of:

I. Helen Maria Douglas - mentioned in her grandmother's will, see above - who m Francis Tucker ICS, and had issue 3 daughters:

a. Isabel, m General Sir Oswald Barnard

b. Marion Douglas, m Herbert Griffith & had 5 children

♦ Francis Huntly

♦ Stella Marion who m -- Magoris, and had a son Michael Magoris, Colonel in the Ghurkas. He has the original of the miniature of Ann Douglas, of which I have a copy, which belonged to Violet Garden.

♦ Hubert Douglas

♦ Helen Monica, who m R E C Adams, and had a dau Jean Awdry, who has been twice married (her first husband was -- Wieser) but without issue

♦ Dorothy Mabel

c. Nell

Notes & Sources:

1. History of the Douglases by --

2. Letter, William Henry Douglas, 1879, to Colonel Archibald Garden, about his family.

3. Edinburgh - Old Parochial Registers. Scots Ancestry Research Society Letters of 21.9.1960 & 22.1.1963

4. Buchan's History of Peebles-shire p.162 states that the lands of Garvaldfoot, which are in the vicinity of the junction of the Garvald Burn with the Medwin, must have been feued in the 17th century and possessed in two halves. In 1706, there is a record of a precept of clare constat to William Douglas of Garvaldfoot of both halves, as son and heir of William Douglas & Lilias Russell, the feu duty payable being 30 merks. William Douglas was succeeded by his son William in 1725, who was then in minority, and from whom the property passed before 1775 to his only child Joanne, who married Sir William Dick of Prestonfield.

5. The Gentlemans Magazine for 1771 record the death on 30th October 1771 of William Douglas Esq of Garwalfoot in Scotland.

6. The Edinburgh parochial registers, ie St Cuthbert's & Canongate, were searched 1738-1741 for any record of Peter's birth, without success.

7. Memoirs of William Hickey HEIC, originally published 1913 in 4 Volumes, ed by Alfred Spencer (Plymouth); shortened version published 1960 by Hutchinson, London, ed by Peter Quennell.

8. Hardy's Register of Ships. National Army Museum Letter 26 Jan 1960

9. Correspondence with Arthur G Tite 1960.

10. Will of Ann Champain & death certificate

11. Correspondence 1986 with Mrs Douglas-Bate.

12. Copy, Obituary, London Courier, 11th December 1813, of Townley Ward Douglas.

13. Letter Muriel Scaife, 3 April 1963

14. Note on the MacLean family

15. Correspondence 1960 about the death & estate of Major Sholto Douglas.

21. **Claud Douglas: 1799-1883**; my great-great grandfather.

He was born on 9th November 1799 in London. He was sent to Eton. His brother William Henry Douglas wrote [ref 2 above]:

> *"Then comes the illustrious Claud, who had a nomination to Woolwich Academy (Military College) and after being there two years, his Colonel so vexed him one day that this creditable young man took himself off the parade ground, and was not sought for!! In 1820, he went to India with a cadetship".*

On 15th February 1877, he recalled his school-days in a letter to his grandson William Melville Douglas:

> *"Dear Willie,*
> *Have you yet mastered the 47th proposition of the first book of Euclid? It is the keystone of science, and I sent you that pocket edition of Horace, that you might read him night and day and always have him by you, and you should learn to repeat by heart some of his charming odes and songs. When I was a boy, my master set me to learn 250 lines of the 4th book of the Aeneid of Virgil as a punishment. I thought it exceeding cruel at the time, for how*

could I ever remember and repeat without an error 250 lines of Virgil; but by dint of perseverance I mastered it and can, though it is about 60 years ago, still repeat the lines. They begin with "conticuere omnes, intentaque ora tenebat" - all were silent and listened with attentive ears; "et iam nox humido coelo precipitat" - and now night falls from the humid sky. My boy youth is the only time to learn and you will never regret, nor I hope forget, what you now learn, and what a prize is before you - the Indian Civil Service. You need no urging - the willing horse needs no whip, and therefore I conclude with my best wishes, and best love to you and your dear mamma, and hoping that you are both quite well, I remain -

> *Always*
> *Your affectionate grandfather,   Claud Douglas".* [1]

His service record was:

Cadet 1818; Ensign 16 August 1819; admitted to the HEIC 10 Feb 1820; Ensign 2/9th Native Infantry 6 Nov 1820; posted as Ensign to 2/10th NI & transferred to 14th NI (late 1/10th) May 1824. Promoted Lieutenant 29 April 1823; on furlough 21 Sept 1824 to 11 May 1827.

Second in command Rangpur NI 14 Sept 1827 to 27 July 1829; Captain 27 Sept 1828; & on furlough 10 Feb 1832 to 8 June 1835.

In charge 13th Rajputana Div PWD 23 Oct 1841 until 1848.

Lieutenant Colonel 56th NI 27 Oct 1848; on furlough 10th April 1848 to 1850.

Transferred to 48th; 60th; 49th; 70th; 56th; 50th; and 32nd NI.

Colonel 1 May 1858 - of 55th NI 25 July 1858; and 65th NI 1854-1860

Major General 4 June 1860

Lieutenant General 25 June 1870

General 1 Oct 1877 [2]

There is no record of his having been on active service; and I think it likely that a generation later he would have been classified as Indian Civil Service, rather than Indian Army.

He was twice married; firstly, on 7th December 1826, at Titchfield, Hants, to **Mary Madelina Bourmaster Collingwood Dickson**, daughter of Admiral Sir Archibald Collingwood Dickson 2nd Bt [Chapter 12: Dickson]. I have a miniature of her, in a heavy gilt mount & frame. She died at Bideford, Devon 18 June 1848. They had 3 sons and 4 daughters.

Secondly, on 22 November 1848, to Eliza Harrison Smith, widow, at St Marylebone Parish Church [3]. She died 24th April 1888 [4]. They had one son (I think) Sholto. He died at Bognor 11th April 1883

His children by Mary Madelina Dickson were:

[i]   Claud Barwell Douglas 1828-187-; Indian Civil Servant; m his cousin Ellen Callow 1834-1925, daughter of Charles Callow, and grand-daughter to his great uncle Richard Jackson, at St John the Evangelist, St Pancras, on 20 Feb 1861. They had an only son:

    I.   William Melville Douglas b 27 Jan 1864; d 13 April 1886 of a fever at Korosko, Egypt, where he was a Lieutenant in the Yorkshire Regiment. I have 2 Commissions of his, both signed by Queen Victoria, the first as Lieutenant, Militia Forces, 24 May 1884, 4th Battalion The Border Regiment; and the second as Lieutenant in the Princess of Wales Own (Yorkshire Regiment) 24 November 1885[5]

[ii]   William Henry Douglas 18-- - 1855; Lieutenant, Royal Navy, was killed at Sebastopol, in the Crimean War. He was an intimate friend of Evelyn Wood, then also in the Royal Navy, but who was to transfer to the Army, and end up as Field Marshal Sir Evelyn Wood. On 11th April 1855, Evelyn Wood wrote in his diary, at HMS Queen, before Sebastopol:

"As I rode into the Battery on my return, I met four men carrying away the body of Douglas, my most intimate friend. The top of his head had been knocked off by a round shot; on his handsome face there was still the pleasant smile which had endeared him to all of us. He was singularly unselfish and by his undaunted courage had attracted the attention of Captain Peel, who had paid him the compliment of asking him to show his indifference to danger. On the 10th, Douglas observed to me at Dinner "You have lost a good many men

today - perhaps it will be my turn tomorrow". I answered laughingly and said "Yes, and mine next day". After dinner, he went over to HMS London Officers' tent and returning said "Our friends are in considerable trouble, for their Mess Caterer, Twyford, was killed today. I shall close my accounts, and you shall all pay up tonight". This he did, in spite of my earnest remonstrances - he insisted on giving back some of the money he ha been keeping for me".

I have a small pencil and wash portrait of William Henry Douglas, in an oval frame, at the age of about 3. My late uncle Donald Stewart had a small oil portrait of him in uniform, and a miniature of the 3 Douglas boys, Claud Barwell, William Henry, and Archibald Alexander, as small children, painted presumably in about 1832-1833.

[iii] Archibald Alexander Douglas 1830 - 1884 [6]. He was a Lt Colonel, Royal Marine Artillery; he fought in the bombardment of Odessa, and served in the breaching batteries before Sebastopol, from 1854 to the fall. He was badly wounded, losing one of his fingers by a shot. His brother, William Henry Douglas, was killed at his side. For his distinguished bravery in the field, he was made a Knight of the Legion of Honour by the then Emperor of the French, and in addition to being decorated with the Crimean medal and clasp, and the Sardinian medal, he was presented by the Sultan of Turkey with the Turkish medal and the Order of the Fifth Class of the Medjidie [10]. He married Fanny Jaques, whose father owned Easby Abbey, nr Richmond, Yorkshire. He had two children:

I.   Frank - who was cut off by his uncle Jaques, who then owned Easby Abbey, because he married the daughter of a local shop-keeper in Richmond, by the name of Spencer. Theirs was a newsagents, stationers, shop, and remained in Spencer hands until it was sold in about 1958. He was a Bank Manager for many years - at one time in Bexhill. After his mother's death, he went to Canada, and was never heard of again, even by his sons. There was a story that he was killed in a sordid quarrel in the low quarter of San Francisco. Frank had 2 sons:

a. Francis Eric Douglas, who m Clarice -- & had a son Alastair Gordon Sholto Douglas - see Correspondence [8].
b. Harold Archibald Sholto Douglas, who was with the Standard Bank, and died in London in 1955 [9] - dsp

II. Mary Madeline, who m 1887 Major Nicholas Stapleton, son of Bryan John Stapleton, who was a half brother of Miles Thomas Stapleton of Carlton Towers, Goole, Yorkshire, in whose favour the abeyance of the Barony of Beaumont was terminated - see Burke's Peerage s.n Norfolk, Duke. The Stapletons were one of the very few families never to have abandoned Catholicism, even after the Reformation. They had 2 daughters:

a. Gwendoline Lavinia 1888 - ; who m 1923, G Francis Mann, of Brooklyn, New York.
b. Ruth Madelina 1889 - who m 1914 Stanley Yates. Their daughter Joan Madeline Dampier Yates b 1920, m Jack Trill, and lives at Gerrards Cross, Bucks.

[iv] **Mary Isabella Douglas 1839-1914**, my great grandmother, who married Brigadier General Frederick John Stuart Adam - see Chapter 9: Adam

[v] Augusta, who married her cousin Henry Campbell Garden, and had one son Douglas who dsp in America in the early 1930s - see above, under descendants of Mary Ann Garden née Douglas 1794-1892. "Aunt Augusta" in widowhood played the role of matriarch of the family. She would travel around the world - India, America, England - spending anything from a month or two, to a year or two at a time with the particular brother or sister, or in-law. She travelled with 20 or more trunks. Mabel Gray, her niece who lived in Virginia, told of how Aunt Augusta used to descend on the family. It was not known for how long

she would stay - that had to be played by ear. If she was particularly pleased on a visit, she would open that trunk which contained family silver, and get it out to use - General Douglas' silver inkstand: jewellery: crested silver spoons and forks. What happened to it all in the end, history does not relate, save that some of the plated cutlery was given by her to her sister Ellen Daniell in Virginia; and her daughter Mabel Gray gave it to me. In those days, around 1900, there were no sidewalks in Washington DC, only duckboards placed over the mud

[vi] Claudine: who m her cousin Peter S Fearon, grandson of Peter Douglas' sister, Mrs Fearon. They had 3 children:

I. James Achmuty Fearon, Col 19th Regiment, Green Howards

II. Peter Fearon

III. Claudine who m -- Fuller

[vii] Lucy Ellen, who m Ralph W Daniell, of the family of Daniell of Trelissick, Cornwall. Some generations earlier, they had married the heiress of Ralph Allan, of Prior Park, Bath. Ralph & Ellen Daniell decided to emigrate to Virginia, and did so shortly after the Civil War had ended. By this, Ralph lost the chance, which would otherwise have been his, of inheriting Trelissick. They bought land and farmed in Fauquier County, Virginia. A year or two after they had gone, Ralph's father, and the rest of his family, emigrated to the same part of Virginia. There was no economising on luggage or space - they took their hunting horses and pack of hunting hounds. In Virginia Ralph founded "Ralph W Daniell's Hunt" - issue

I. Charles, who died unmarried in Feb 1961; aged 88

II. Alice, who died in the same week, unmarried and aged 85

III. Mabel Daniell Gray, who m John Chilton Gray (he died 5th May 1961). We visited her in 1964, in Warrenton, Va, when

Andrew was a babe in arms. She was a splendidly larger than life character. Her house was full of photographs of the Douglas and Garden families. There we found a photograph of the miniature of Mary Madelina Douglas, née Dickson. Mabel knew who it was of - her grandmother Douglas. My mother, who had the miniature after my father died, was confident that my grandmother Freda Stewart had said that it was of her Adam, rather than Douglas, grandmother.- It illustrates how fallible human memory can be. She gave us then the Douglas plate spoons and forks that we have; and she gave for Andrew an emerald ring (in need of extensive repair) ex Mary Madelina Douglas, née Dickson. Andrew & Valerie have it now. [10] Shortly before her death, Mabel wrote asking me to visit her so that she could give me "Uncle Sholto Douglas' watch", and some other things. Sadly, she died only a week or two before I got to the USA in 1967, so the gift never took place. Mabel had no children, so the line of Ellen Daniell is extinct.

Notes & Sources:

1. Letter 15.02.1877 General Claud Douglas, to his grandson William Melville Douglas.
2. Officers of the Bengal Army 1758-1834, Vols D-K, by Major V C F Hodson; Constable, London, 1928.[his father is wrongly named as Patrick]
3. Burke's Peerage 1923, s.n Islington B
4. Base, Eton College Lists, G.N 1826 II 556; 1849, i, 148
5. The Times 17 April 1883
6. Certificate of Marriage Claud Douglas to Eliza Harrison Smith, 22 November 1848
7. Certificate of Death of Eliza Harrison Douglas, 24 April 1888.
8. Marriage Certificate, Claud Barwell Douglas & Ellen Callow, 20 Feb 1861
9. 2 Commissions of William Melville Douglas, 1884 & 1885, signed by Queen Victoria; and his sailing orders dated 4th January 1886; & letter to his mother about his death from Surgeon, Medical Officer, J Russell; together with a further letter from General Claud Douglas to Willie about studying the Classics.
10. Death Certificate of Archibald Alexander Douglas, 16 March 1884
11. Correspondence with Eric Douglas, in 1970, & with others about the family of Archibald Alexander Douglas.
12. Letter Standard Bank 1970
13. Correspondence, miscellaneous, from Mabel Gray.

The Garden Family:

This family came from Aberdeenshire.

1. John Garden, portioner of Latheris or Dorlatheris 1480-1510, died before 1555, leaving issue:
2. George Garden, portioner of Dorlatheris & Laird of Banchory 1555. m Isabel Keyth, d the Laird of Troup. He had 2 children

    [i]   Alexander, who succeeded him

    [ii]   Beatrix, who m Finla Mor, ancestor of Farquharson of Invercauld & Finzean

3.   Alexander Garden of Banchory, m Elspeth dau Gordon of Gight, and had 2 sons:

    [i]   Alexander, last laird of Banchory, d before 25th October 1639, leaving 2 sons

        I.   Alexander Garden, afterwards of Troup, from whom descend the Gardens of Troup

        II. Captain George Garden

    [ii]   Rev George Garden, of whom hereafter

4.   Rev George Garden, 1633-1677 Minister of Clath, had 4 sons:

    [i]   Rev Alexander, Minister of Gartly and then at Deer

    [ii]   William, farmer at Taveltie, Kinkell 1696

    [iii]   John, of whom hereafter

    [iv]   Rev Thomas, Minister of Clath 1669-1681

5.   John Garden, farmer of Fowllartoune Kinkell 1696 had issue 2 sons:

    [i]   Rev Alexander, Minister of Kinerny, then of Birse; b 1680; d 1778, who had 2 sons:

        I.   Dr Alexander Garden, 1739-1791, of Charleston, South Carolina, after whom the Gardenia is named.

        II. John Garden, Army Accoutrement Maker, London.

    [ii]   George, of whom hereafter.

6.   George Garden, farmer of Heugh Head, Keith; & then Bandley, Alford; 1710-1791; had issue 3 daus [Agnes d unm 1831; Elizabeth d unm 1831; & Elspet m --Milne & d 1831] and a son:

7.   Alexander Garden 1752-1804, farmer Bandley, m Grizel McCombie dau Alexander McCombie, Lynturk, Leochel, Cushine, and had issue:

[i]   George Garden, farmer Bandley; 1758-1858; m Agnes Patterson 1783 - 1856 + issue

[ii]   Colonel William Garden CB, ADC to Queen Victoria; 1790-1852;

[iii]   *Hugh Garden* 1794-1851, Army Accoutrement Maker of Piccadilly. An executor of the Will of Ann Douglas or Champain, 1838. left issue

[iv]   *Dr Alexander Garden 1795-1845*, Presidency Surgeon, Calcutta, who married *Mary Ann Douglas* & had issue - see above.

[v]   Elizabeth, m Alexander Cowie of London + issue

[vi]   Jane m George Yeats, merchant in Aberdeen

[vii]   John, Lieutenant HEICS 1797 - 1821. Violet Garden had a small oil portrait of this John, which went with the other Garden portraits to Troup House.

A NOTE ON MRS GEE née Wilhelmina MacLean

(Grandmother of Violet Garden- we have a portrait)

Mrs Gee was the daughter of a Mr MacLean and a Hanoverian lady, who fell into distress about the year 1805. The Duke of Cambridge, who was then Viceroy in Hanover, recommended Mrs MacLean to come to England, since her husband's father was an old soldier of 60 years' standing in the 95th Regiment, who for his services had been made a "Poor Knight of Windsor".

Mr & Mrs MacLean had two daughters:

Louisa, was befriended by Lord & Lady Harrington, Lady Harrington being one of Queen Charlotte's Ladies in Waiting. When Lord Harrington went to Ireland as Lord Lieutenant, Princess Elizabeth, daughter of George III "adopted" Louisa MacLean, who went with the Princess to Germany when she married the Duke of Hesse Homburg. On the Princess' death she was awarded a pension of £100 pa, and given the William IV salt cellars.

Wilhelmina [Mrs Gee] - the subject of the portrait - who was taken under the protection of Queen Charlotte in 1806, and remained at Windsor, Claremont, or Frogmore, under the care of Miss Pole. When she was grown up, she was sent for two or three years to a school at Bristol. Queen Charlotte allowed her £20 a year pocket money. On the death of the Queen in 1818, she was given a pension of £20 a year. She then went back to Lady Harrington as companion, till she married Mr Gee, the son of one of the oldest tenants on Lord Harrington's property in Cheshire. From 1832 until her death in 1849, Mr Gee was one of Queen Adelaide's pages, at a salary of £240 pa and a lodge in Windsor Park. After Queen Adelaide's death in 1849, until his own death in 1856, Mr Gee had a pension of £80 pa.

Mrs Gee had 2 children:

[i] Adolphus, who after training as a Surgeon at St George's in 1847, joined the Hon[ble] East India Company's Service, in the Bengal Presidency. He used to make his mother an allowance of £100 pa plus many gifts. He died of a "disease of the liver" on 6th December 1858. As a result, Mrs Gee was left entirely unprovided for.

[ii] Louisa, who m 1857 Colonel William Alexander Garden, Indian Army 182- - 1884. [His parents were Dr Alexander Garden HEICS Presidency Surgeon Calcutta, and Mary Ann dau Captain Peter Douglas HEIC Navy]. Col W A Garden was a first cousin of my great grandmother Mary Isabella Adam née Douglas. They had several children, none of whom left issue. The last survivor of this family was VIOLET HELEN CATHERINE GARDEN, b 1871/2 d 1962. This portrait, of her maternal grandmother, was in her possession until her death. It then came to me.

Chapter 11: Jackson including Hartshorne & Rothery

The Jackson & Hartshorne families both came from Roston, Church Broughton, Derbyshire. The link is through **Ann Jackson** who m **Captain Peter Douglas** HEIC Navy, in 1792. Both families were Millers & Maltsters at Roston for some time.

Church Registers for Church Broughton include the following Jackson marriages:

27 Jan 1551:   Wyllyam Jackson & Izabell Jackson

16.Jan 1552:   Henry Jackson & Margaryt Bullyvant

18 Feb 1554:   Rychard Jackson & Angnis Bullyvant

29 Jan 1583:   Robart Jackson & Grace Hall

12 Feb 1587:   Wyllyam Jackson & Angnis Bullyvant

26 June 1610:   Robarte Jackson & Joone Sante

Jackson gravestones still visible at Church Broughton include:

William Jackson d 11 April 1759, aged 51
Sarah Jackson, his wife, d 10 May 1789, aged 80
Penelope Jackson d 24 March 1821, aged 70

Among benefactors of the County of Derby, there appear:

> 1690; Henry Jackson: (places) Marston, Montgomery, Norbury & Church Broughton. Will dated 25th June 1690; land at Roston, nr Church Broughton, Derby; 10/- per annum to the poor in bread.
>
> 1752   Henry Jackson (place) Ideridgehay

Marriages:

On 1st December 1701 **Henry Jackson** m **Susannah Hartshorne**. He died 1752.

Robert Jackson, Miller & Maltster of Roston, who was probably the father of:

Robert Jackson, Attorney at Law of Mark Lane, Eastcheap, London; who m **Mary Hartshorne** dau Robert Hartshorne 1717-1779, Miller & Maltster of Roston. They had issue one son and one daughter:

Richard, of whom hereafter

> [i] **Ann** 1765-1838, who m (1) **Captain Peter Douglas HEIC Navy** - they were my great-great-great grandparents; and (2) James or John Champain HEIC

Richard Jackson 1768-1845 was an importer of brandy from France, during the Napoleonic Wars, and rose to great wealth and prosperity by this. He lived in a large house in Mark Lane, Eastcheap, in the courtyard of which a coach and 6 could be driven round without difficulty. He also used to drive a tandem. It is related that the Prince Regent, later George IV, so admired the horses, that he sent word that he would like to buy them. Richard replied regretting that they were not for sale.

On the ending of the Wars, Richard was overstocked with brandy. The price collapsed and he was ruined. He retired to the "village of Paddington". He died on 5th June 1845, at 27 Upper King Street, Bloomsbury, his son Robert being there at the time.

He married Ruth Alderson. She was the second daughter of John Alderson & his wife Mary Leake. Mary Leake was the daughter of Rev Robert Leake BD, MA Cantab, Vicar of Great Snoring, Norfolk. He was the heir to the Earldom of Scarsdale, but could not afford to take it up, and contented himself with the baronetcy that went with it; as did his son.

Mary Leake eloped with John Alderson in 1766 to Gretna Green, but her father soon forgave them, and had them married (for the second time) in Church - at Epperstone, Notts, on 28th February 1768.

The elder daughter of John Alderson & Mary Leake, Mary Alderson, married *Martin Samuel Callow* of Brenchley, Kent, gentleman. This family intermarried with the Jackson, Scaifes, and Douglases several times over a few generations:

1822:   John Scaife m Sarah Frances Callow

Their son, Reginald Scaife, married as his second wide Mary Isabella Callow.

Ellen Callow m Claud Barwell Douglas.

I am not sure of the precise Callow relationships, save that they were closely related.

Richard Jackson & Ruth Alderson had issue:

Robert Christopher, who was described as "a great trial" to his family. I do not know why. At one time, he entered his father's brandy importing business; alive at the time of his father's death in 1845.

[i]   ? Christopher, who died young?

[ii]   Anna Margaretta. She was engaged to her first cousin Townly Ward Jackson - but he was killed in action off Denmark, in 1813. She subsequently m Charles Callow, who was probably her first cousin - ie son of her aunt Mary Alderson & Martin Samuel Callow. She inherited the portrait of her aunt, Mary Ann Douglas; and gave it to her first cousin William Henry Douglas. This is the oil portrait that I have. She had issue:

I.   Elizabeth Callow, d unmarried - dsp

II.   Ellen 1834-1925; m her cousin Claud Barwell Douglas, son of General Claud Douglas - qv Chapter 10: Douglas. Their only child was William Melville Douglas b. 1864, who dsp in Egypt 1886, as a Lieutenant in the Yorkshire Regiment.

III. Mary Isabella married as his 2nd wife Reginald Scaife. [Reginald's father, John Scaife, had m Sarah Frances Callow in 1822]. The Scaifes are an old family from Westmorland, some of whom sat as Members of Parliament in the 14th century. Apparently, Reginald Scaife, at the age of 22, was jilted by a girl (? one of the Callows?). He met a girl at a party given for that purpose, who was in the same sad condition. She duly became his first wife; and they had 7 daughters and 1 son. Mary Isabella Callow & Reginald Scaife had issue one son and one daughter:

a. Harry Scaife dsp

b. Muriel Scaife 1879-1969. She was a great source of information about the Jackson and Douglas families; and an amusing raconteur of stories about them. She gave me several family possessions, salvaged from her house in Putney during wartime bombing, including:

♦ a mahogany dressing case which had belonged to **Ann Douglas** née Jackson

♦ the 2 small watercolour portraits of Richard Jackson and his son Robert.

In the bombing, a miniature that she had of Mrs Peter Douglas was destroyed; and a small oil portrait of a Miss Ward, on copper, décolleté, was stolen along with a japanned deed box.

Both Muriel Scaife and her mother were god daughters of Mary Anne Garden. With her death, the descendants of Richard Jackson became extinct.

Notes & Sources:

Muriel Scaife was the source of all tales about the Jackson family

The Hartshorne & Rothery families:

1. **Robert Hartshorne** 1717-1779 was a Miller & Maltster of Roston, nr Ashbourne, where he lived & died [2]. He was twice married. Both his wives were beautiful, and both died of small pox. By his first wife he had 2 children:

[i]   Thomas Hartshorne, also a brewer and maltster at Ashbourne, who lived to an advanced age. Like his father, he was twice married & had several children, including:

    I.   Thomas, who became prosperous & well to do. He lived at Silksmore, and became influential in the neighbourhood. He had 3 daughters - Mrs Harland, Mrs Shorthose, & Mrs Hagg.

[ii]   **Mary Hartshorne**, who was also twice married (1) to Robert Jackson and (2) to Mr Butler. By Robert Jackson she had:

    I.   Richard Jackson - see above

    II.   **Ann Jackson** who m **Captain Peter Douglas HEIC**.

By his second wife, he had:

[iii]   Prudence 1741-1839 - who m 1772 John Rothery; of whom hereafter

[iv]   Anne, a pretty, fair, delicate looking lady, who became the wife of a Mr Hine

[v]   Monecai, who m Mr Hards, and had one daughter Julia, who eventually m Sir David Brewster [Brewster's Edinburgh Encyclopedia]

[vi]   William Hartshorne; a fine looking, easy going, man; who m a Miss Waring of Ashbourne. He brought up a large family, under great difficulties.

2.   Prudence Hartshorne 1741 - 1839; m. 1741 John Rothery, at St George's Southwark

The *Rothery* family came from Yorkshire, or even Northumberland. John's father was well to do "whether farmer or gentleman, I know not". John & his brother Joseph ran away from their father's house when aged 16 or 17, each riding a horse taken from the stables. They went slowly to London, and by the time that they got there, they were penniless & had to sell their horses, and take the first offer of a livelihood. Never again did they hear of their parents or their home.

Prudence Hartshorne & John Rothery has 12 children, including:

[i]   William, of whom hereafter, b 1777

[ii] Thomas, RN, commander of HM Sloop "Snapper"

[iii] Joseph, some of whose descendants were living in Congleton in 1897.

[iv] a dau, who became Mrs Boulton, later Mrs Thompson

[v]   Mary, who d young

[vi] Margaret Esther, the 12th & youngest child, 1789 - 1877; m 1822 at Bloomsbury Church, John Roberts of Foxhale, Henllan, Denbighshire. Their only child *Margaret Anne Roberts* compiled the manuscript on which this Appendix is based.

3. William Rothery 1777-1864; m 1798 Frances Cadogan, dau of a Dr Cadogan of Cardiff; and had 15 children:

[i]   William b 1800; m Harriette Hendrie + issue, Robert & a dau who m Rev Abbott

[ii] John, in the Army, d young

[iii] Frances m Captain Teed + issue

[iv] Mary Ann d unm

[v]   Georgina, m Sam Smith & died in childbirth

[vi] Stephen, a Judge in Trinidad. d there of yellow fever c 1838

[vii] Alexander, RN, d in Haslar Hospital when young

[viii] Augusta who m Felix Belloc, the Procureur Imperial at Lyons. They had 3 daughters [Louise, Augusta a nun, & Emma who d unm] & a son Peter, who m, it is thought, in Australia. Felix Belloc's grandmother had been a lady in waiting to the Empress Josephine. ?This family was that of *Hilaire Belloc*.[3]

[ix] Emma, d unmarried

[x]   *Henry Cadogan Rothery of Ribsden, Windlesham*; a Barrister at Law & Wrecks Commissioner, who m his cousin *Madelina Douglas Garden*.

[xi] Charles Frederick, Queen's Commissioner in the Bahamas; m a Miss Simpson

[xii] Douglas d young

[xiii] Agnes, his twin, d young

[xiv] Archibald Huntly d young

[xv] a baby d young

4. There was a John Rothery, a surgeon, wounded & taken prisoner at Culloden 1746 - a Jacobite. Margaret Roberts thought it very likely that he was related, because

> *"My grandfather and grandmother (John Rothery & Prudence Hartshorne) were staunch Jacobites; and when my grandmother was young and still Prudence Hartshorne, being i London on the 10th of June, she wore - as she should - a White Rose at her breast, and so recent then (this was about 1759 or 1760) were Jacobite bitter feelings that some passers by tore the rose out of her dress and stamped upon it. - Grandma told me about this when I was little in hushed tones, and said that if they had a portrait or a relic or a book about the Prince, they used carefully to hide it away, so long did the old feeling against Jacobites continue. I believe the very first thing I can remember about Grandmama was finding her coming home from Church on a weekday - "Why to Church, Grandma, this is not a Sunday?" says I, "My love, it is the day of King Charles the Martyr (30th January). We all ought to go to Church.*

She goes on to describe a present from Andrew Lang, the literary celebrity: an oval medallion about 2" by 1½", of silver gilt: on the front an "admirable" head of Charles I in armour; and on the obverse are the Arms of France and England, quarterly, with the garter and motto. From the bottom depends a pear. It is "original 1649", one of several made in France for Queen Henrietta Maria, which she gave to her friends and household. "They were called 'Tear Tokens' or 'Tear Pieces' ".

Notes & Sources:

1. This Appendix is based entirely on a manuscript by Margaret Roberts of Orchard Street, Portman Square, London, written for her then young cousin, Muriel Scaife.

2. Hartshorne marriages recorded at Church Broughton include:

   1735, 14 April, Thomas Hartshorne to Ann Blood
   1768, 26 May, Thomas Hartshorne to Elizabeth Spurrier of Scropton.

3. (Joseph) Hilaire Belloc, the author, was the grandson of Hilaire Belloc. This first Hilaire Belloc m Louise Swanton, dau of a Colonel Swanton, an officer in the Berwick Regiment of Napoleon's Army. He died in or before 1867. Their son, Louis Belloc, was an invalid and qualified barrister. He m Bessie Parkes, whose grandfather was Dr Joseph Priestley. They lived at Celle Saint Cloud, 12 miles outside Paris, and in London. Louis d in 1872, leaving issue [1]: Joseph Hilaire Belloc (the author) b 27.07.1870, d 16.07.1953; and [ii]: a daughter Marie b 1868 who after her marriage was known as Mrs Belloc-Lowndes

Chapter 12: Dickson and Collingwood

On 7th December 1826, **Mary Madelina Bourmaster Collingwood Dickson** married **Claud Douglas**, then a Lieutenant, and later a General in the Indian Army. They were my great-great grandparents. The marriage was at Titchfield, Hants - the home of her [Bourmaster] maternal grandparents.

Of all the families from which we descend, this is the one of achievers: from rags to riches in the first half of the 18th century: then in the 150 years or so after achieving wealth, the family produced 5 Admiral*s*, one of whom was made a Baronet: 3 Generals - one of whom was one of the earliest holders of the Victorian Cross - General Sir Collingwood Dickson; & a Governor General of New Zealand who was made a peer Sir John Dickson-Poynder, Lord Islington [1910]. The Dickson family motto was "fortes fortuna juvat" - "Fortune helps the brave". They showed it.

The history of the Dickson family can be traced back to the early years of the 18th century, to two brothers, **James Dickson** 1713-1771 and **Archibald Dickson**, who were apprentices in Kelso, Roxburghshire.

Prior to that there is mention of various Dicksons in and around Kelso. *William Diksoun* in Ednam, Roxburgh, was one of the parties mentioned in a caution from Hume of Aytoun, 5th August 1591.

In 1607, *William Diksoun* gave an obligation to *John Diksoun* at Ednam, both being described as being in Ednam.

I do not know who was the father of James & Archibald Dickson. *James Dickson*, born in 1713, was a Saddler's apprentice in Kelso. Archibald was also apprenticed there; in what trade, I am not sure. In an escapade, James and Archibald broke up the lamp on the pant well in Kelso, a local "sacred" spot. Rather than stay to incur the wrath of the local inhabitants, they wisely decided that discretion was the better part of valour, and left Kelso.

James Dickson made his way to London, where he became a Navy Agent - in effect an Insurer of ship's cargoes. The Navy Agent bought the cargo wherever it was. If it reached its destination port safely, the Navy Agent did very well. If on the other hand it fell to the Spaniards or was otherwise lost, then the Navy Agent bore the entire loss. James made a very substantial fortune, particularly on one ship, The Havannah. Having made his fortune, he returned to Kelso, where he bought extensive landholdings, part in Kelso, and part in Ednam. He built himself a fine house in Kelso, which he named "Havannah House", but which acquired the name "Ednam House". It has been described as one of the finest examples of Georgian architecture in Scotland, though alas it has been somewhat ruined in its conversion into an hotel (The Ednam House Hotel).

It is curious that James built his main house in Kelso, a little way away from his main landholding; but this did not detract in any way from his interest in his estate. Apart from building the Cross Keys Hotel in Kelso, he drained land extensively; rebuilt his village of Ednam; built a mill and a brewery; and laid out a bleachfield. He was a progressive landowner, with a wide range of business activities.

He became Senior Grand Warden of the Grand Lodge of English Freemasons; and Member of Parliament for Peebles. In 1766, he was elected Grand Master of Kelso Lodge of Freemasons, and built them a Meeting Place.

Together with Sir Alexander Don, he founded the Society of "Bowmen of the Border"; and he started the Kelso Races, owning the grey horse Cheviot, which ran at Caverton Edge in 1765.

James died in 1771, aged 58, He had no children, and entailed his property on his nephew, **William Dickson**, the son of his brother Archibald.

1. **Archibald Dickson**, brother of James, left Kelso at the same time as James. He went to Pontefract, Yorkshire, where he was a one-time

baker. He married a Miss Smith, whose sister was the mother of Dr Thomas Mein RN of Eildon Hill, Roxburghshire, and the grandmother of Mrs Susan Sibbald, whose Memoirs were published in 1926, and contain many references to the Dickson family [1]. They had 3 sons & a daughter:

[i]   **William Dickson** Admiral of the Blue, 17-- - 1803, of whom hereafter

[ii] *Archibald Dickson*, Admiral, 17-- - 1803; created a baronet 21st September 1802, for his services during the Napoleonic Wars, with special remainder in default of issue, to his nephew **Archibald**, son of his older brother **William**. He lived at Hardingham Hall, Norfolk - which he rented, rather than owned. He had an only daughter, who married her first cousin William Dickson 1770-1795, Captain 22nd Regiment, eldest son of Admiral William Dickson of Sydenham.

[iii] *John Dickson*, Lieutenant General, 17-- - 1816. He married Elizabeth, daughter of Alexander Collingwood of Unthank, Northumberland. Her sister Jane, married John's brother, Admiral William Dickson. Elizabeth was born 1745; the marriage took place on 12th April 1771 [2]; they lived in Newcastle upon Tyne; and she died 25th February 1801 [3]. John Dickson died 14th April 1816. They had 2 children:

  I.   Captain Archibald Dickson 1772 1836, who m. 1801, Jane, daughter of Admiral William Dickson of Sydenham, and lived at Morpeth.

  II. Helen, who m. Captain Soane.

[iv] A daughter, Mrs Smail, of Mains, Berwickshire, who in widowhood, 1801, lived in Dublin Street, Edinburgh.

2. **William Dickson**, Admiral of the Blue, 17-- - 1803; eldest son of **Archibald** and heir to his Uncle James Dickson of the estates in Kelso and Ednam - to which he succeeded in 1771. He played quite a

material part with his uncle in forming the estate, sharing the negotiating and buying of the land - Outfields & Infields & Tiend Sheaves, & Riggs, & Gowksknowe - which thereby formed the estate, one half in Ednam, the other in Kelso. He also bought Kaimsknowe [now Pylestead] for £3,050.

Because of his business ventures, James died owing considerable cash sums, which he had borrowed for working capital. These debts totalled £27,040:8:11d. William did not risk carrying on his uncle's business ventures, and chose instead to pay off the debts by selling Ednam House in Kelso. This left the estate without a main house. So a small house was taken over and enlarged. It was named "Sydenham House" after the village near London. The name Sydenham was given to the whole estate, and the family itself was called DICKSON OF SYDENHAM.

He was twice married - firstly to **Jane**, daughter of **Alexander Collingwood** of Unthank (later called Collingwood House) Alnham, Northumberland, on 11th November 1765 [5]. She was baptised 21st May 1740, and died on 12th April 1782. They had 3 sons & 2 daughters:

[i] William 1770-1795; Captain 22nd Regiment; m his first cousin, the only daughter of Admiral Sir Archibald Dickson, 1st Bt. He dsp.

[ii] **Sir Archibald Collingwood Dickson** 2nd Baronet, 1772 - 1827, Rear Admiral of the Red, RN, of whom hereafter.

[iii] Alexander 1777-1840. He was in the Royal Artillery, and became a Major General, and Director General of Artillery. He was made a KCB, and became ADC to King William IV. He was conspicuous in the Peninsular War and at Waterloo. I have an engraving of his portrait. He m a Minorcan lady, Eulalia dau Don Stephani Briones & had 2 sons:

I. William, Lieutenant RE, 1805-1827; dsp

II. General Sir Collingwood Dickson VC - one of the earliest holders of the Victoria Cross. He followed his father into the Royal Artillery, and was a most distinguished soldier. He dsp. I know of 2 portraits of him - one at the Royal Artillery Mess at Woolwich. The other was bought at the sale of his effects by Sir John Dickson-Poynder Bt (later Lord Islington).

[iv]   Nelly

[v]   Jane, who married her cousin Captain Archibald Dickson of Newcastle upon Tyne.

Admiral William Dickson's second wife was Elizabeth Charteris (or Chatres, per the footnote in "The Memoirs of Susan Sibbald") daughter of James Chatres of Eton College, and they had 3 sons and 2 daughters:

[vi]   David John 1790-1870, Commander RN

[vii]   Rowland Cotton 1793-1832, Captain Bengal Artillery

[viii] Robert who served under his half brother Sir Archibald Collingwood Dickson Bt, ran away more than once, and was eventually dismissed from the Navy.

[ix]   Mary Anne

[x]   Louisa.

3.   **Rear Admiral of the Red, Sir Archibald Collingwood Dickson 2nd Bt 1772-1827.** b 30 June 1772; d 18 June 1827. Succeeded to his father's estate of Sydenham in 1803, and to his uncle's baronetcy under the special remainder, later in the same year.

He married 17th August 1797 Harriet, daughter of **Admiral John Bourmaster** RN [6], of Titchfield Hants. She died 8th Jan 1865. They had 6 sons and 2 daughters.

[i]   Vice Admiral Sir William Dickson, 3rd Bt, b 10 June 1798, dsp 5 Jan 1868

[ii]   Colonel Sir Colpoys Dickson, 4th Bt, Bengal Army. b 21 August 1807, dsp 21 May 1868. He was named after the famous Admiral of the Napoleonic Wars, Sir John Colpoys [of whom I

have an engraving]. Whether there was any relationship, I do not know.

[iii]   Captain Sir Alexander Collingwood Dickson 5th Bt, RN: b 1 May 1810, dsp 1886

[iv]   Rear Admiral John Bourmaster Dickson CB, RN, b 29 April 1815, d 11 Feb 1876; married a Miss Poynder, an heiress to Wiltshire estates, & had issue one son and 3 daughters:

    I.   Sir John Poynder Dickson-Poynder 6th Bt, of whom hereafter

    II.   Mary Harriet Isabella Cumberland, b 1857, who m (i) Frederick Amelius Beauclerk, and (ii) Lt Col Robert F M Johnstone [Johnstone Bt colls] dsp

    III.   Caroline Matilda b 1860 dsp

    IV.   Isabella Emily b 1862 dsp

[v]   Captain George Collingwood Dickson 1817-1853, 23rd Madras NI. m Henrietta Emma dau W H Frampton of Hall House, Frome, & had 2 daughters

    I.   Ellen Amelia m 1877 Alfred Henry Burton JP, DL, & had 3 sons:

        a. Stephen John b 1882
        b. Robert Cecil b 1882
        c. Maurice Walter George b 1884

    II.   Florence m 1886 Major General Richard Steele Rupert Fetherstonhaugh CB [Roche Bt]; lived at Gwydir, Ryde, IOW; & had 2 sons & 1 dau

a. Richard Collingwood b 1893

b. George Rupert Alexander b 1894

c. Kathleen Florence

[vi]   Captain Francis Farrill Collingwood Dickson 1822-1884, Madras Fusiliers, m Frances Murtagh dau Thomas Turner of Arcot, India, & had issue

I.   Francis Colpoys Dickson

II.   4 daus.

[vii]   Harriet b circa 1800 d 21 December 1859; m Admiral Thomas Carter RN

[viii]   **Mary Madelina Bourmaster** b circa 1800-1805; died at Bideford, Devon, 14th June 1848.; m at Titchfield, Hants 7th December 1826 **Claud Douglas**. They were my great-great grandparents - their daughter **Mary Isabella Douglas** m. **Brigadier General Frederick Adam**; and their grand-daughter **Freda** married **Robert Barton Stewart**. I have a miniature of Mary Madelina Douglas, née Dickson.

4.   Sir John Poynder Dickson-Poynder 1886-1936: 6th Bt, only son of Rear Admiral John Bourmaster Dickson, succeeded to the baronetcy and entailed estates of the Dicksons of Sydenham, on the death of his uncle Sir Alexander Collingwood Dickson 5th Bt in 1886.

In 1888, he succeeded to the Poynder estates in Wiltshire of Hartham, Corsham, and Hilmarton Manor, Calne. He sold these, and Sydenham. His wife, a Dundas of Dundas, was one of the pioneer lady decorators of the inter-war years. They occupied a number of historic houses, including Glynde Place, Sussex, all of which she redecorated with great flair and an advanced understanding of historic details. "She adored all beautiful things and never did I meet with more ecstatic enthusiasm for houses, furniture and works of art than hers" according to Philip Tilden, whom the Islingtons employed as their architect to modernise Home House, including the installation of bathrooms on the second and third floors. They took the lease of Home House, Portman Square, London W.1 in 1919. This was a "beautiful and untouched example of Robert Adam's work at its best .... But there were no bathrooms" wrote Philip Tilden in his autobiography entitled "Time Remembrances. In 1926, they were succeeded in the lease by Mr and Mrs Samuel Courtauld. Samuel's brother, Sir Stephen Courtauld had 47 Grosvenor Square and Eltham Palace, Kent. The last home that the Islingtons had together was Rushbrooke Hall, Bury St Edmunds. After Lord Islington's death in 1936, Anne Islington rented and refurbished Dyrham Park, Gloucestershire. [see Country Life, December 21/28 2000, pages 43-45.

He began his political career as a Conservative, but was for many years a Liberal MP, and was appointed Governor General of New Zealand in 1910; and created a Baron, as *Lord Islington*. He married 1896 Anne Beauclerk, dau Robert Henry Duncan Dundas, Field Marshal the 1st Baron Napier of Magdala. After his death in 1936, his widow gave the last piece of Dickson land in Kelso, to the Town as a playing field, named, somewhat inappropriately Poynder Park. As a widow she lived at, and restored, Dyrham Park, Glos. They had an only child:

[i]   Joan Alice Katherine 1897-1987. John Singer Sargent drew her portrait 3 times in charcoal, and offered to paint a full length portrait of her free of charge, but her parents refused, insisting that she got on with her schooling instead. She m 1923 Colonel Sir Edward Grigg 1897-1955, who in 1945 was created a Baron, as Lord Altrincham. He was Governor of Kenya 1925-1930. During that period Joan Grigg founded a maternity hospital for African women in Nairobi, at Pumwani, which has since grown to impressive dimensions; and one at Mombasa, which still bears her name. In the Second World War, Sir Edward Grigg was Minister Resident in the Middle East, after the assassination of Lord Moyne. She lived at Tormarton Court, Badminton, Glos, and had 3 children:

I. John Edward Poynder Grigg; b 1924; succeeded as 2nd Baron Altrincham, but disclaimed the title q.v Burke's Peerage sub nom Altrincham. A journalist and historian, biographer of Lloyd George.

II. Anthony Ulick David Dundas b 1934, m March 1964 Eliane, dau the Marquis de Miramon

III. Annabel

The many Dickson portraits are now the property of John & Anthony Grigg.

Arms of Dickson of Sydenham:

Arms: Azure, between an Anchor erect or, encircled with an oak wreath vert, between three mullets pierced or; on a chief paly of seven of the last and gules, a mural crown argent.

Crest: Over an arm brandishing a falchion proper, a trident and spear in saltire or.

Motto Fortes fortuna juvat.

Notes & Sources:

1. Memoirs of Susan Sibbald, pub 1926
2. On the Dickson family, see generally Burke's Peerage & Baronetage.
3. Register of Morpeth
4. Monumental Inscriptions, St Andrews, Newcastle upon Tyne.
5. Register of Morpeth
6. Admiral John Bourmaster; Lieutenant 19 Oct 1759; C R 30 May 1776; C A 9 Sept 1777; Rear Admiral of the Blue 23 Oct 1794; Rear Admiral of the Red 1 June 1795; Vice Admiral of the White 14 Feb 1799; Vice Admiral of the Red 1 Jan 1801; Admiral of the Blue 23 April 1804.

Collingwood Of Great & Little Ryle & Unthank

Later called Collingwood House, Parish of Alnham, Northumberland

The Collingwood family have long been landowners in Northumberland. Branches were seated at Eslington, Chirton, Dissington, Lilburn Tower, Glanton Pyke, Great & Little Ryle etc. In 1553, Sir Robert Collingwood of Eslington made a large purchase of monastic lands in Northumberland, on behalf of Robert and Alexander Collingwood, presumably his kinsmen. The land of Brinkburn Priory in Little Ryle was included in this purchase.

1. -- Collingwood of "Bewett" [Bewick] had a son **Alexander Collingwood of Little Ryle**, who was called "my cozen" in the will dated 12th June 1556, of Robert Collingwood of Eslington. He m a dau of -- Forster, and had issue:

    [i]   Thomas of whom hereafter

    [ii] John, aged 60 in 1625, m Katherine -- (dead by 1625) + issue

       I.   John

       II. Ephraim

       III. Daniel

2. **Thomas Collingwood of Little Ryle,** to whom the manor of Hedgeley was conveyed by Sir Cuthbert Collingwood 20th December 1587, died 1st May 1624, seised of many lands in Little Ryle, Carsley, Hedgeley, Alnham, Screnwood, Reaveley, St Margaret's Grange in Alnwick, & Rugley. He m (1): a dau of Robert Clavering of Callaly & had issue:

    [i]   Alexander 1593, alive in 1663. By deed of 20 Sept 1658, he limited Little Ryle & other lands to himself for life, remainder to his half brother John. Had the King's pardon 1660-1661.

    [ii] Thomas m (2) Fortune, dau Henry Collingwood of Great Ryle + issue

    [iii] Cuthbert, under age 1624

    [iv] John, of whom hereafter

    [v]   Several others

3. **John Collingwood** under age 1624, d 1689; of Reaveley, had issue:

4. **Thomas Collingwood** of Reaveley, Hedgeley, Little Ryle, & Great Ryle 16-- - 1727 m Jane ?Ker?, + issue

5. **Alexander Collingwood** of Little Ryle 1664-1744, built a house at Unthank, Alnham; m Dorothy, dau Wilfrid Lawson of Brayton, and had issue

   [i]   Alexander, of whom hereafter
   [ii]   Jane
   [iii] Elizabeth
   [iv]   Sarah, who m 1716 George Reid of Hethpool

6. **Alexander Collingwood** of Little Ryle, bapt 8th September 1700, of Queen's College, Oxford. Settled lands in Little Ryle, Hedgeley, Carsley, Alnham, and Screnwood tithes 1754. d 1758; m Eleanor, dau Robert Blake of Twizell 1702-1777. They brought up his great niece Sarah Roddam [2] [daughter of Robert Roddam, postmaster of Berwick, by Sarah Reid; who was daughter of Sarah Collingwood & George Reid of Hethpool]. Sarah Roddam m John Erasmus Blackett of West Matfen. She died July 1775, leaving 2 daughters, one of whom, Sarah 1762-1819, married Cuthbert Collingwood, later Admiral Lord Collingwood.

   Alexander Collingwood had issue:

   [i]   Alexander, of whom hereafter
   [ii]   Robert 1725-
   [iii] Thomas 1726/27; Captain RN, m Mary dau Sir Thomas Hughes 1st Bt
   [iv]   Gilfred 1728-1793
   [v]   George 1729-1795, succeeded to Unthank, & Little Ryle
   [vi]   Fraser 1731 - ; of Jamaica
   [vii] a dau bapt 1724
   [viii] Sarah bapt 1724/25
   [ix]   Dorothy bapt 1732, m 1754 Walter, eldest son of John Strother Ker of Fowberry

[x]   Sarah, bapt 1735; m 1766 Captain, later Admiral, Robert Hughes of Portsmouth; d 1774

[xi] **Jane** bapt 21st May 1740, m 11th November 1765 Captain, later Admiral of the Blue, **William Dickson of Sydenham.** She died 12th April 1782. He died May 1803. They had issue inter alia **Admiral Sir Archibald Collingwood Dickson 2nd Bt** 1772-1827, whose daughter **Mary Madelina Bourmaster Collingwood Dickson** m General **Claud Douglas** (my great-great grandparents).

[xii] Eleanor

[xiii] Ann

[xiv] Elizabeth; 1745-1801; m General John Dickson (her brother in law's brother]

7.   **Alexander Collingwood** of Little Ryle & Unthank b 1723/24; of Queen's College, Oxford; high sheriff 1761-62; d Oct 1795. His widow renamed his house at Unthank, Collingwood House. He had 3 daughters:

[i]   Eleanor 1753-1764

[ii] Margaret 1766-1841, co-heir, m Captain Charles Michell, 49th Regiment

[iii] Isabella 1768-1830, co-heir, m John Tarleton of Liverpool. He bought out his sister-in-law's moiety of the Collingwood estates, which were sold by his trustees 1848.

Arms

Argent a Chevron between 3 stags heads erased sable (sometimes gules)

Crest: A stag at gaze in a holly bush ppr. [A stag's head erased is sometimes used].

8.   **Admiral Lord Collingwood**. Cuthbert Collingwood 1748-1810 was one of the Collingwoods of East Ditchburn. They were cousins of the Collingwoods of Great & Little Ryle, & of Eslington; but the precise

relationship in 16th century Northumberland, is almost impossible to work out. He always treated the family of Little Ryle & Unthank as "cousins" [3]. Edward Collingwood of East Ditchburn, Shipley & North Dissington, his great grandfather's brother, had a son, Edward, who was Recorder of Newcastle, and owned Chirton, which he left to the Admiral & his heirs male. Edward died in 1806.

Cuthbert Collingwood therefore inherited Chirton. But since he left only daughters, his brother John inherited Chirton. From John descend the Collingwoods of Lilburn Tower.

Our connection with the Admiral is twofold. Firstly he was a "cousin". Secondly, his wife's mother, Sarah Blackett née Roddam, was brought up by her great uncle, and our direct forebear, Alexander Collingwood of Little Ryle & Unthank 1700-1758.

Engravings:
I have 2 Collingwood engraved portraits.

1. The first is of George Collingwood of Eslington who was "out" in the '15, captured, and condemned for treason. He was hanged, drawn, and quartered at Carlisle.
2. Cuthbert, Admiral Lord Collingwood.

Notes & Sources:

1. Northumberland County History Vol XIV pp 550-552
2. Archaeologica Aeliana - Transactions of the Newcastle Society of Antiquaries 4th Series Vol 32
3. Letter Sir Edward Collingwood of Lilburn, 16th October 1967.

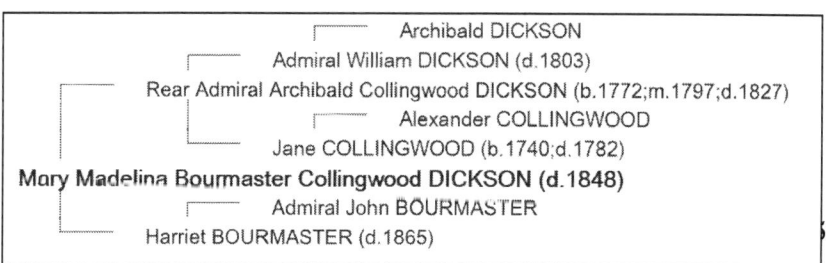

Figure 2: Dickson and Collingwood

Chapter 13: Earengey, including Steel

On 26th July 1930, my father, **Guy Milton Stewart,** married **Elaine Oenone Earengey.** She was the only child of **William George Earengey** by his wife **Florence** née How.

The Earengey family is by tradition Norwegian[1] in origin. A Norwegian once suggested to me that the name would originally have been something like Åreng -oy. "Oy" means "island"; thus the name would indicate that the family haled from an island with a name like "Åreng". The spelling of the name used in England, of "Earengey", would thus have given a reasonable phonetic rendering of the Norwegian original; though the Norwegian Åreng would have sounded like the English "ng", whereas the "g" in the name as pronounced in England, is like a soft "j". Sometime in the early 18th century, or even in the late 17th Century, the Earengey progenitor left Norway and settled in Ireland. In the 19th century they were settled in Limerick (or possibly Cork). When I visited Dublin in the mid 1970's (being then involved in a case about the painting of steelwork for Dublin Airport), a search of the telephone book for Eire revealed an "Erangey"[2] then living in County Cork. [Australian relatives have shortened it to "Earngey" [3]

Early in the 19th Century one of the family came from Ireland to England, and settled in Wiltshire, at Malmesbury. From there, they moved to Castle Combe [5½ miles north west of Chippenham] or Grittleton [which is a mile or so further away from Chippenham]. The father of Thomas Earengey was a Surgeon; whose surgical instruments descended to my grandfather, but alas they were stolen. It was either the Surgeon or his father who was the first to settle in England.

1. **Thomas Earengey**, who was born about 1815-1820, was Superintendent of Police, in the early days of Sir Robert Peel's "Bobbies" in Malmesbury. He was my grandfather's grandfather.

   James Earengey left Ireland in about 1820, to go to Australia[3]. I think it likely that he was a brother of Thomas Earengey's father, the Surgeon.

   It seems that at the same time, a third brother stayed in Ireland. It was probably in the next generation that Samuel Earengey left Ireland and settled in America.

   Thomas Earengey's father achieved some affluence, for my grandfather heard tell of the big house that they lived in, at or near Malmesbury. But if they had money in that generation, it evaporated during the 19th century. Thomas himself lived in either Malmesbury or Grittleton, nearby.

   Thomas had 4 children - I do not know the name of his wife:

   [i]   George, a Grocer in Cheltenham, who d unmarried of tuberculosis.

   [ii] Thomas, who m -- and was a lay preacher, and, I think, in the Salvation Army.

   [iii] James, of whom hereafter, b 1846.

   [iv] Minnie, who m John Noel, of Castle Combe, Wiltshire, and had 4 children:

        I.   Mary Ann

        II. Bessie

        III. Katie

        IV. Harry

   Thomas was dead before 1870, the date of his son James' wedding.

2. **James Earengey 1846-1889:** He was my great grandfather [4].

James was a boot maker (cordwainer) as were a number of the members of his wife's family [Steel]. He had the reputation of being extremely knowledgeable about hides, and one of the best leather cutters in the business. He ended life as a boot maker's manager.

On 27th July 1870, he married at Salem Baptist Chapel, Clarence Parade, Cheltenham, **Emma Steel**, daughter of John Dunn Steel, then a farmer at Taunton[5]. Early in their married life, James wanted to emigrate to America. But his wife's mother got him to promise to return to England frequently. They settled in or near Pittsburgh, Pennsylvania. After one of their visits back to England, Emma Earengey would not go back to America with James. So he returned to Pittsburgh for a short time on his own. On his return journey to England, a chill exacerbated the tuberculosis from which he suffered. He went from one sanatorium to another in England, and eventually died in Croydon in 1889. His widow spent the remainder of her life living in Cheltenham, save for the period 1899-1901, which she spent in Colorado Springs, looking after her oldest son, Jim, in his final illness with tuberculosis.. She died in Cheltenham in 1940, aged 91 [6].

James & Emma Earengey had 3 sons and 2 daughters:

[i]   James "Jim": 1871-1901; b 8th December 1871, in either Allegheny or Pittsburgh, Pa. He returned to America in about 1889, at the age of 17. He settled in Pittsburgh, taking the first job offered to him, of freight elevator boy. He gained rapid promotion, on showing how good he was at figures, and was soon in charge of 60 men. The manager then took a holiday, leaving Jim in charge. He worked night and day, in intense heat, which proved his undoing, for he developed tuberculosis. He was advised to go out to Colorado, and there he remained for the rest of his life.

On one occasion in Colorado, he was held up by a bandit, but managed to escape by shooting the bandit first. Jim was wearing English trousers, the pocket of which was in a different place to that on American trousers. Thus he was able to get his hand in his pocket, without the bandit realising it; and shoot through the pocket. After this, he joined the US Army for a period. He became involved in gold mining, making and losing several fortunes. He sent back to England a nugget of gold that he had mined, from which my grandparents' wedding rings were made. This gold was used later to make wedding rings for our daughters in law, Jenny and Emma.

His last fortune was spent in trying, in vain, to cure his tuberculosis. In September 1899, my great grandmother, Emma Earengey, went to Colorado Springs, with Aunt Nan (& her husband Sid & daughter Win) and Aunt Min, to look after Jim. There they stayed until Jim died in February 1901. They left for England in July 1901. Jim dsp.

[ii]   **William George**, my grandfather, 1876-1961; of whom hereafter.

[iii]   Frederick Thomas 1877 - 1882(?). dsp.

[iv]   Annie "Aunt Nan" 1874-1968. She m Sidney Harris & lived in Cheltenham. They had an only daughter, Winifred who m Leslie Carrick, a commercial artist. Winifred dsp. Aunt Nan lived for some 20 years in the same house as Leslie Carrick's mother. But true to their Victorian upbringing, they never got beyond calling each other "Mrs Harris" and "Mrs Carrick". Aunt Nan was a remarkable old lady. She was meticulous in remembering each birthday of every relative; and she would always send a small present to every niece, nephew, great niece or great nephew as the case may be, though she had but little means. She continued this right up to her death at the age of 94.

[v]   Minnie b 1880 - 1975 "Aunt Min". She m Albert Wehlisch, an American, and consequently settled in the USA. She had disappointed her family by refusing an offer of marriage from an Englishman with "excellent prospects", for the more dashing but less stable Albert Wehlisch. The disappointed Englishman went off to Australia, where he became a millionaire from sheep

farming. Aunt Min in contrast had few pennies to bless herself with.

For many years, Aunt Min lived at Tonapah, Nevada, high up in the desert. Water was brought up by pack, once a week. If anyone ran out earlier, it was too bad: there was no alternative source. It was a lesson in domestic economy that she never forgot. Just before the war, Aunt Min came back to see her ageing mother. The War started, and she remained in England until it ended, living with Aunt Nan. Neither would take any step, or make any decision, without first consulting their brother (my grandfather) then a County Court Judge: often seeking his advice on such simple and obvious matters as to become almost a nuisance to my grandparents. Aunts Nan and Min were the sole beneficiaries of their mother's will. Reluctantly she had omitted my grandfather, at his request because he was far more affluent than his sisters; save to appoint him her executor.

After the war, Aunt Min returned to the USA, and settled in Tyler, Texas. In 1957, I spent a couple of days staying with her and her family, at 222 South Peach Ave, Tyler. The contrast with England was dramatic - the heat: the houses of the oil millionaires: the enormous long straight highways built on oil money: the nearby town where virtually every house had an oil well in its back yard. It was an incredible contrast to the neighbouring, poverty stricken, state of Arkansas. Aunt Min had incredible energy and a zest for life. She played a major role in cooking and keeping the house well into her 90s; and loved watching wrestling on television at breakfast time.

She had an only child, Joan, who met & married Ken Reed in Cheltenham, towards the end of the War. They had 6 children:

I.   Angela Moya b 1946

II. Heather Dawn b 1952

III. Donna Celeste b 1954

IV. Rhonda Charmaine b 1956

V. Monica Chere b 1958

VI. Nigel Philip b 1960.

3. **William George Earengey**: 1876 - 1961

My grandfather was born at Cheltenham 10th January 1876; and was aged 13 when his father died. He could remember until his dying day the financial struggle his mother had in widowhood, to bring up her family: and of how uncomfortable he used to be in suits of clothing that did not fit. This background made him determined throughout his life to work and save, so as to provide financial stability and independence for his family.

He was educated at Cheltenham Grammar School; and was a classic example of the product of the old English Grammar Schools, which set out to provide the best of education to children no matter what their financial status. He was a classical scholar, keeping Latin and Greek texts on his bookshelves all his life: well read: and a generally cultured and cultivated man. He was a kindly man, who rarely showed any outward sign of anger. He had the ideal judicial temperament - wholly courteous, intelligent, and fair minded.

He always wanted to go in for the law, but could not afford the Bar until he had first made money. So he became a Solicitor, and joined the family firm of Steel & Broome in Cheltenham, where he was articled to his cousin Robert Steel [son of Edward Steel, an older brother of my grandfather's mother]. His Aunt Jane Steel funded him while he was in articles, by way of loan - which he repaid in full within a few years of qualifying. He was admitted a Solicitor on his 21st birthday.

He did not go to America with the rest of his family in 1899, for that was the year in which he married **Florence** daughter of **John How** of Cheltenham- on 2nd September 1899, at Salem Chapel, Cheltenham [7]. The witnesses to the marriage were John How & his wife Hannah, their daughter Ethel, and Grandpa's mother Emma Earengey.

Early in their married life my grandparents espied in a local antique shop a walnut & sycamore writing table, English c 1845, but in the Louis XV style; and a walnut commode of similar date and style. They paid in weekly instalments until the total was paid. Only then would they take delivery, even though offered it earlier. These 2 pieces remained among their most treasured of possessions all their lives. I now have the writing table.

In 1906, he obtained the degree of Ll.D from London University [8]. During the First World War, he made many attempts to enlist in the Army, but was always turned down because of poor eyesight. Eventually, he was accepted as a Recruiting Officer, and served at Stourbridge and Reading.

After the War, my grandparents moved to London, and Grandpa read for the Bar. He was admitted to the Middle Temple on 12th May 1919, aged 43. In October 1919, he was placed in the First Class and awarded the Certificate of Honour by the Council of Legal Education [9]. He was called to the Bar on 17th November 1919, and was pupilled to Sir Hugh Fraser, one of the greatest experts in libel and slander at the Bar; and joined the defamation Chambers at 1 Brick Court, Temple, where he was eventually Head of Chambers. He took Silk in 1931; became Recorder of Tewkesbury in 1930 [10], and Recorder of Dudley in 1931 [11]. On 1st September 1934, he became a County Court Judge [12] - much to the disappointment of his wife and colleagues, who expected him to reach the High Court Bench. His base Court until his retirement was Clerkenwell [13].

My grandmother, **Florence Earengey,** née **How**, was a more extrovert and less quiet or measured a person than my grandfather; but the perfect foil for him. She was educated at North London Collegiate School for Girls; and got a BA from the University of Aberystwyth. She was as well read and cultured as my grandfather.

She was admitted to the Middle Temple 6 years after my grandfather, on 13th May 1925, and was called to the Bar on 26th

January 1928. She became a Magistrate - one of the first women to be appointed a JP after the passing of the Sex Disqualification (Removal) Act 1919. On her own description she was an "unrepentant suffragette", and a key figure in the National Council of Women of Great Britain, of which she was National President 1949-1951, and Honorary Legal Adviser until her death [14].

He died at Camberley, Surrey, on 12th April 1961, aged 85 [16 & 17]. His widow, **Florence Earengey** died on 29th December 1963, aged 86 [15 & 18].

Their only child was my mother **Elaine Oenone Stewart, née Earengey,** b. 20th February 1904, d. 8 October 2002 in Alton, Hampshire.

****

Earengey family in Australia: known there as "Earngey".

[i] **James (or Richard) Earengey** emigrated from Ireland to Australia in about 1820. He had 3 sons:

I.   George, of whom hereafter

II. James (Jim), who had a son

III. Harold, who had a son

IV. Peter

V.   Thomas (Tom) who had a daughter.

[ii] George Earengey or Earngey had 2 sons and several daughters. The sons were:

I.   Stan, who had issue

    a. Edison

    b. 6 daughters

II. Thales, who had issue:

a. George, d before 1950.

b. John, b. 1928, a dress designer in Sydney, NSW, who visited the UK in the 1949 and 1951.

c. David

Earengey Family in America:

In about 1860, **Samuel Earengey** (who may also have spelt his name in the Australian way, without the middle 'e') left Cork, Ireland for America. It is thought that he settled in Pittsburgh, Pa, and possibly later in Virginia. He had 4 children:

III. Samuel - died in his early 20s of typhus

IV. Frank - died in his early 20s of typhus "

V. Jessie

VI. Willard

[iii] **Willard Earngey I** had 3 children:

I. Shirley, d 1968

II. Willard II

III. Jane

[iv] **Willard Earngey II** had 3 children

I. Willard Earngey III - stationed in North Carolina in the Marine Corps in 1970

II. Lynne

III. Martha

Erangey Relatives in Ireland:

In 1975, I got in touch with John B Erangey, of Glebe House, Castle Martyr, Co Cork [2]. One of the Erangey family who remained in Ireland was responsible for a masterpiece of a stucco ceiling at St Mary's Church in Cork City, which was built in 1840; and also for a ceiling in a church in

Mallow, Co Cork. He married into a family from Mallow, co Cork. He had a son:

John Erangey 1850-1919, who stayed in Cork, who had four sons:

    IV. **Stephen Erangey** 1875-1945, who had an only son:

    V. John B Erangey, of Castle Martyr, Cork

    VI. Thomas

    VII. James

    VIII. William

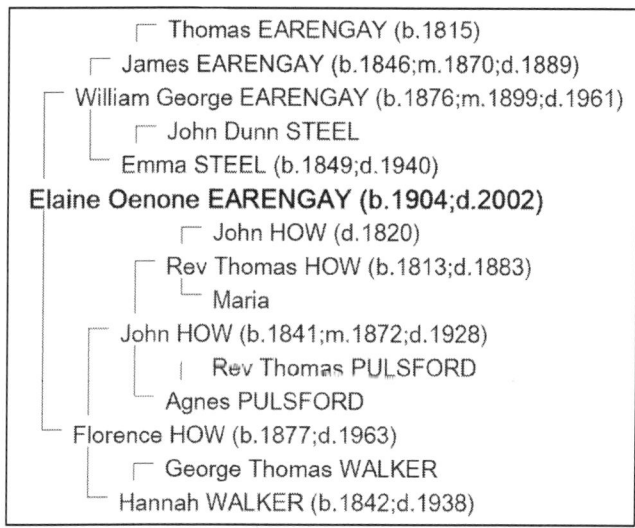

Figure 3: Earengay Ancestry

Notes & Sources:

1. Tradition of descent from Norway comes from my grandfather. He at one time had a tree of the family; but it was lost. John B Erangey of Co. Cork was told of an origin in Holland - see Note 2.
2. John B Erangey of Glebe House, Castle Martyr, Co. Cork.
3. Correspondence 1949 onwards from John Earngey, of Sydney, NSW.
4. Correspondence from Aunt Min, from Tyler, Texas.
5. Marriage Certificate, James Earengey & Emma Steel, 27.07.1870
6. Will of Emma Earengey
7. Marriage Certificate, William George Earengey & Florence How, 2.09.1899
8. W G Earengey - Ll D Certificate 1906
9. W G Earengey - Certificate from Council of Legal Education 1919
10. W G Earengey - Appointment, Recorder of Tewkesbury 1930, signed by King George V.
11. W G Earengey - Appointment as Recorder of Dudley 1931, signed by King George V.
12. Appointment as County Court Judge, 1934, signed by Lord Sankey LC
13. Times Obituary W G E
14. Times Obituary Florence Earengey.
15. Death Certificate Florence Earengey 29 Dec 1963
16. Death Certificate W G Earengey 12.04.1961
17. =Will of William George Earengey
18. =Will of Florence Earengey

A Note on the Steel Family

My great grandmother, **Emma Earengey**, was the daughter of **John Dunn Steel**. She was born 5th April 1849, and died 31st December 1940.

Admiral Herbert of Wisanger Manor, Miserden, Glos had a son:

Captain Edward Herbert RN of Wisanger Manor, b 1760, d 1820 [1]. He was said to be an extremely harsh and autocratic man, so much so that his son, John Dunn Herbert, could take him no further, ran away from home, and changed his name to Steel [2]. Thus by tradition, this Captain Herbert was the father of:

1. **John Dunn Steel, I** of Bristol, a Cordwainer, b 1790. There is some question whether his proper surname was "Herbert" -see above, "Dunn" or "Steel". He m a Miss Trebreh --. She was born 1786/87 at Porton, Wilts, the daughter of Ann Woolford (bapt. 7 Sept 1763). Her father's name is not mentioned; but since her name is an anagram of Herbert, this may be the true origin of the "Herbert" connection. She m in widowhood (2) 1828 George King; and after his death (3) William Clark [3]. At the marriage of her second son James Dunn Steel in 1839, she was a witness who "made her mark" rather than signed. So presumably she was illiterate. They were the parents of:

[i]   John Dunn Steel II, of whom hereafter

[ii] James Dunn Steel, b ante 22.12.1818, m Ann Twigg, 23.12.1839, issue

   I.   Ann, b 6 Feb 1841

[iii] a dau who m -- Parry + issue

2. **John Dunn Steel II**, b 1815 in Bristol m Sarah Ann Skay c 1833 (she died 1894). He was brought to Cheltenham at about the age of 5, schooled there, and apprenticed as a bootmaker. He founded a bootmakers shop in the High Street, which was carried on after his death under the name "Steel & Son". An early supporter of the Chartists, and later a Liberal, he formed a cooperative farm at Taunton. For many years he was one of the Poor Law Guardians, and sat on many non conformist bodies. He objected to the compulsory payment of Church Rate; and year after year he defaulted: he would display the summons in his window: and goods would be seized to be sold to pay for the Church Rates. The public in Cheltenham would not buy them, because they were so hostile to compulsory Church Rates. So they had to be sent elsewhere to be sold. He was Town Councillor in Cheltenham. I had always understood that he was a

founding Member of Cheltenham & Gloucester Building Society - though this is not mentioned in his obituaries[4]. He died 6th January 1898 at 2 Sandford Terrace, Cheltenham. His estate was finally sworn at £6,347.12.2. + issue:

[i] John Dunn Steel III, m Anna -- + issue:

    I.   Gertrude, who m -- Brown, + issue Donald Brown (in Glasgow)

    II. Ernest, dsp

[ii] Edward Steel: + issue

    I.   Eva

    II. Robert, had 3 daus, Emma, Mina, & ?

[iii] Thomas b 1837, + issue

    I.   Sidney Thomas: a jeweller in High Street, or The Parade, Cheltenham; I have a clock, which was my grandparents', which was "examined by S T Steel, Cheltenham".- issue 2 daus

    II. Frank, a shoemaker with 2 shops in Cheltenham - issue Marjorie & Frank jr (disappeared)

    III. Maud

[iv] Jane b 1840 dsp unmarried in 1911 [5]. She was the Aunt who loaned my grandfather the money to enable him to become a Solicitor. Thereafter she treated herself as having the right to point out to him any indigenous relatives whom she thought he should help. She lived with her youngest, unmarried, brother Charlie - whose great love of life was the work of Charles Dickens. The delicate mahogany arm chair in our hall, with the needlework seat, was Aunt Jane's chair - her gift to my grandparents.

[v] Robert b 1842 m (1) Annie James; (2) May How; (3) Mary Lance; issue (by his first wife)

I. Fred, who had a son Norman

II. Harry, m Maud Hiram + issue

    a. Leslie, who had a son Robert Steel

    b. Robert

III. 2 daus

[vi] James b 1844, had 2 daus Bessie & Emmie

[vii] Ellen b 1846

[viii] **Emma 1849-1940**, who m **James Earengey**

[ix] William Columbus Steel b 1851, had 2 daus & a son William

[x] Sarah Ann b 1853; m 1874 Frederick Henry Lane, issue (inter alia):

    I. Ellen, whose dau Margaret Hulbert drew the tree

    II. John Dunn Lane, Solicitor in Cheltenham + issue

[xi] Charles b 1856, dsp unmarried.

Notes & Sources:

1. The grave of Captain Edward Herbert is at Miserden Church. He was buried 18th May 1820 aged 62; Mary his wife died in 1845.

2. Miserden parish registers record:

Burials:

1738:Aug 31:   John Herbert

1747: Oct 3   Sarah Herbert

1757: Jan 14th   Mary Herbert

1769: April 13   Elizabeth Herbert

1770: March 3   Margaret Herbert aged 70

1771: March 19:Mary Herbert (infant)

1776: Sept 26:   Peter Herbert aged 72

1777: March 19:Sarah Herbert junior

1791: Nov 8th   Anne Herbert, pauper

   Births

   1729: May 17th, Mary dau Peter & Margaret Herbert

   1731: May 26th, Jane dau   "   "   "   "

   1733: June 29, Peter son   "   "   "   "

   Christenings

   1738:   2 Sept, William Hamblin, son Peter & Margaret Herbert (he d 24 April 1791, aged 52)

   1791:   3 July, Anne, dau Thomas & Jane Herbert

   1799:   17 Nov, Peter, son Peter & Jane Herbert

   1801: 12 April, Peter, "   "   "   "   "

   1803: 31 July, William Hamblin, son Peter & Jane Herbert

   1805: 6 Jan, Sarah Hamblin, dau Peter & Jane Herbert

   1807: 25 Feb, Jane, dau Peter & Jane Herbert

   1808: 30 Oct, Patience Hazel, dau Peter & Jane Herbert

   Marriages

   1744: 3 Oct, John Owen & Ann Herbert

   1799: 3 Feb, Peter Herbert & Jane Blackwell

   1779: 13 Oct, William Smith & Sarah Herbert

   1791: 22 May, Thomas Herbert & Jane Snow

1802: 12 Oct, Henry Herbert (widower of Brimpsfield parish) & Mary (illegible)

3. Correspondence from Aunt Min - see Notes under Earengey above
4. Steel Family tree compiled by cousin Margaret Hulbert.
5. Obituaries of John Dunn Steel II, 1898.
6. Will of Jane Steel.

Chapter 14: How

My maternal grandmother, **Florence Earengey**, née **How** 1877-1963, was the daughter of **John How** of Cheltenham 1841-1928, by his wife **Hannah Walker** 1842-1932.

The How family was formidable - well educated: well read: highly intelligent: and fighters of causes great and small. It was a family of strong, non-conformism (in fact, both my maternal grandparents were brought up as Baptists). My grandmother's parents lived in Cheltenham, but the family descends from a line of yeomen farmers in Torrington, Devon.

By tradition, they are descended from a 17th Century Curate of Great Torrington, Devon, **Rev John Howe** 1630-1705, who was domestic chaplain to Oliver Cromwell. The Kneller portrait of Rev John Howe, in the National Portrait Gallery, shows a clean shaven face; with large, slightly hooked, nose; and firm, prim, lips, suggesting that his puritanical soul is offended by a slight odour of corruption. The nose, lips, and indeed the expression, are characteristic of the How / Howe family of my immediate forebears. If looks are anything to go by, the link is clear. However, it is still to be proven.

Ancestry & Family of Rev John Howe 1630-1705:

1. **Rev William Howe** born late 16th century had 2 sons:

    [i]   Rev John Howe, of whom hereafter

    [ii] Rev Obadiah Howe 1616-1683; MA Magdalen College Oxford 1638; incumbent of Stickney, Horncastle, & Gedney; Vicar of

Boston 1660-1683; published several controversial works. [DNB@ Vol 28, p.92]

2. **Rev John Howe**, born presumably c 1600, Curate of Loughborough, ejected 1634 under the Laudian Regime; m. Anne --, and had issue:

[i]   Rev John Howe 1630-1705, of whom hereafter

[ii]   Ann, b July 1628

3. **Rev John Howe 1630-1705:** b Loughborough 17 May 1630; d 2 April 1705 at St John Street, Smithfield; buried at Church of All Hallows, Bread Street. BA Christ's College, Cambridge, where he was intimate with Henry More 1614-1687 [see DNB]; MA Magdalen College, Oxford 1652; fellow and chaplain of Magdalen College; Perpetual Curate of Great Torrington, Devon, 1654-1662 & ejected for refusing to comply with the Act of Uniformity 1662. As domestic chaplain to Oliver Cromwell, the Lord Protector, he preached against fanaticism; he befriended Fuller and Seth Ward; he was Chaplain to Richard Cromwell; preached at houses in the West after ejection; was joint pastor at Haberdashers Hall, London, 1676; began the controversy on predestination 1677; answered a sermon on schism by Shillingfleet 1680; expostulated with Tillotson 1680; refused to support dispensing power; advocated mutual forbearance of conformists and dissenters 1689; prominent in happy union of Presbyterian and congregationalists 1690; controversy with Defoe on occasional conformity 1700; conferred privately with William III before his death; was visited by Richard Cromwell in his last illness. Chief works "The Living Temple of God" 1675; collected works 1724, enlarged 1810-22, and 1862-63. [see DNB].

He m Katherine Hughes & had issue:

[i]   George 1655-1710, MD; m Laetitia Foley, probably dau of Thomas Foley of Witley Court, Worcs; issue

    I.   John

    II. Philip, both dsp before 1729

[ii] James 1653-1714; Barrister Middle Temple; m Mary dau Samuel Saunders Esq of Little Ireton & Caldwell, Derby [son of Col Thomas Saunders, a distinguished Parliamentary Officer in the Civil War]. issue:

    I. John 1708-1769; of Hanslop, Bucks; m Caroline dau Scrope, 2nd Viscount Howe [see para 10 below].

    II. Samuel

    III. James

[iii] John, of whom no particulars exist, save that he had two sons:

    I. John

    II. James

[iv] Obadiah, b 1661 at Torrington; probably d inf

[v] Philippa, b 1664, m Matthew Collett & had issue John & Matthew

Our line (so far as it has been researched) goes back to **John How** 17--, d circa 1820;

John How was a yeoman farmer of Huntshaw, near Torrington, Devon. His wife was Maria --. I do not know her surname, though it may have been Beer, for an "Aunt Beer" helped to bring up John How's 2 sons.

I have a pair of (copy) miniatures of John & Maria How; and a pair of (copy) miniatures of his parents, whose names I do not know. The identifications are presumptive; but on physical looks and period they are very likely to be right. The originals were in the ownership of Rev Harold Howe of Kemsing, Kent, and date from around 1800-1810. In particular the older man has the characteristic How nose, lips, and expression.

John How died in a kicking match on a public holiday - a rather barbarous, public house, sport, to modern thinking, but apparently of great popularity in the early 19th century. Since his 2 sons were both young when their father died, I would put his death to around 1820.

John & Maria How had issue:

Thomas How 1813-1883, my great-great grandfather, of whom hereafter
[vi]   George Howe 1815-1899, of whom hereafter - see para 8 below.

Both these sons started life as Anglicans, and both became
somewhat straight laced, non-Conformists - both indeed became
Baptist Ministers. Whether there was an element of rebellion against
the sort of pasttime that had cost their father his life, history does not
relate. George was the first of the two brothers to be baptised as a
Baptist - he came under the influence of Rev Thomas Pulsford, pastor
of the Baptist Chapel in Great Torrington, when he was only 16, in
1831. Thomas followed, and in due course married Rev Thomas
Pulsford's daughter, Agnes.

Thomas, the elder son, retained the spelling "How"; whereas
George, the younger son, added a final 'e' and spelt his name "Howe".

4.   **Rev Thomas How** 1813-1883, the elder son of John & Maria How.

He was born 16th August 1813 and baptised 27th August 1813 at
Little Torrington Parish Church. He followed his brother George into
the Baptist Church, starting to preach in the villages around
Torrington. In 1836, he came closely under the influence of Rev
Thomas Pulsford.

He married Agnes, daughter of Rev Thomas Pulsford. Her family
came from Torrington; and in Great Torrington Churchyard there is a
gravestone of a Thomas Pulsford who died 2 Jan 1768 in the 68th year
of his life; and of Mary his wife who d 13 November 1791 aged 88
They are believed to be related.

He was a Baptist Minister at Padstow 1837; Chipping Sodbury
1839-1849; Cheltenham 1849-1852; Shrewsbury 1852-1866; and
Roade, Northants, 1866-1877. He retired to Cheltenham in 1877,
where his son John was in business as a grocer, and died there on 4th
July 1883. Agnes How died in Cheltenham on 5th November 1887.
They are buried in Cheltenham Cemetery (in the same grave are their
son, John, 1928; and John's wife, Hannah, 1932).

In 1937, my great uncle Herbert How, and his sister Aunt Edith, visited Roade, and met the oldest inhabitant, a Mrs Foddy, then aged 87. She had a photograph of Rev Thomas How, whom she remembered as "much respected, perhaps feared rather than loved, as he seemed a stern man". Agnes How was an invalid with a spinal complaint and had to spend much of her time on a sofa, so a window was cut in her room in the manse, next to the church, for her to look out. Every day, she would have the floor under her sofa washed out with cold water.

They had 5 children:

[i]   Emma 1836-1899, who m Rev Richard Littlehales 1839-1891, and had issue:

    I.   Richard How Littlehales 1872-1952; m 1896, M A Scott & had 2 daughters:

        a. Marjorie Alice, who m first -- Eadington, but was divorced; and second Christopher Bilton: no issue.
        b. Dorothy, m 1930 Michael McConnell. She died Dec 1930. dsp.

    II.   Florence Emma 1875 - 19--; m 1900 Thomas Hubert Hardinge Vowles (he d 1946) & had issue:

        a. Florence (m Malcolm Bone: no issue)
        b. Hubert Henry m. 1935 Lucy Hunter + 2 children - Richard Henry b 1940; and Hazel b 1944
        c. Richard Guy m 1945 Winifred Andrews + 2 children Andrew b 1946; and Pamela b 1949

[ii]   Rebecca 1839-1859, d & buried at Shrewsbury
[iii] **John 1841-1928, my great grandfather**
[iv]   Agnes 1842-1847, d & buried at Chipping Sodbury
[v]   Maria 1846-1899; m Robert Steel of Cheltenham - an uncle of my grandfather William Earengey - see Chapter 13.

A rather primitive portrait of Rev Thomas How shows him with the typical How face - large, slightly hooked, nose; firm, prim, lips; and the puritanical look. It is now in the possession of Nicholas How, grandson of my Uncle Bert.

5. **John How 1841-1928**, my great grandfather:

Born at Chipping Sodbury. He m 12th January 1872, at Salem Chapel, Cheltenham, Hannah dau of George Thomas Walker, then a Surveyor's Assistant, of Bristol. She was b 1842, and died aged 90 in 1932.

His father had little money, but managed to settle John into partnership with a tea importer. Disaster befell the business, when the partner absconded with all the money. This left John almost penniless. So he set up a grocery business. By dint of hard work, combined with a shrewd head for business and investment, he built up a sizeable business in Cheltenham, ending as a Master Grocer and general man of property - he would have provided Galsworthy with a model for a country Forsyte.

His was a typical somewhat strict Victorian household. The weakest minded of the daughters, Lil, was expected [as often happened in Victorian families] to stay at home to look after her parents, rather than lead her own life and marry. Alcohol was only allowed into the house for "strictly medicinal purposes". A little Brandy was "strictly medicinal".

At the age of 40, he was seen by 2 London medical specialists, who told him that he had but weeks to live, and should return home and put his affairs in order. Nothing deterred, he lived for a further 47 years, continuing in business, and building up his property interests.

I have a pair of oil portraits of John and Hannah How. After their deaths, they were left with Aunt Lil who had lived with and looked after her parents. Then they went to my grandmother, and then to me. They are a sombre pair, painted in 1879 and 1880, by Beynon & Co of Cheltenham - done, so repute has it, to settle a debt owed to John

How. It is difficult to see much character in them: - the John who so disliked one of his wife's dresses that he took a pair of scissors to it in the wardrobe, and then when the damage was discovered, suggested that a mouse must have been nibbling at it. Hannah looks stern and prim, but was in fact a kindly woman who used to cosset her husband after the prognostication of his early death at age 40, and would wrap several sheets of brown paper on his chest before he went out to take his constitutional walk.

In 1879, John & Hannah How were on holiday in Scotland; and, as was fashionable, had seats booked to go by train over the Tay Bridge at Dundee. On the morning that they were due to go, John had a premonition that something was to happen, and refused to go. His dutiful wife remained with him - he giving no reason for his refusal. The train on which they had seats booked was the one involved in the Tay Bridge Disaster [when the bridge blew down, and many passengers on the train were killed]. He would never say what it was that put him off taking the booked trip.

John & Hannah How had 8 children:

[i]   Arthur 1872-1951; m 1900 Catherine Jane Brooks 1873-1956. They had one son, Jack who was scatter-brained, b 1903. When both he and my mother were children he hit her hard on the head with a croquet mallet, to kill a wasp or fly, quite oblivious to harm that it might cause her. Jack was married twice (i) to P. Tebbutt (divorced); (2) to Miriam Spicer by whom he had 3 daughters Jean Mary b 1942; Judy Margaret b 1944, and Ann June b 1946. Jack just disappeared.

[ii]   Thomas b & d 1872, a twin with Arthur.

[iii] Edith 1874 - 1954 (d in Australia). She was a brilliant, but very masterful and dominant character - by no means unusual for this family. She was a suffragette; imprisoned for her activities; an ardent Socialist; an early woman Labour Candidate for Parliament; one of the first women to get an M Sc at London University; and a one time lecturer in Science at the University.

She m in 1899, Herbert George Martyn; after which they hyphenated their surnames together as How-Martyn.

Her determination and domination became misplaced when she tried to filch all of her mother's jewellery after Hannah How's death. Hannah How had divided it before her death, but my grandmother and Aunts Ethel and Lil declined to take their shares during their mother's lifetime. A Court case was brought, which Edith lost. This caused a family rift, that was only repaired shortly before Edith died, when she wrote out of the blue to my grandmother. Edith also tried to dominate the rather weak willed Lil over the property left to her. My grandmother & Aunt Ethel persuaded Lil to have her money put in the Public Trustee's hands, to stop Edith getting her hands on it. This also was part of the rift in the family.

[iv] Ernest 1876-1957; m 1903 Mildred Stevens 1882-1938, by whom he had 5 daughters:

I. Joyce b 1905, m George Harkness; had 2 adopted girls, Margaret Joan b 1940; and Joyce Stella b 1944; lives in Dumfries.

II. Vivian b 1907; m (1) Kenneth Shaw 1892-1938, by whom she had Ann b 1931; and David Kenneth, & Nigel, twins b 1934. She m (2) Donald L Simmons b 1900, and had a daughter Jennifer.

III. Mary b 1912

IV. Stella b 1914; m 1947 George Bramham Bence b 1910; & has 2 sons, Thomas How b 1948; & Christopher George b 1950.

V. Ruth b 1918.

[v] Florence 1877 - 1963, my grandmother, of whom hereafter.

[vi] Lilian 1878-1957. In complete contrast to the rest of the family, she was weak willed and easily dominated. She was persuaded that she should stay at home to look after her parents, rather than have an independent life. She lived and died in Cheltenham.

[vii] Herbert 1880-1963 "Uncle Bert". He was a Surveyor. He was the only one of my grandmother's brothers whom I met - he was on the other side of the family rift, and only met up with my grandmother again at Aunt Lil's funeral. He must have been unhappy about the rift, for he was deeply interested in his relations, and was a charming, courteous, and kindly man. He was twice married (i) to Dorothy Vere Goodland 1886-1928, by whom he had an only son

I.   Peter Goodland How 1915 - 1991 (?); a surveyor like his father, and almost a caricature of his father, in looks, hand writing, and speech. He m 1946 Nellie Elizabeth Armstrong 1908-1976; and had issue one son:

a. Nicholas Peter b 1949, m + 1 dau.

Uncle Bert m (2) in 1933 Mabel Elizabeth Messenger 1895 - 198-.; by whom he had a son Frank Thomas b 1937 & died in infancy.

[viii] Ethel 1883-1977. A nurse; m 1911 Eustace James Carey Dicks 1883-1954, a doctor. She was the closest in the family to my grandmother - much like her though more given to making outrageous comments or demands, simply to provoke a lively and humorous atmosphere. Though outwardly less tolerant and more autocratic than my grandmother, in fact she had a heart of gold, and was a most kindly and sympathetic person. She had 2 children:

I.   Jean b 1914; m 1938 Richard Baic who d 1965. Dick was a highly gifted engineer and draftsman; but unstable in character, and ended an alcoholic. Issue:

a. Paul b & d 1942

b. Michael, b 1943

c. John Richard 1944-1990; a solicitor, who died of multiple sclerosis; m Hilary dau Very Rev Robert W Pope[1,] one time Dean of Gibraltar; and had issue

◆ James b 1974

II. Eustace 1918-1925; killed in a car accident in his father's car, driven by his father when there was a sudden steering failure. This was in Framlingham, Suffolk, where his father was in practise as a Doctor.

6. **Florence How** 1877-1963 - my grandmother.

A person of remarkable intellectual vigour, well read, and of strong character, she was educated at North London Collegiate School for Girls, and at Aberystwyth (a College of the University of Wales) where she got the degree of B.A.

She was a suffragette, and a life long fighter for women's causes. On her own description she was an "unrepentant suffragette" and a key figure in the National Council of Women of Great Britain, of which she was National President 1949-1951, and Honorary Legal Adviser until her death. Unlike her socialist sister, Edith, she was a strong Conservative. However, she took pride in her Non Conformist roots, and would never slavishly follow any line, unless she had satisfied herself that it was right.

She was admitted to the Middle Temple 6 years after my grandfather, on 13th May 1925, and was called to the Bar on 26th January 1928, and practised for a short time. She became a Magistrate - one of the first women to be appointed a JP after the passing of the Sex Disqualification (Removal) Act 1919.

At the age of 22, on 2nd September 1899, she married my grandfather, **William George Earengey** - then a Solicitor. They built a

---

1 Rev Bob Pope officiated at the wedding of Andrew Stewart and Valerie McQuiston in 1992

house on Battledown, Cheltenham, which they named Ashley Rise. The sale of this was one of their regrets when they moved to London for my grandfather to go the Bar after the First World War. In London, they lived in Belsize Park, and Hampstead.

I remember my grandmother as an indefatigable, very active, vivacious, loving, and generous person; of great principle, but at the same time of great fun. Her writing was immaculately neat, and her diction was always clear and concise. Physically, she was a typical How - with the large, slightly hooked nose, and the firm, prim, lips. She had grey blue eyes, and her hair was originally brown - but tinted to a bluey grey when I knew her. She only gave up her very active life in the last year or two of her life. Even when living in old age in Camberley (to be close to my mother) she would travel regularly to London, and always by coach.

****

A Note on the Life & Family of Rev George Howe 1815-1899 [2nd son of John & Maria How]:

An extract from Memoirs of Ministers of the Baptist Church, supplied by Baptist Church Headquarters, says of him:

> *"He was one of the oldest Ministers of our Denomination. He was born at Little Torrington, North Devon, in the "year of Peace" 1815. He came of a worthy stock and was brought up in the Church of England; but at an early age his convictions underwent a change, and he became a non-conformist and a Baptist. He was baptised in 1831 at Torrington by Rev Thomas Pulsford, entered Bristol College in 1837, and outlived nearly all his fellow students. In 1840 Mr Howe accepted a Call from the Church at Warminster and there spent 16 years of devoted service. His removal to Cardiff in 1856 was the occasion of an outburst of loving feeling on the part of those he was leaving, seldom surpassed, and the parting scene was never effaced from his memory. It was chiefly due to his earnest ministry in Cardiff that the existing Bethel Chapel in Mount Stuart Square was built. Mr Howe removed to Ross in 1866 and after a pastorate of 6 years in that town accepted a call to*

Countesthorpe. In 1876 he entered what was to prove his final pastorate at Newbury, where he laboured until 1884, when he retired to Lee, Kent. He was pre-eminently a man of prayer, and withal a man of his word. Of great tenacity of purpose, he was strong and definite in his convictions, but he sowed true catholicity of spirit by instituting monthly united services among Free Churches in the several localities where he ministered. He was a lifelong abstainer and an ardent temperance advocate from his earliest years. In politics he was a pronounced Liberal and a devoted admirer of Mr Gladstone. He was also deeply interested in all forward movements, especially in the federation of Free Churches and in the Twentieth Century Fund, but the cause that lay nearest his heart and claimed the greatest share of his sympathy was Foreign Missionary enterprise. Mr Howe was full of force and fervour which advancing years could not diminish, and continued preaching occasionally until within 18 months of his death. His sermons to the last were characterised by brightness and enthusiasm. He was one of the hundred ministers who visited Ireland about 1853, and his career may be summed up in the testimony of a friend shortly after his departure, who said "His was a useful life". He fell asleep after a day's illness on 26 February 1899".

George Howe m Charlotte (Foster?) & had issue:

[i]   John Foster 1845-1931 m Caroline Presland 1852-1931 & had issue 12 children:

    I.   Arthur John 1873-1966 m Mary Griffith & had 6 daus, all m + issue

    II.   Dora Winifred 1875-1967, m Howard Jenkins + had one son, m + issue

    III.   Ethel 1879-1887 dsp

    IV.   Rose 1880-1886 dsp

    V.   Eirene 1883-1889 dsp

    VI.   Wilfred 1884-1885 dsp

    VII. Foster Garfield 1881-1956 m Anna Milhoff + issue:

a. Frances, 1914-1968, m Alan Kitching + issue Colin b 1941

b. Mira 1918 - m (1) Denis Matthews, the world famous pianist, + issue Rachel b 1943; Miranda b 1947; Sophy b 1949; James b 1952; she m (2) Michael Henderson

c. Michael 1927 - ; m Pamela Wingrove + issue Roger, Denis, & Catharine.

d. Gabrielle 1929 - m Patrick Merton.

VIII. Percival Presland 1886-1954 m Edith Stobart + issue:

a. John 1914 - ; m A Whyman + issue Diana; & Ian

b. Anthony 1916 - m E Shaw + issue Michael

c. Josephine m + issue

d. Angela m + issue

IX. Charles Kingsley 1889-1916, killed in action dsp.

X. Arnold Ewart 1893-1917, killed in action dsp.

XI. Harold Wilberforce 1890-197-; Vicar of Kemsing, Kent; m Margaret Bell + 4 daus. He had the originals of the 2 pairs of How miniatures of John & Maria How & his parents - see para 4 above.

XII. Eric Graham 1897-1975 m Nora Blaxill, issue 2 daus, one d in infancy; and one m + issue.

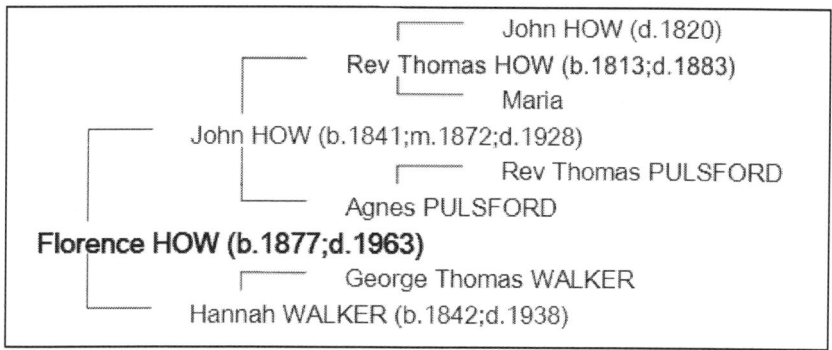

Figure 4: Ancestors of Florence How

Notes & Sources:

1. On Rev Thomas How & his ancestry - predominantly my Uncle Bert
2. On the family of John How 1841-1928, my Uncle Bert & my grandmother
3. On the family of Rev George Howe - Mira Henderson, and her Uncle Rev Harold Howe.

****

How of Balnacarron, Fife:

This family also come from Devon; and also have a tradition of descent from Cromwell's Chaplain, Rev John Howe. Their pedigree is set out in Burke's Landed Gentry 1952 edition.

John How 1838-1885, of Bideford, Devon, JP, [there is still a firm of John How & Co in Barnstaple] m Mary Jane Lovering Evans & had issue:

John Herbert How 1856-1930, Major 3rd Bn Devon Regiment, JP Bideford; m 1887 Madeline Ellen dau Lt Col R T Boothby of St Andrews Fife & had issue:

[i] William Fitzherbert How 1888 - 1949 of Balnacarron House, St Andrews 1888-1949 m + issue:

Hope and Faith

I. William Sawbridge How, of Hillhouse, Kirknewton, Midlothian b 19--; m Ludivina Frances, dau Sir W F Stuart-Menteith 5th Bt; + issue Stuart Sawbridge How b 1950

II. Major John Edward 1916-1948

III. Robert Boothby How 1918 - [issue see Burke's L G]

IV. [Silvia Jean b & d 1921

[ii] Everard John Boothby 1890 - ; m Mary Lawrence Kintzing of New York; & (2) 1949 Elizabeth Francis [who owns the Edinburgh Silver Dealers How of Edinburgh]

[iii] Madeline Dorothy 1890 - m Henry Alexander Trotter.

Arms:
Arg on a fesse between in chief 2 wolves heads erased pean, collared gu., & in base a rose of the last barbed & seeded ppr, 5 bezants.
Crest: Upon a billet fessewise sa., charged with five bezants, a wolf's head pean, collared gu.
Motto: Justus et propositi tenax
From the heraldry, this family looks as though it is connected with that of Viscount, later Earl, Howe.

Family of Viscount, later Earl, Howe:

Whether this family is related, is not known. But heraldically, the How family of Balnacarron [who, as set out in para 9 above, come from Devon & also claim descent from Cromwell's chaplain] should be kin.

Henry Howe, living temp Henry VIII had issue:

John Howe of Hunspell de la Heies, co Somerset d 1574; had issue:

John, m Jane heir of her brother Sir Richard Grubham, knight, of Wishford, Wilts; & had issue:

[i] Sir John Howe 1st Bt, of whom hereafter

[ii]   Sir George Howe 1594-1647, of Cold Berwick, Wilts, who had issue:

    I.   Sir George Grubham Howe 1st Bt cr 1660, of Cold Berwick, who had issue

    a. (Sir James, 2nd Bt dsp.

1. Sir John Howe 1st Bt cr 22 Sept 1666, m Bridget dau Thomas Rich Esq of North Cerney, Glos, Master in Chancery; obtained the Manor of Compton from his uncle Sir Richard Grubham; + issue

[i]   Sir Richard, 2nd Bt of Compton; & had issue:

    I.   Sir Richard Grubham Howe 3rd Bt of Compton; dsp 1730

    II. John, obtained the Manor of Langar, Notts, by his wife, Annabella, illeg dau & co-heiress of Emanuel Scrope, Earl of Sunderland, + issue:

    a. Scrope, cr Viscount Howe 1701; d 1712 at Langar; m (1) Anne dau John Manners, Earl of Rutland + issue

    ♦ John Scrope dsp
    ♦ Annabella
    ♦ Margaret
    He m (2) Juliana dau William, Lord Allington & had issue

    ♦ Scrope 2nd Viscount Howe & 3 daus

2. Scrope, 2nd Viscount Howe had issue

[i]   1st Earl Howe
[ii]   Caroline, m John Howe, of Hanslop, Bucks [see para 3.3 above]

Arms:
Or a fesse between three wolf's heads couped sa.
Crest: Out of a ducal coronet or, a plume of 5 ostrich feathers az.
****

How Family in Devon:

In the 1960s, my Uncle Bert was in touch with a Herbert How, farmer of Little Bowden, nr Torrington; likely to be kin, but the relationship had not been sorted out.

Chapter 15: Medhurst

On 8th September 1962, I married **Lynda Grace Medhurst** at St Paul's Knightsbridge, London SW1. She was born 4th January 1939 at Leigh on Sea.

1. **Albert Medhurst** b circa 1855; a blacksmith at Storrington, Sussex. He m Sarah Jane Boniface, dau Thomas Boniface. (She d. 194- at Storrington). Issue:

2. **Arthur Medhurst** 1885-1961, a Grocer, latterly at Southend, Essex. He m Grace Muggeridge, b 1884 at Ardingly, Sussex, d 1969 at Burham, Kent. She was the daughter of Thomas Muggeridge, Blacksmith at Peas Pottage, nr Crawley, Sussex, and Sarah Louise Grace. For some reason, the families disapproved of the marriage, and Arthur Medhurst cut himself off from his Medhurst relations. They had issue:

   [i]   Arthur Thomas Albert Medhurst of whom hereafter.
   [ii]   Charles m Ada + issue a dau. Charles d. 2000

3. **Arthur Thomas Albert Medhurst** b 27 Dec 1906 – 5 Dec 1976. Arthur was a highly intelligent man, who won a scholarship to a Grammar School. Had he taken it up, his career would have been very different. But it would have meant daily travel from his home in Holmbury to Guildford; and his mother would not countenance it. So his education and achievements suffered. He was a highly skilled engineer, who could maintain a motor car to a smoother pitch than

anyone else. For a number of years, he kept a general store at Burham, Kent; and died in Hexham, Northumberland in December 1976.

On 10th June 1934, he married Laura Annie Dobson b 29 Nov 1915. She was the daughter of Francis John Dobson 1880(?) - 1955 by Ellen Thrush 18-- - 26.12.1950(?). He was a professional gardener, who moved around the country as a Head Gardener. For some time they lived in Derbyshire at Eyam. Latterly he was Head Gardener at Hylands, Chelmsford (?Cunard family?). He came from Hungerford, Berkshire (his mother's first name was Thursa. Ellen Thrush's family came from Lyneham, Wiltshire (her mother's first name was Sarah). Laura Annie died in Thirsk on 16th December 2008.

Their only child was **Lynda Grace**, b 4th January 1939 at Leigh on Sea, Essex.

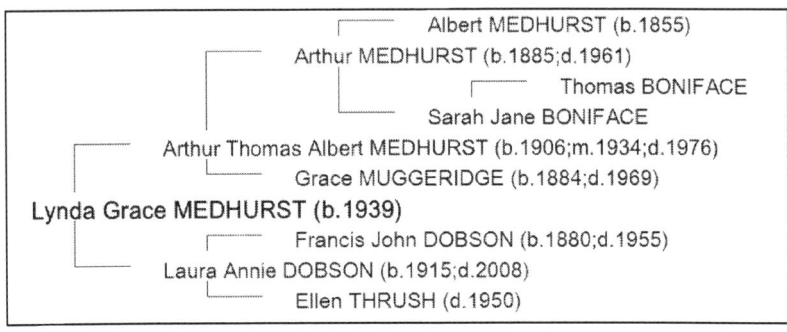

Figure 5: Medhurst Family

Printed in Great Britain
by Amazon.co.uk, Ltd.,
Marston Gate.

Telegraphy

R N Renton, CGIA, CEng, FIEE

Pitman Publishing

First published 1976

Sir Isaac Pitman and Sons Ltd
Pitman House, Parker Street, Kingsway, London WC2B 5PB
PO Box 46038, Banda Street, Nairobi, Kenya

Pitman Publishing Pty Ltd
Pitman House, 158 Bouverie Street, Carlton, Victoria 3053, Australia

Pitman Publishing Corporation
6 East 43 Street, New York, NY 10017, USA

Sir Isaac Pitman (Canada) Ltd
495 Wellington Street West, Toronto 135, Canada

The Copp Clark Publishing Company
517 Wellington Street West, Toronto 135, Canada

Cased edition   ISBN 0 273 40846 1
Paperback editition   ISBN 0 273 00085 3

Text set in 10/12 pt. IBM Press Roman, printed
by photolithography, and bound in
Great Britain at The Pitman Press, Bath